D1327005

OXFORD STUDIES IN THEOLOGICAL ETHICS

General Editor
Oliver O'Donovan

OXFORD STUDIES IN THEOLOGICAL ETHICS

The series presents discussions on topics of general concern to Christian Ethics, as it is currently taught in universities and colleges, at the level demanded by a serious student. The volumes will not be specialized monographs nor general introductions or surveys. They aim to make a contribution worthy of notice in its own right but also focused in such a way as to provide a suitable starting-point for orientation.

The titles include studies in important contributors to the Christian tradition of moral thought; explorations of current moral and social questions; and discussions of central concepts in Christian moral and political thought. Authors treat their topics in a way that will show the relevance of the Christian tradition, but with openness to neighbouring traditions of thought which have entered into dialogue with it.

The Family in Christian Social and Political Thought

BRENT WATERS

OXFORD

UNIVERSITY PRESS

OXFORD
UNIVERSITY PRESS

Great Clarendon Street, Oxford OX2 6DP

Oxford University Press is a department of the University of Oxford.
It furthers the University's objective of excellence in research, scholarship,
and education by publishing worldwide in

Oxford New York

Auckland Cape Town Dar es Salaam Hong Kong Karachi
Kuala Lumpur Madrid Melbourne Mexico City Nairobi
New Delhi Shanghai Taipei Toronto

With offices in

Argentina Austria Brazil Chile Czech Republic France Greece
Guatemala Hungary Italy Japan Poland Portugal Singapore
South Korea Switzerland Thailand Turkey Ukraine Vietnam

Oxford is a registered trade mark of Oxford University Press
in the UK and in certain other countries

Published in the United States
by Oxford University Press Inc., New York

© Brent Waters 2007

The moral rights of the author have been asserted
Database right Oxford University Press (maker)

First published 2007

All rights reserved. No part of this publication may be reproduced,
stored in a retrieval system, or transmitted, in any form or by any means,
without the prior permission in writing of Oxford University Press,
or as expressly permitted by law, or under terms agreed with the appropriate
reprographics rights organization. Enquiries concerning reproduction
outside the scope of the above should be sent to the Rights Department,
Oxford University Press, at the address above

You must not circulate this book in any other binding or cover
and you must impose the same condition on any acquirer

British Library Cataloguing in Publication Data
Data available

Library of Congress Cataloging in Publication Data
Data available

Typeset by SPI Publisher Services, Pondicherry, India
Printed in Great Britain
on acid-free paper by
Biddles Ltd., King's Lynn, Norfolk

ISBN 978–0–19–927196–2

1 3 5 7 9 10 8 6 4 2

In Memoriam

MABEL E. LIEBERG

(1918–1978)

WILLIAM C. LIEBERG

(1920–1977)

DONNA L. WATERS

(1918–1991)

CHARLES F. WATERS

(1912–2001)

Preface

A number of 'culture wars' are being waged over the family. Some of the battles are contested along the fronts of legal policies and social mores. Critics contend, for instance, that taxation laws favouring married couples over cohabiting couples and single parents caring for dependent children (or vice versa) are inherently discriminatory. Moreover, maintaining traditional marriage and family as the norm is unrealistic and unwarranted. Given the rapid growth of cohabitation, divorce, and single-parent households, inclusive social practices and legal codes are now needed. More aggressively, the family is characterized as a needless distraction in addressing larger questions of social and political ordering. It is alleged, for example, that marriage and family comprise special relationships that divert attention away from issues of social justice. The family has little to tell us about how we should live our lives in civil communities comprised of autonomous individuals, for it constricts our moral vision given the stunted range of its relationships. More pointedly, the nuclear family is attacked as a regressive institution preventing individual members from realizing their true potential. Given the patriarchal, misogynist, and heterosexist principles upon which the traditional family is based, it is an anachronism that has little to offer in constructing a pluralistic, humane, and just society.

A number of counter-arguments are offered in defence of 'family values'. Some defenders, for instance, cite numerous studies indicating that children thrive within traditional families, and married persons tend to be happier, healthier, and more productive than their single, cohabiting, or divorced counterparts. Consequently, a privileged status for marriage and family is justified because they promote the common good. More expansively, it is argued that social order, if not the survival of civil society, depends on stable families. It is within families that citizens learn basic social skills which provide the foundation for civic virtues and practices. More radically, a dominant male role may be defended on the basis of a 'natural' family structure. Drawing on evolutionary psychology, the so-called patriarchal structure of the traditional family reflects the culmination of survival advantages that have benefited the human species. Traditional gender roles that many critics decry are grounded in our genes. Consequently, if the human species is to flourish the family must be defended against the assaults of alternative lifestyles and parenting arrangements.

Although some Christians are partisans in these culture wars, they do not adopt any uniform position. While some churches have defended marriage and family along traditionalist lines, other ecclesiastical documents have endorsed or embraced a variety of lifestyles and parenting arrangements. Modern Catholic social teaching, for example, contends that lifelong, monogamous marriage provides the only normative foundation for procreation and childrearing as propounded in scripture and natural law. A number of fundamentalist movements are recovering a 'biblical model' in which men play a dominant role as heads of their families. Some liberal Protestant statements, however, propose that the church should endorse a broad spectrum of family structures that reflect a diverse range of experience characterizing the contemporary world. The principal consideration is not a biological bond among parents and offspring, or the presence of two parents of different genders, but the depth and quality of love forming the parent–child relationship. More radically, some theologians have argued that the church should abandon its support of the nuclear family, given its legacy of abusing women and children. More moderate options decry the 'culture of divorce' because of its adverse effects upon children, while simultaneously stressing a fundamental equality between spouses.

These conflicting claims about the family are not espoused within theoretical vacuums. Rather, they both reflect and reinforce a series of disparate presuppositions regarding the nature, goals, and tasks of social and political ordering. If it is assumed, for instance, that human associations consist of autonomous individuals, then social and political ordering is primarily an act of corporate will. The common good is thereby the sum total of individual goods of which it is comprised. Consequently, individuals may find the family to be either a useful tool or impediment in pursuing their interests. Although such a scheme implies no inherent hostility towards the nuclear family, nor are there any obvious or compelling reasons for granting it a privileged status. It may be argued that the interests of many individuals are best served through traditional familial structures, but a case might also be made that the tasks of perpetuating civil society from one generation to the next could be achieved as effectively by ordering reproduction and childrearing through alternative institutions other than marriage and family.

If it is assumed, however, that human associations are grounded in human nature, then social and political ordering consists of upholding natural bonds. The family, with its nexus of biological and social affinities, is the most basic form of human association upon which all other private and public affiliations are based. In the absence of strong families the common good is diminished. Thus it is incumbent upon the state to promote and support the 'traditional' family. Although this naturalistic account of social and political ordering seemingly offers an alternative to that premised on the primacy of the corporate will, it is rarely given much credence in the current debates on 'family values'. There are two reasons why this position is dismissed. First, given the late liberal context where most of the culture wars are waged, naturalistic accounts of the family are confined to the private sphere. Individuals are free to entertain whatever moral beliefs they choose about familial relationships, but no larger implications for social and political ordering may be derived from them. Individuals may impose normative restrictions upon themselves regarding their families, but they are not options to be considered in political debate and public moral deliberation. Second, naturalistic accounts of social and political ordering often couch their arguments in late liberal rhetoric. Late liberal civil community, with its emphasis on the freedom of autonomous individuals, marks the crest of human evolution. The freely chosen bonds of human associations take into account an aggressive and selfish human nature that is in turn being mastered and aimed in a more constructive direction through the power of an evolving human will. The 'traditional' family may not be imposed because of any normative convictions regarding its foundational status for promoting the common good, but it may be commended for the competitive advantages it offers to its members pursuing their respective goods.

Consequently, there are no normative arguments in defence of the family that may be admitted to the public arena. Its defenders are

reduced to pragmatic appeals in behalf of the benefits families offer
to its members, especially children. This tactic, however, is unsatis-
factory in terms of Christian social and political thought. Although
Christians may commend the family because it benefits its individual
members, this cannot be the only reason for affirming the family.
Rather, the involuntary social and biological bonds imposed by the
family disclose suggestive clues for the social and political ordering
of larger spheres of affinity. Reducing the family to a means of
individuals pursuing their private interests may have far-reaching
and troubling implications for broader spheres of human association,
such as nationality and citizenship, that also include involuntary
bonds.

Moreover, there are theological reasons why Christians may affirm
a particular, normative account of the family. As the most basic form
of human association, the family is part of a vindicated creation being
drawn towards its destiny in Christ. Familial affinities that are ordered
in accordance with this *telos* do not turn in upon themselves, but
evoke an unfolding love that is drawn towards more expansive spheres
of association. Or more prosaically, the love of neighbour that lies
at the heart of the gospel is rooted in a properly ordered love for kin.
This claim is not overlaying a thin veneer of theological jargon over
a naturalistic argument. Rather, it acknowledges that familial relationships are not solely matters of personal or private interests, but
that their inherent strengths and weaknesses disclose some important
clues for how humans should order their lives and life together under
the sovereignty of God. Social and political thought that claims to
be Christian, cannot ignore or dismiss the family as an irrelevant
consideration, especially in respect of the involuntary nature of its
affinity. To do so is to place the entire burden on a voluntary human
will which transforms social and political ordering into a project to
be undertaken, rather than faithful stewardship of a gift entrusted
to humans by their Creator. In the absence of an overtly normative
account of the family's significance for social and political ordering,
'family values' become ideological weapons to be used against op-
ponents in resolving underlying social, economic, and political issues.
Politicizing the family has effectively stripped it of any genuine social
and political significance.

It is in response to the paucity of theological accounts of the family that prompts this book. Its purpose is twofold: (1) to examine critically the role the family plays in traditional and contemporary Christian social and political thought; and (2) to develop a constructive account of the family that may inform current Christian social and political thinking.

The principal critical thesis is that historically Christian social and political thought drew heavily on an understanding of the family as the most basic form of human association. Although this strand was developed in tension with the church's eschatological witness, a teleological ordering of the family nonetheless informed a Christian vision of civil society that is grounded in a created order. It is with the rise of modern liberalism that the family disappears as a formative feature in Christian social and political thought. Coincidently, a voluntaristic vision of civil society emerges, portraying human associations as outcomes of the corporate will of autonomous individuals. Examining selected historical and contemporary sources test this thesis.

The principal constructive thesis is that the virtual disappearance of the family has diminished contemporary Christian social and political thought. In order to correct this weakness, some salient philosophical and ideological foundations of late liberalism are subjected to a critical analysis regarding its understanding of the nature of human association in general, and the familial association in particular. Building upon this critique an alternative set of philosophical and theological presuppositions is proposed. These presuppositions provide the basis for developing a normative account of the family that may in turn inform a contemporary Christian vision of civil community.

Chapter 1 initiates the critical analysis by examining biblical and historical sources. The first two sections place Jesus' teaching against the family, Paul's indifference toward marriage and family, and the New Testament's household codes against the backdrop of the Graeco-Roman emphasis on the family as the fundamental social cell. The following sections assess Augustine's affirmation of marriage in light of ambiguous patristic teaching, and medieval efforts to institutionalize marriage and parenthood as Christian vocations roughly on a par with singleness. The final sections examine Reformation and Puritan themes, and nineteenth-century attempts to bolster the family.

Chapter 2 continues the critical analysis by examining the rise of modern liberalism, and assessing the works of selected theorists and their critics. The first section summarizes the origins and subsequent development of modern liberalism by examining the works of Hugo Grotius and Johannes Althusius, followed by their contractarian (Thomas Hobbes and John Locke) and Kantian revisions. The following two sections contrast the works of leading liberal theorists John Rawls and Susan Moller Okin with such critics as Peter and Brigitte Berger and Christopher Lasch.

The following chapter concludes the critical analysis by examining three types of Christian responses to liberal accounts of the family as depicted in Chapter 2. These responses include: reformulation (James Nelson and Adrian Thatcher); resistance (John Paul II and Germain Grisez); and critical adaptation (Don Browning, Rodney Clapp, and David Matzko McCarthy).

Chapter 4 is the transition from the critical to constructive phase. The problematic liberal themes that need to be addressed in a more systematic manner are identified, and the principal theological resources drawn upon in constructing a Christian normative account of the family in subsequent chapters are noted.

The following chapter initiates the constructive inquiry by developing alternative philosophical, theological, and moral themes. Alternative philosophical themes are developed by examining the relationship between nature and history as representing two related spheres of human activity. This examination is followed by a largely sympathetic portrayal of Herman Dooyeweerd's account of sphere sovereignty as a means of relating nature and history, but it is also argued that there are severe limitations in respect to developing a normative account of the family that must be corrected by employing supplemental theological themes. The subsequent section develops these themes by asserting the primacy of a vindicated created order, and discussing the relationships between providence and eschatology, and dominion and stewardship. The final section develops a series of themes directly related to the moral and social ordering of the family as a form of human association. These themes include the household as a place of timely belonging within the temporal confines of a created order, an unfolding and enfolding familial love that orients the family toward broader forms of human association, and a teleological ordering of the familial association to its destiny in Christ.

Chapter 6 describes the normative contours of the family in respect to its teleological and eschatological orientation toward larger spheres of affinity. The principal foci of this account are the temporal and timely ordering of affinity, the providential movement of the family through history, and the providential witness of the family within a vindicated creation being drawn towards its destiny in Christ.

The subsequent chapter examines the tension between the church as eschatological witness and the family as providential witness. It is argued that the distinctive and complementary nature of each respective witness applies this tension in a constructive manner. The principal indicators of this tension are identified in an overview of the eschatological witness of the church, followed by discussions contending that the church is not a family, and the family is not a church.

The final chapter explores how the tension between the providential witness of the family and the eschatological witness of the church informs a Christian vision of civil community. It is argued that both the family and the church disclose the principal characteristics of the social and political ordering of a vindicated creation, namely, that the multiple bonds of human association, as well as the foundations of freedom, consist of a series of created, natural, imposed, social, and political relationships. Subsequent sections examine selected implications of these relationships by focusing on the gift of social ordering, the relation between destiny and the common good, and what the nations (should) desire and judge.

Although significant portions of this book are dedicated to reclaiming traditional theological themes that may inform a contemporary understanding of the social and political significance of the family, it should not be presumed that the book is motivated by a nostalgic desire to recover a family structure from a simpler era, or reassert a patriarchal model. Appeals to a so-called 'traditional family' are rejected, for they often mark reactions to economic and political issues that are inconsistent with or opposed to Christian

social and political thought. Rather, Christian contributions to public disputes over the fate of the family should be welcomed, but if
these voices are to be genuinely Christian then they must draw widely
and deeply upon the church's biblical and theological traditions. This
book marks an attempt to offer a modest contribution to this
enterprise.

To speak of the family entails exploring a wide range of philosophical, theological, and moral texts, because it embodies a unique
nexus where the social and political ordering of human life converges
across generations. To speak of the family, then, also engenders
controversy, for it lies at the heart of human communication and
association. Ambrose once wrote that

the piety of justice is first directed towards God; secondly towards one's
country; next towards one's parents; lastly towards all. This, too, is in
accordance with the guidance of nature. From the beginning of life, when
understanding first begins to be infused into us, we love life as the gift of
God, we love our country and our parents; lastly we love our companions
with whom we like to associate. Hence arises true love, which prefers others
to self, and seeks not its own, wherein lies the pre-eminence of justice.   (*On
the Duties of the Clegy* 1.27(127). 22)

In the centuries preceding and following Ambrose, it has been debated whether this list is too long or too short, whether the priorities
are ordered correctly, whether the family promotes or hinders the
justice envisioned, and if it is to be found in nature or imposed by
human will. The culture wars now being waged over 'family values' is
yet another chapter in this enduring argument over the moral, social,
and political ordering of these loves, and it is hoped that this book
will provide some perspective on their just ordering.

In writing this book I have been the beneficiary of many excellent
teachers. The best ones were my parents-in-law, Mabel and William
Lieberg, and my parents, Donna and Charles Waters, to whose
memory this book is dedicated. The former taught me that being
welcomed into a family did not depend on bonds of blood, while
the latter taught me that it is precisely because of those bonds that
a home should be a place of unconditional belonging. Together
they embodied the primacy of love which orders the passage of life

from one generation to the next, a teaching being re-enacted and reinforced once again in my own family. My wife, Diana, and daughter, Erin, serve as constant reminders that we are inescapably embedded in familial lineages and histories which locate us in the juncture between past and future. And more importantly, that it is love which binds us together over time. Substantial portions of this book are adapted from my D.Phil. thesis supervised by Oliver O'Donovan. He was not only a wise and patient teacher, but as will become apparent in the following pages, I am deeply indebted to him in respect to this theological reflection on the family. It is a debt that I happily acknowledge, and fear that I can never fully repay. I am also grateful for the Oversees Research Student Award that I received from the Committee of Vice-Chancellors and Principals of the Universities of the United Kingdom (CVCP) while studying at the University of Oxford. Steve Long, David Hogue, Gilbert Meilaender, Sondra Wheeler, and Robert Song read portions of initial drafts, and their critical comments and conversations are appreciated. Each will no doubt find something to quarrel with, and they are quarrels I will welcome, for I have not written this book as a definitive statement but as an invitation to further conversation and debate. Finally, I would also like to thank Dong Hwan Kim, Jason Knott, Julie Smith, Donna Techau, and Andy Watts, current or former students at Garrett-Evangelical Theological Seminary, for their insightful comments and essays which have enriched my thinking on the family. They are the kind of students which make teaching a joy instead of a burden.

B.W.

Contents

1

Biblical and Historical Sources

What is *the* Christian family? This question defies any definitive answer, given the often disparate themes and emphases which are present in the Bible and Christian doctrinal teaching. A comprehensive survey of the biblical and historical sources that have shaped various understandings of the family, particularly in respect to social and political thought, is beyond the scope of this chapter. Some representative characteristics can be identified, however, by concentrating on selective developments. Although the structure of the family has changed over time, there are nonetheless some continuous strands that may inform present-day deliberation.

GRAECO-ROMAN CONTEXT

Rome may have vanquished its enemies with apparent ease, but at home it waged a desperate war against death. The greatest threat to its security lay within its borders, namely, that a time might come when Rome could not produce enough offspring to defend its empire. Due to high infant mortality rates, it is estimated that each woman had to give birth to at least five children to maintain a stable population.[1] The human body, particularly its reproductive capacity, was a crucial public resource, and 'the ancient city expected its citizens to expend a requisite proportion of their energy begetting and rearing legitimate children to replace the dead'.[2]

---

[1] See Peter Brown, *The Body and Society* (1989), 5–7.   [2] Ibid. 6.

The greatest burden fell inevitably upon young women, whose plight was compounded by 'scientific' views and social mores that offended contemporary sensibilities. It was not uncommon for women of elite classes to marry at the age of 14 to maximize their childbearing potential.[3] They were brought by their husbands into households controlled by men who had grown up, in Peter Brown's words, 'looking at the world from a position of unchallenged dominance. Women, slaves, and barbarians were unalterably different from him and inferior to him.'[4] This presumed superiority was propounded in a hierarchical understanding of both reproductive biology and household ordering.

The birth of a boy, for instance, indicated that a man had generated sufficient 'heat' and 'vital spirit' for a fully formed foetus to develop in the woman's womb. The birth of a girl, however, disclosed that an insufficient quantity of heat and vital spirit had been deposited in the womb, resulting in an underdeveloped foetus.[5] Not only was there pressure upon women to bear as many children as possible, but more importantly to produce healthy males. Although reproductive 'failures' could be corrected through infanticide or adoption, women nonetheless endured an unremitting anxiety to achieve both quantitative and qualitative reproduction goals.[6] Women played a crucial role in perpetuating both a man's lineage and the larger society, but they were viewed as inferior vessels for accomplishing such important tasks.

It should not be assumed, however, that men were spared the burdens and contradictions of offering their bodies as a public resource, albeit in a less demanding and demeaning manner. Men refusing to marry or failing to produce legitimate offspring were often subject to legal sanctions and public scorn. Although lifelong continence by an eccentric philosopher could be indulged, even

---

[3] The average age was slightly higher in some cities such as Sparta.

[4] Brown, *Body and Society*, 9.

[5] For overviews of ancient Roman and Greek understandings of human reproduction, ibid. 10–12, 17–21. See also Susan B. Pomeroy, *Families in Classical and Hellenistic Greece* (1997), 95–8.

[6] Although infanticide was permissible under both Greek and Roman law, the extent to which it was practised is unknown. Pomeroy contends that most Athenian families, for example, raised only one daughter (ibid. 73–4). Sparta, however, restricted infanticide to males, and few Spartan families had any surviving sons (ibid. 54–5).

he might be chided to perform his public duty to marry and leave a copy of himself for posterity. Yet the same heat and vital spirit needed to produce offspring were also the source of a man's physical strength, intellect, and emotional wellbeing. A balance had to be struck between the demands of producing progeny and performing other public duties, for there was a finite limit to the physical resources that could be expended. Consequently, some athletes contemplated castration as a competitive advantage, and men who spent too much time in brothels were thought to be womanly. Contrary to popular portrayals of pagan decadence, men (at least among the ruling classes) subjected their passion and bodies to rigorous self-control in fulfilling their myriad duties and responsibilities.[7]

The fate of the Graeco-Roman world, however, could not be assured through haphazard breeding. The procreation and education of children must be pursued in an orderly manner if the requisite quantitative and qualitative population goals were to be achieved. This responsibility fell squarely on the institutions of marriage and family. Arranged marriages were negotiated between heads of households, and desirable mates were selected both by their reproductive potential, and the size of the dowry they might fetch. Although the so-called nuclear family based on monogamous marriage had, by the second century, become the norm within the Roman Empire (at least among the privileged classes), an intimacy among its members characterized its modern, idealized counterpart cannot be presumed. Since a man in his late twenties was often wed to a girl in her early teens, her husband often treated her as both wife and daughter. Men were frequently absent from their homes for long periods of time, and in many Greek cities men dined exclusively outside the household with other men. Philosophers urged men to take the time to train their wives to be shrewd household managers so they could devote their own time to public affairs or intellectual pursuits.

Marriage provided the legal and social foundation of the Roman *familia* and Greek *oikos*. These terms can be translated as institutions

---

[7] See Brown, *Body and Society*, 17–25. This control, however, did not extend to the double standard of adultery in which wives were subjected to severe punishment for any infidelity, whereas husbands suffered no legal punishment sanctions as long as they confined their exploits to household slaves.

comprising a family, household, and estate, composed of people related by blood, marriage, or adoption, and holding property that included slaves. A typical *familia* or *oikos* consisted of a husband/ father/master, wife/mother, dependent children, one or more married sons with their wives and children, other kinfolk, and varying numbers of servants and slaves.[8] A household was also an institution of economic production, requiring adequate space for agriculture, manufacturing, and storage. Consequently, marriages were often arranged within loosely knit kin groups or among allied households, in order to maintain property control.[9]

A familial association extended beyond a particular *familia* or *oikos*. Individuals were related to larger networks of relatives, such as clans, and associations formed around common tasks or interests were often described in familial terms. In Athens, for example, a man's business or political associates might be regarded as brothers (a *phratry* or brotherhood), and the *polis* could be perceived as a 'family of men'.[10] More importantly, it was through the *familia* or *oikos* that individuals were inducted into the *polis* as citizens. Although rituals and customs for admitting children into households exhibited regional variation and change over time, the basic elements of this process included: (1) the head of a household accepting a child into his family; and (2) presenting his child publicly to a larger familial association such as his *phratry*. The *polis* was not a state composed of individual citizens, but more akin to a family of families, capturing Aristotle's adage that the family is the seed or foundation of the *polis*.[11] As Susan Pomeroy contends, 'as part of an effort to create a cohesive, loyal group of citizens, the *polis* usurped the terminology of the family in order to appropriate its affective relationships'.[12] By the second century, marriage and family took on an even more central role, representing the central social and political

---

[8] See Beryl Rawson, 'The Roman Family', in Rawson (ed.), *The Family in Ancient Rome* (1992), 8–15.

[9] Roman marital arrangements tended to be more exogamous than endogamous Greek practices.

[10] See Pomeroy, *Families*, 17–18; cf. Jean Bethke Elshtain, *Public Man, Private Woman* (1991), 19–54.

[11] See Aristotle, *Politics* 1. 2.   [12] Pomeroy, *Families*, 18.

virtue of *concordia*.[13] It was within well-ordered households that children learnt the requisite virtues enabling them to govern the *polis* in an equally orderly manner. As Brown has observed: 'By the beginning of the late antique period . . . the vast weight of Empire had ensured that the Roman ideal of marital concord had taken on a crystalline hardness: the married couple were presented less as a pair of equal lovers than as a reassuring microcosm of the social order.'[14]

Given this heavy burden, it is not surprising that the lines separating the family's private and public dimensions appear nearly incomprehensible to present-day eyes.[15] Although the lives of women and the relationship between masters and slaves were not routinely subjected to public scrutiny, the fact that households were units of economic production, models of social order, schools of political virtue, and the foundation of the *polis* rendered them as indispensable social institutions ensuring the survival of the *polis*. How could it be otherwise if the fate of civilization (and for a Roman to contemplate a world without Rome, for example, was to ponder an uncivilized future[16]) depended on an orderly marshalling of its superior reproductive capacity? How could men govern wisely and protect society against inferior barbarians if they could not first rule their own households? It is not too fanciful to suggest that well-ordered families were drawn naturally towards larger, public spheres of social and political association, at least for men of a superior caste.

The world of this idealized portrayal of marriage and family was haunted by the spectre of Sparta, or at least the counter-ideal it represented.[17] Sparta was not so much a family of families as it was *the family* writ large. The king was regarded as a common father, and natural fathers treated all children as if they were his own. Although Sparta also waged a constant war against death, its eugenic policies required that the *polis*, rather than the household, regulated reproduction. Consequently, there was little need for stable marriages. Married men, for instance, were free to select more promising

---

[13] See Brown, *Body and Society*, 16.   [14] Ibid. 16–17.

[15] See Hannah Arendt, *The Human Condition* (1998), 22–78, and Elshtain, *Public Man*, 11–16.

[16] See Charles Norris Cochrane, *Christianity and Classical Culture* (2003).

[17] The following summary draws extensively on Pomeroy's analysis (*Families*, 39–66).

women to bear their children. Moreover, 7-year-old boys left home to spend most of the remainder of their lives in military training and campaigns. The Spartan household thereby consisted primarily of women, daughters, young sons, and serfs (*helots*), and many families had no surviving sons because of frequent warfare.

Spartan social and political ordering presented two troubling implications. First, women controlled the *oikoi* due to the extended absence of their husbands. Women exerted a great deal of control over the wealth and economic transactions of households, and benefited from more egalitarian inheritance laws in contrast to their Athenian counterparts. Second, there was an implicit equality, at least at a functional level, that eroded the natural bonds of marriage and family. Spartan women, for example, were required to engage in competitive sports and tests of strength, because it was believed that two strong parents would produce healthier offspring. It was the qualitative outcome of reproduction, not marital and familial stability, that was the paramount concern. As Pomeroy suggests, in 'a system of aristocratic endogamy the haphazard selection of spouses is a symptom of equality. One spouse is as good as the next.'[18]

Aristotle denounced Sparta as a city dominated by women, and therefore contrary to nature.[19] There could be no more damning indictment of a polity than this failure to honour a natural hierarchy in its social and political ordering, especially at the foundational level of marriage and family. Moreover, the vehemence of his denunciation, echoed by later generations of philosophers, may help us to better understand why early Christianity, with its doctrine of equality in Christ and preference for continent singleness, was treated as a seditious movement.

NEW TESTAMENT THEMES

There is no systematic teaching on marriage and family in the New Testament, but some important themes are introduced which

---

[18] The following summary draws extensively on Pomeroy's analysis (Families, 60).
[19] See Aristotle, *Politics* 2. 9.

set a pattern for subsequent Christian thought. The initial development of these themes, however, must be placed in their formative Jewish context. Although aristocratic Jewish families also waged an unremitting war against death, unlike their Greek and Roman counterparts the most pressing objective was not to organize their bodies as a public resource. Rather, the goal was to order their lives under the sovereignty of God with a 'singleness of heart'.[20] Using modern terminology, the principal task was not to assert the primacy of the human will over anatomy, but to devote one's entire being to the dictates of God's will. Although women in general, and procreation and the responsibilities of parenthood in particular, might pose tempting distractions, familial solidarity, especially in terms of lineage and larger networks of kinship, reflected the special status of a covenanted people serving God with single-hearted devotion. In contrast to modern categories, they were the *people* (not a collection of autonomous individuals) of God.

Maintaining this distinctive solidarity proved highly challenging. A lengthy history of foreign occupation, resettlement, and colonization, punctuated by relatively brief periods of political independence or limited autonomy, was deeply imprinted upon the Jewish consciousness. By the time of Jesus and Paul, Jews were already spread widely throughout the Roman Empire. The task was to preserve an ethnic and religious identity in the midst of indifferent, and at times hostile, political regimes. For many, if not most, Jews the solution was to master social practices centring on the household and larger community. Marriage, parenthood, and the 'traditional norms of Jewish life' reinforced a patient expectation that God would restore Israel's fortunes through a deliverer or Messiah.[21] A more radical solution was to blame Israel's misfortune on its loss of piety, requiring a requisite practising of more demanding virtues in recovering a single-hearted devotion to God. Communities of single men and married couples practising sexual abstinence were formed to provide a foundation for austere, disciplined lives of ritual purity. It would be through such communities that Israel would be prepared for the approaching messianic age. It should be noted, however, that continent singleness was not promulgated as a superior, or even

[20] See Brown, *Body and Society*, 33–44.   [21] Ibid. 42–3.

equivalent, option to marriage and family. It marked a temporary, though necessary, response to a desperate set of circumstances, with the eventual goal of strengthening familial bonds with more robust religious convictions and practices.

Consequently, the tension between singleness and marriage that would underlie early Christian thought was already explicable within its earliest social and religious contexts. This tension can be seen if we examine selected New Testament themes, namely, the teachings of Jesus, Paul, and the household codes.

Jesus

The life, ministry, and teaching of Jesus, as recorded in the Gospels, seemingly weigh heavily against marriage and family. Jesus never married, preferring instead a life of continent singleness, and he pursued an itinerant ministry in which he had no place he called home. Many of his closest disciples left their homes and families to follow him, and he was often in the company of drifters and social outcasts unencumbered by familial ties. Jesus is portrayed as foretelling an approaching time of trouble in which individuals will be unable to fulfil their familial responsibilities, and members of families will turn against each other. Moreover, Jesus' teaching implies that familial bonds are irrelevant to God's impending reign. In answering his own rhetorical question, he proclaims: 'My mother and my brothers are those who hear the word of God and act upon it.'[22]

Does not the pattern of Jesus' life, ministry, and teaching suggest that marriage and family are impediments to be avoided in serving God with single-hearted devotion? His life offers a model of a man free to wander where he will in proclaiming the good news of God's kingdom. He attracts a following among those who have little at stake in maintaining a household or perpetuating a lineage, and his closest disciples have admitted to leaving everything for the sake of his message. With imminent calamity looming on the horizon, parents, siblings, spouses, and offspring are little more than sources

---

[22] Luke 8: 21; see also 8: 19–20. Cf. Matt. 12: 46–50, and Mark 3: 31–5.

of suffering and grief to be avoided. Most importantly, blood ties offer no advantage in hearing and acting upon God's word. Indeed, familial bonds present a barrier that must be overcome, for one must hate one's parents, spouse, children, and siblings before becoming a disciple.[23] Can we not conclude that Jesus simply dismisses the family as an institution with no role to play in the kingdom he has come to establish? Two factors must be taken into consideration, however, that militate against this conclusion.

First, it is not recorded that Jesus forbade marriage or condemned familial ties. Indeed, he commends marriage in prohibiting divorce, insisting that its one-flesh unity embodies a mutual and lifelong fidelity,[24] and his love of children conveys a blessing upon parents.[25] Marriage and family are not inherent barriers to loving God with all of one's heart, mind, and soul. What Jesus denounces is any partial loyalty preventing one from serving God with single-hearted devotion, and these partial loyalties may in some instances include an unwarranted attachment to a household or lineage. It is out from all such partial loyalties that Jesus is calling together the subjects of God's new, universal reign, and familial bonds are condemned only when they prevent, instead of permitting, this more expansive loyalty. It is those who do the Father's will that Jesus embraces as family. Blood ties do not convey any advantage in hearing and acting upon the word of God, but nor do they pose an inherent disadvantage —Mary and Jesus' brothers may also become his disciples. Admittedly, there is an inevitable tension between the temporal qualities of family life and bearing witness to the in-breaking of God's new kingdom, but the tension need not be debilitating.

Second, the portrayal of Jesus' life, ministry, and teaching takes on a particular edge due to the social and political contexts underlying the compilation of the synoptic gospels. Most New Testament scholars contend that Matthew, Mark, and Luke were compiled shortly after the Jewish revolt in 66–74, roughly forty years after Jesus' death. Rome crushed the revolt through a series of military campaigns, leading to mass executions, confiscation of property, and banishment for

---

[23] See Luke 14: 26.   [24] See Mark 10: 2–12; cf. Matt. 19: 3–12.
[25] See Matt. 19: 13–15, Mark 10: 13–16, and Luke 18: 16–18.

many Jews from Jerusalem.[26] Rome's brutal occupation policies, however, were not confined to Jerusalem. Military campaigns were also conducted in the Judean countryside to eliminate future opposition, resulting in the destruction of many villages, and the virtual disappearance of social and economic structures that had been relatively prosperous and stable. The rural population was displaced and stripped of its traditional means of providing its livelihood. Under these circumstances, it became increasingly difficult to maintain households that had been tied to the land for generations. Moreover, these desperate circumstances dictated that the ministry of the fledging church could only be conducted by itinerants who, unencumbered by such concerns as a family, could move easily among a population that was largely displaced, impoverished, and homeless.[27] This does not suggest that the editors of the synoptic gospels took the liberty of placing words in the mouth of Jesus in response to their immediate social and political context. Rather, the sayings of Jesus that had been preserved through oral tradition took on a greater urgency in the gospel accounts *because* of the circumstances faced by the audience. The teachings against the family are harsh only to an audience that has placed its hope and confidence in a social, economic, and political order derived from stable households. To an audience that cannot presume such stability, these same words are received as reassurance that their present state does not exclude them from God's new reign. Their lack of familial belonging is more than compensated by their fellowship in the church, for it is water and spirit, not flesh and blood, that will inherit God's kingdom. The dispossessed and homeless are reminded that their destiny is in Christ rather than the fate of their households and lineage.

Yet how is early Christian thought on the family developed when the context shifts from one that is predominantly rural, Jewish, and characterized by social and political instability, to one that is largely stable, urban, and gentile?

[26] See Richard A. Horsley (ed.), *Bandits, Prophets and Messiahs* (1999), 43–5, and James D. Newsome, *Greeks, Romans, Jews* (1992), 304–10.

[27] See Brown, *Body and Society*, 41–4, and Gerd Theissen, *Social Reality and the Early Christians* (1993), 33–93.

Paul

It should be kept in mind that Paul's letters predate the synoptic gospels by roughly two decades. Paul's immediate context was not the aftermath of the Jewish revolt, although he was probably aware of the underlying social and political tensions leading up to it. He was a highly educated Diaspora Jew born in Tarsus, fluent in Greek, and claimed to be a Roman citizen. Thus he was familiar with both a Jewish emphasis on single-hearted devotion to God, and the Graeco-Roman preoccupation with maintaining familial stability. Moreover, his claim to apostolic authority was not based on a faithful recalling of Jesus' sayings, but a direct encounter with the risen Lord, and his mission was not directed towards a largely rural, Jewish population, but to gentiles in such major cities as Corinth, Ephesus, Thessalonica, and Rome.

What is most striking about Paul's teaching on the family is his apparent indifference. He neither condemns nor commends marriage and parenthood. The reason for his ambivalence is his belief in Christ's imminent return. Marriage and family are part of an age that will soon come to an end. He counsels those who are single to remain single, and those who are married to remain married. This does not reflect a cavalier attitude on Paul's part. He is not suggesting that it doesn't matter whether one is single or married. Rather, he is guiding recent converts on how to live out their new lives in Christ within the practical constraints of their current circumstances. A Christian husband, for instance, should not leave his unbelieving wife but perform his spousal and paternal responsibilities in service to the Lord, and a single woman is no longer under any obligation to marry and procreate, but is free to devote her entire time and energy to the Lord's work. Christians may serve their Lord faithfully regardless of their particular situations or stations in life.

Paul's concern is simultaneously theological and practical. He had to explicate the doctrine of radical equality in Christ within social and political categories of his day. How could he account for the fact that, although Christ had removed the distinctions between Jew and Greek, slave and free, male and female, these divisions were nonetheless perpetuated by the current social and political order?

Paul's solution was to assert that equality in Christ did not necessarily remove functional differences that appeared to conform to the conventions of the present, but passing, age. Although equality in Christ displaced a hierarchy reflected in these 'natural' distinctions, the corresponding social roles were not obliterated in a present age not yet fully subject to God's new reign. Christians by necessity remained *in* a world that they were not *of*. This does not mean that Paul merely spiritualized radical equality in Christ, thereby stripping it of any real significance. To the contrary, Paul is keenly aware that the gospel he proclaims strikes at the very foundation of Roman social and political order, but he adopts a strategy of subversion over confrontation. Married Christians are to conduct themselves in outward conformity to the conventions of their neighbours, but their households are based on their equality in Christ rather than on temporal distinctions perpetuating familial concord in support of Rome's imperial power. This does not mean that Paul was counselling hypocrisy or duplicity. Rather, he had to take into account the practical consideration that the largely gentile households of his churches were under tremendous pressure to conform to prevailing social and political expectations. Attracting attention through what might be perceived as unconventional or dubious behaviour would risk scrutiny or even persecution that might jeopardize his mission to the gentiles, a mission that was heavily dependent on the patronage of a few influential households.

Yet despite Paul's scrupulous effort not to disparage marriage and family, there is nonetheless a thinly veiled preference for singleness that permeates his teaching. He wishes that all could be like him, while admitting that continence is a rare gift given to few, and his support of marriage is not based on any inherent value but as an expedient means of keeping lust at bay, forcing his concession that it is better to marry than to burn. To be married meant that one had not received the gift of a superior way of life, and could not, practically speaking, serve the Lord with an undivided heart. Paul's subtle preference and the example of his own life did not go unnoticed in the early church, leaving many converts (as well as subsequent generations of Christians) at a loss on what to make of their inferior lives. It is instructive to note Brown at some length in this regard:

The married person, whose heart was inevitably divided, was almost of necessity a 'half-Christian.' Ascetic readers of Paul in late antiquity did not mis-hear the tone of his voice. The apostolic gift of celibacy was too precious a thing to extend to the Church as a whole. Paul made that clear. But he had not been greatly concerned to defend marriage. He left the world of the married householder a long way behind, bobbing in the stormy wake of his own urgent call to live a life of 'undistracted' service before the coming of the Lord. Marriage... was a 'calling' devoid of glamor. It did not attract close attention as the present age slipped silently toward its end. The 'shortening of the time' itself would soon sweep it away.[28]

Yet time did not sweep marriage away, and despite Paul's preference the married householder became the mainstay of the church. The task of helping these households navigate Paul's stormy wake would be undertaken by other Christians.

Household codes

The so-called household codes of the New Testament reflect such a navigational aid.[29] A rapid proliferation of married converts, as well as Christians marrying and starting families, required instruction for governing households in ways that were acceptable to the Lord. The severe tension between marriage and singleness implied by Paul's life and teaching was lessened by depicting familial roles as ways of serving Christ, thereby giving marriage and parenthood an inherent value instead of tolerated as an encumbrance. The structure of the family outlined in these codes is nearly identical to that of a typical Graeco-Roman household, consisting of a series of relationships between husband and wife, father and child, master and slave. As James Dunn has observed, 'the patriarchal character of the times is clearly evident' in the man asserting his authority over his wife, children, and slaves.[30]

---

[28] Brown, *Body and Society*, 55–6.

[29] See Col. 3: 18–4: 1, Eph. 5: 22–6: 9, 1 Pet. 2: 18–3: 7, 1 Tim. 2: 8–15, 6: 1–2, and Titus 2: 1–10.

[30] See Dunn, 'The Household Rules in the New Testament', in Stephen C. Barton (ed.), *The Family in Theological Perspective* (1996), 48.

The striking qualification of these codes, however, is that, unlike the Greek and Roman models from which they are derived, they are directed to *both* the weaker and stronger members of each relationship 'as equally members of the assembled congregation'.[31] Why did congregational equality have a bearing on household ordering? Early Christian congregations were often associated with particular households, leading to inevitable overlap and confusion between ecclesial and familial relationships.

This overlapping space, both household and house church, of course, had already created the possibility of some dissonance and tension between the roles: what was 'fitting' and 'acceptable' within the 'neither male nor female' ethos of the house *church*, might be at odds with what was deemed 'fitting' and 'acceptable' within the house*hold.*[32]

Whereas Paul had blurred familial relationships in bearing witness to the in-breaking of God's eschatological kingdom, the household codes attempt to clarify them in a manner bearing witness to the temporal and providential dimension of this new reign. In this respect, Christian households resembled their traditional Graeco-Roman counterparts that contributed (male) citizens to the hierarchically based *ekklesia* (assembly) of the *polis*, but they were actually aligned to Christ's equality-based *ekklesia* (congregation) of God's eschatological reign.[33]

According to Dunn, the household codes separate and codify familial and ecclesial roles by emphasizing their complementary, rather than antagonistic, qualities. Instead of pulling believers in antithetical directions, the family and the church 'should feed into, reflect, and indeed enhance the other'.[34] A well-ordered family provided an evangelistic and apologetic witness. 'The fact that the Christians used similar household codes would thus indicate to their neighbours that they too shared the same concern for society and its good order.'[35] This shared concern was qualified by an overriding

[31] See Dunn, 'The Household Rules in the New Testament', in Stephen C. Barton (ed.), *The Family in Theological Perspective* (1996), 52.

[32] Ibid. 57 (emphasis original); cf. Stephen C. Barton, *Life Together* (2001), 17–36.

[33] See Richard A. Horsley, *Paul and Empire* (1997), 208–9.

[34] Dunn, 'Household Rules', 57.

[35] Ibid. Cf. Brown's contention that the household codes 'provided Christians with an image of unbreakable order that the pagan world could understand. In the church,

loyalty to Christ. Equality in Christ enabled Christian households to bear an explicable witness 'within the social constraints of the time' which were 'often inimical to the gospel'.[36] Although Christians lived in households resembling those of their pagan neighbours, they were ordered to a different *telos*, bearing witness to the destiny of God's kingdom instead of Caesar's empire. Rather than interpreting the household codes merely as a conservative reaction against the radical teachings of Jesus and Paul,[37] Oliver O'Donovan contends that their purpose is not to promote 'accommodation to current norms; it is to show how social situations are retrieved within the new context. The roles of household life are to be reconceived.'[38] And reconceived in ways stressing mutual responsibilities and a 'fundamental equality'.[39] Although a sharper line was drawn distinguishing the family and the church, there were nevertheless ecclesial images reflected in the household, while a glimpse of familial belonging could also be seen in the church. Moreover, the chief contribution of the household codes is that they afforded 'fixed points for a continuing Christian ethic'[40] that shaped the parameters of much subsequent Christian thought on the family, and in turn its significance for social and political ordering.

AUGUSTINE AND THE PATRISTIC LEGACY

Although throughout the patristic period[41] the 'silent majority' of Christians lived in families ordered along the lines set forth in the New Testament's household codes, there was little 'doubt that for most of the Fathers marriage and family life were definitely second best, preferably to be avoided, and certainly not the place for the

---

as in the city, the concord of a married couple was made to bear the heavy weight of expressing the ideal harmony of a whole society' (*Body and Society*, 57).

[36] Dunn, 'Household Rules', 63.

[37] See e.g. Browning *et al.*, *From Culture Wars to Common Ground* (1997), 141–9.

[38] Oliver O'Donovan, *The Desire of the Nations* (1996), 183–4.

[39] Ibid. 184.   [40] Dunn, 'Household Rules', 63.

[41] This section is comprised of a more extensive presentation of material that appeared in Waters, *Reproductive Technology* (2001), 61–5.

leaders, heroes and saints of the church'.[42] The degree to which the
early patristic writers exalted singleness, or conversely denigrated
marriage and family, reflected a great deal of regional variation. In
Rome, Hermas portrayed virginity as an ideal reflecting a pure heart
that resisted being seduced by worldly temptations. Yet he took it
for granted that the survival of the Roman church would depend on
the patronage of influential households, and he worried about
the worldly fortunes of his own family. Tertullian praised sexual
abstinence as a means of gaining spiritual clarity, but he presumed
it would be practised primarily by elderly widows and widowers or by
younger married couples for short periods of time. Similar to Rome,
the church at Carthage was a 'confederation of believing households,
in which married persons predominated'.[43] Along with Hermas,
Tertullian had no intention of challenging the social structure and
conventions these households supported. It was in the eastern, rural
regions of the Empire that the Encratites, influenced by the works of
Marcion and Tatian, required converts to renounce sexual intercourse (even if married), and to abandon unbelieving spouses or
family members. Marriage and family were the basis of a corrupt and
evil society that Christians should resist by withdrawing their bodies
as a public resource, freeing them to form celibate and more spiritual
communities.

Reacting against the Encratites, Clement of Alexandria provided an
extensive defence of marriage and family, commending marriage as a
means of exerting self-control in the 'begetting of children, and in
general behaviour',[44] exclaiming that a monogamous household is
'pleasing to the Lord'.[45] His affirmation of 'married Christian laity' as
the bulwark of both the church and civil community was prompted
by Stoic influences, as well as his reaction against radical attempts to
displace the leadership of 'well-to-do married householders who
protected and endowed the Christian community'.[46] Moreover,

[42] C. Harrison, 'The Silent Majority: The Family in Patristic Thought', in Stephen
C. Barton (ed.), *Family in Theological Perspective* (Edinburgh: T. & T. Clark, 1996),
87.

[43] Brown, *Body and Society*, 79.

[44] See Clement of Alexandria, *Miscellanies* 3. 46.   [45] Ibid. 3. 108.

[46] Brown, *Body and Society*, 137–8.

Clement believed that a well-ordered household reflected God's providential care for his creation.

Clement, however, would prove to be a minority voice, for following his death there was a pronounced shift in the patristic literature favouring continent singleness and virginity at the expense of marriage and family.[47] The desert fathers, for instance, believed that a single-hearted devotion to God could never be achieved unless the worldly distractions of running a household were cast aside. The desert, where one could live a solitary life devoted to God, was portrayed as the place where one fled to escape the world.[48] This effectively denigrated marriage and parenthood as less than praiseworthy ways of life in comparison to continent singleness, where one's time and energies could be devoted fully to the church. Gregory of Nyssa argued that marriage and family were institutions created out of a fear of death, and unworthy of Christians who placed their hope in the Lord of life. Virginity was the only sure road to heaven, because marriage is 'the fire of inevitable pain',[49] and children are doomed to suffer 'so the power of death cannot go on working, if marriage does not supply it with material and prepare victims for this executioner'.[50] Echoing similar themes, John Chrysostom dismissed the household as a doomed institution of a passing age. The human body and offspring were not public resources to be ordered for the common good, but liabilities in serving Christ in expectation of his return, and he envisioned Christian families which modelled the monastery rather than the household.[51]

Although much of the earlier patristic literature asserted the superiority of the single life, it assumed that it would be undertaken largely by older Christians, especially widows, who had raised families and no longer felt any compulsion to maintain a household. In the third century, however, lifelong virginity was portrayed as the ideal Christian life. The advantages of virginity were contrasted with the physical rigours of pregnancy, childbirth, and running a household,

---

[47] Ibid. 122–39; cf. Carolyn Osiek and David L. Balch, *Families in the New Testament World* (1997), 148–55.

[48] See Brown, *Body and Society*, 213–40.

[49] See Gregory of Nyssa, *On Virginity* 3. [50] Ibid. 13.

[51] See Brown, *Body and Society*, 305–22.

leading frequently to exhaustion, ill health, and premature death. Ambrose, for instance, admonished Christian parents to commend holy virginity to their daughters, reminding them that if they were willing to 'entrust their money to man' then how much more honourable it would be to loan their daughters to Christ who would reward them with 'manifold interest'.[52] Jerome would go so far as to assert that even in marriage sexual intercourse was intrinsically evil. In short, a social and political order based on marriage and family had become so corrupted in the fall that they were now virtually irredeemable, better to be abandoned than preserved.

These contrasting assessments of marriage and virginity were complicated by a number of ecclesiastical, political, and social factors. Established households were becoming the church's mainstay, raising generations of children within its fold. How could Christian moral teaching continue to malign this wellspring of the faith by praising a vocation disrupting familial stability? With Christianity emerging as the dominant religion, Christian households took on greater political significance. How was this new prominence to be reconciled with a preference for sexual renunciation? To what extent should Christians be encouraged to abandon ascetic practices for the sake of promoting social stability? The church was also besieged by various heresies, sharing a belief that the human body was evil or polluted, but holding disparate conclusions on whether this suggested sexual abstinence or indulgence. Yet how could the church teach authoritatively on sexual conduct if the body had little religious significance, as often implied by the church fathers? In short, the patristic literature had failed to explicate a normative relationship between marriage and singleness.

It was against this background that Augustine established *both* marriage and continent singleness as Christian vocations.[53] The task he undertook was not an easy one. On the one hand, he had to portray the intrinsic worth of marriage in a manner that did not challenge the superiority of sexual continence as set forth in Jesus' life and ministry, as well as Pauline and patristic teaching. On the other

---

[52] See Ambrose, *Concerning Virgins* 1. 64.
[53] See Augustine, *City of God* 14, *On the Good of Marriage*, *Of Holy Virginity*, *Of Continence*, and *On Marriage and Concupiscence*.

hand, he also had to affirm the supremacy of virginity in a way that did not deprecate marriage and family, while at the same time refuting heretical doctrines on sexual indulgence or renunciation.

The strategy Augustine employed marked a shift in emphasis on how marriage and singleness were related. Instead of contrasting them, to the detriment of the former, he compared them as lesser and greater goods. Both are praiseworthy vocations, but one denotes a higher, more difficult way of life than the other. Accordingly, Augustine argued that marriage is the lesser good because of its association with sexual intercourse and procreation that had become disfigured in the fall. Coitus, however, is not inherently evil, nor is procreation a consequence of original sin, for Adam and Eve had been created with bodies designed for producing offspring. Prior to the fall sexual intercourse had been subject to the will without the disruptive influence of lust; sexual organs were willed to perform their procreative functions undeterred by concupiscence. Moreover, because of their spiritual and physical harmony, Adam and Eve enjoyed a perfect delight and fellowship in their mutual and embodied presence. With the fall, the delight of sexual intercourse was corrupted into shame, reflecting the disordering of human life following in the wake of Adam's rebellion. The bodily means of procreation, which was intended to be subject to the will, was now out of control. The anarchy ensuing from the fall was especially pronounced in this loss of control, because sexual intercourse became corrupted by a divided will unable to master its desires and body.

Although marriage does not remove the shame associated with sexual intercourse, it does mitigate its disruptive influence by channelling lustful desire toward the goods that marriage enables. When a woman and a man are made one in marriage, they are accompanied by Christ's grace in encountering the necessities of an embodied existence distorted by sin. Augustine uses the example of a lame man to illustrate his argument.[54] A lame man attains a good by limping after it. Securing this good is not evil because the man's condition is evil, but nor is his disability good because he achieves a good end. Likewise, marriage, through the good of procreation, for instance, should not

---

[54] See Augustine, *On Marriage and Concupiscence* 1. 8.

be condemned because lust is evil, but nor is lust good because marriage 'effects some good out of evil'.[55] Rather, marriage 'permits a little
limping'[56] in respect to the lust and shame that accompanies sexual
intercourse. Augustine portrays marriage as a means of achieving good
despite evil, while acknowledging that shame cannot be removed in
pursuing this good, given the evil conditions of a fallen world. Sexual
limping enables a reordering of life, so the good of marriage may be
differentiated from ignominious lust.

Augustine's commendation of marriage is based on what has
become known as its three goods: *proles*, faith, and sacrament. Faith
channels lust in assisting a married couple to pursue the good of
propagation. A faithful couple help restore the rightful place of sexual
intercourse in God's created order. Marriage is not a license for
sexual pleasure, but a way of directing human love and anatomy
more in line with the kind of life God wills for his creatures. A chaste
wife and husband are following, albeit in a limping manner, their
creator and redeemer. Marital fidelity expresses charity (*caritas*) for
one's spouse, recognizing that lust is part of their fallen condition, but
chastening it to achieve a good end. The sacramental bond carries the
most weight, for Augustine does not argue for lifelong marriage
because it assists procreation and faith. Rather, its permanence is
intrinsically and independently good. It was the will, not marriage
and family, that was disfigured in the fall. A household based on
friendship and concord is still a bond of human association ordained
by God that in turn provides a solid and faithful foundation for social
and political ordering in anticipation of Christ's kingdom.

Since Augustine held marriage in relatively high esteem, why
did he continue to insist on the superiority of virginity? With the
incarnation, the providential value of procreation decreased while
the eschatological significance of singleness increased. Before the
birth of Jesus procreation was necessary to prepare the time when
the Word would be made flesh. After Jesus' birth this purpose was
eliminated, elevating virginity as a vocation bearing witness to
Christ's return. History is divided into the eras of marriage and

---

[55] See Augustine, *On Marriage and Concupiscence* 1. 8.

[56] Paul Ramsey, 'Human Sexuality in the History of Redemption', *Journal of Religious Ethics*, 16/1 (1988), 66.

continence, and Christians live in the latter, rather than former, age. Virginity's lofty status not only reflects the practical consideration that unmarried individuals may devote themselves single-mindedly to Christ, but more importantly it signifies the highest form of sanctity. Although marriage is good because it bears witness to God's providential love for creation, it nonetheless retains a compromised relationship with a fallen world. Continent singleness is greater because it provides an admittedly imperfect foretaste of life in Christ's new creation. It is one's second, rather than first, birth that is of greater importance.

To fully appreciate Augustine's argument, it is crucial to keep in mind that in contrasting marriage and singleness he is *not* comparing evil with good, but ordering the relationship between ordinary and extraordinary goods. Both are good but virginity is better, in the same way that a mountain is greater than a hill.[57] Marriage and singleness are both Christian vocations, but the former retains a close association with the children of Adam, while the latter enjoys a closer fellowship with the heavenly host of the new Adam. Augustine established a way of perceiving these two vocations as bearing a distinct, but complementary, witness to creation's redemption, vindication, and perfection in Christ. Marriage is naturally oriented to temporal concerns, so its goods afford an ordering of human life in accordance with God's created order. Singleness, however, serves as a reminder that creation's destiny transcends these temporal concerns as it is drawn toward its transformation in Christ. Augustine simultaneously affirmed marriage as a providential witness, while upholding singleness as an eschatological witness.

In addition to clarifying a normative relationship between marriage and singleness, Augustine provided a context for discerning the theological significance of these mutually exclusive vocations. He argued that only sin, not grace, is transmitted from parents to offspring; all humans carry Adam's sin in their bodies.[58] In procreation, children are given the 'carnal birth, of their parents, but cannot receive their spiritual rebirth'.[59] What is born of the flesh is a child of the world, and a

---

[57] See Augustine, *Of Holy Virginity* 18.
[58] See Augustine, *On Marriage and Concupiscence* 1. 7.
[59] Ibid. 1. 37.

child of God is only born through baptism. This is why godly parents may give birth to unregenerate offspring, and why the children of notorious sinners may be among the elect.[60] The only hope for healing one's sin is through baptism in Christ's resurrection, for it is not flesh or blood but water and the Spirit that will inherit the kingdom of God.[61] Hope lay solely in God's grace, and not in the progressive perfection of the human body through generations of Christian offspring.[62] More tersely, there is no salvation through procreation.

Augustine was refuting a notion that was evidently prevalent enough to spark his ire, namely, that if Adam's original sin was transmitted from parent to child, then so too was Christ's grace transferred among the elect. The elect carried in their bodies something akin to a 'godly seed' that was passed on to offspring. Yet this implied that humans could engineer their grace over time through the progressive breeding of the most spiritually fit. The fruition of God's kingdom would be, after all, a matter of flesh and blood. Through this original infusion and subsequent transmission of grace across generations, humans could eventually achieve their own perfection.[63] Moreover, this implied that humankind was the architect of its own destiny.

The most obvious way of constructing this destiny was through offspring, so children embodied practical objects of hope. Rome was a splendid example, for the Empire could only perpetuate, and perhaps eventually perfect, itself through its children. Augustus, for instance, enacted laws penalizing childless couples or men who did not marry by a certain age, while rewarding married couples producing at least five legitimate children. Additional legislation discouraged, and in some cases, prohibited marriage among individuals of differing social strata in the belief this would help preserve, if not improve, the physical and mental vigour of the aristocracy.[64]

According to Augustine, however, it is God alone who determines human destiny. Since the kingdom of God will displace all earthly empires, children can never be proper objects of hope because they

---

[60] See Augustine, *On Marriage and Concupiscence* 1. 21.

[61] Ibid. 1. 38.   [62] Ibid. 1. 20.

[63] See John Passmore, *The Perfectibility of Man* (1970), 94–115.

[64] See Eva Maria Lassen, 'The Roman Family: Ideal and Metaphor', in Halvor Moxnes (ed.), *Constructing Early Christian Families* (1997), 103–20; see also Rawson, *Family in Ancient Rome*.

merely magnify the futility of the passing age. Since Christians are subjects of a heavenly, rather than earthly, realm, they have little interest in helping temporal regimes achieve their quantitative and qualitative population objectives. This is one reason why early Christians relativized the need for procreation, for since in Christ *the* child sealing the world's destiny had already been born, there was no urgency to produce any more offspring.[65] If God is the true object of hope, as Augustine contended, then grace is a divine gift given to every generation instead of a possession imparted from one to the next.

Augustine is a pivotal figure in this inquiry, for he sets the deliberative parameters on the moral ordering of marriage and family, and in turn their foundational roles in subsequent Christian social and political thought. Although marriage and singleness emphasize different ways of ordering human life, together they bear witness to the common origin and destiny of creation's temporal ordering. These two ways of life need each other in offering a complete witness to both the providential and eschatological dimensions of God's creation. Hence, the need for maintaining their distinctive qualities and mutually exclusive virtues and practices.

Medieval themes

Subsequent generations of theologians refined and elaborated an essentially Augustinian framework of marriage and family. The works of Gratian, Hugh of St Victor, Peter Lombard, and Thomas Aquinas in particular offered more systematic theological and legal accounts.[66] Although there were severe disputes over specific issues, such as what constituted a lawful marriage, a consensus emerged regarding three basic characteristics.

1. Marriage is a natural association subject to the laws of nature. God created Adam and Eve with a natural and mutual inclination to form a familial association. Although this proclivity was distorted

[65] See Augustine, *On Marriage and Concupiscence* 1. 14; see also Ramsey, 'Human Sexuality', 56–86.

[66] See e.g. Gratian, *The Treatise on Laws*, Hugh of St Victor, *On the Sacraments of the Christian Faith* (part 11), and Thomas Aquinas, *Summa Theologica*, Part III (supplement), qq. xli–lxviii.

in the fall, humans were still under a divine mandate to be fruitful and multiply. The purpose of sexual intercourse, therefore, was procreation rather than pleasure. Consequently, adultery and fornication were forbidden, and the medieval church condemned contraception, abortion, and infanticide.

2. Marriage is a consensual contract subject to civil law. Since stable households promote the peace and common good of civil society, marriage should be a publicly sanctioned and regulated institution. Most theologians eventually argued against the validity of clandestine unions, insisting that vows be exchanged in a public setting or ceremony, preferably presided over by a priest. A valid marriage also required the mutual and uncoerced consent of the contracting parties. In addition, a number of impediments to marriage, such as monastic vows, consanguinity, affinity, and physical or psychological disability were identified and explicated, often in painstaking detail.[67]

3. Marriage is a sacrament subject to spiritual laws. Although marriage was still portrayed as a means of channelling the lust associated with sexual intercourse towards the good of offspring, friendship between spouses and a parental desire for children received greater, as well as more positive, attention. The marital bond was not merely an antidote to concupiscence, but was also a means of receiving grace, thereby emphasizing the sacramental quality more heavily. The shift in emphasis was subtle but decisive, for a couple's one-flesh unity embodied Christ's fidelity to the church. Augustine, for instance, had called marriage a sacrament to 'demonstrate its stability'; thirteenth-century theologians used the same designation to express the 'spiritual efficacy' of marriage.[68] This shift in emphasis ensconced the indissolubility of marriage. The spiritual bond between wife and husband could no more be broken than could the relationship between Christ and the church. Whereas previous generations of Christians believed that a marriage *should* not be dissolved, it was now asserted that a valid marriage *could* not be broken. Consequently, an important distinction was made between

---

[67] See e.g. Aquinas, *Summa Theologica*, Part III (supplement), qq. xli–lxviii.
[68] See John Witte, *From Sacrament to Contract* (1997), 29–30.

annulment and divorce. An annulment declared that a marriage was invalid because a genuine spiritual bond had never been formed, and the innocent party was free to marry. A divorce, however, involved a separation in which 'bed and board' was no longer taken together.[69] Although a couple's physical bond was broken, their spiritual bond remained intact, and neither spouse was free to remarry until one of them died.

As the church gained jurisdiction over marriage, many of these principles derived from the laws of nature, civil law, and a sacramental understanding of the marital bond were incorporated into canon law. The Council of Trent may serve as a convenient signpost marking a 'systematic distillation' of 'biblical, patristic, and medieval' themes on marriage and family.[70] Echoing a distinctly Augustinian accent, the purposes of marriage were defined as companionship, a remedy for lust, and a desire to raise children in faith and service to God. A faithful marriage enjoyed the blessings of offspring, fidelity, and sacrament. Admittedly, this cursory overview of the medieval refinement of an inherited Augustinian framework does not capture the rich and complex fabric of the principal theological and legal arguments. Given the restricted scope of this book, however, two salient observations can be made.

First, the church's growing control over marriage coincided with social and economic changes that transformed the family. Centres of production and economic exchange shifted from large manorial households dependent upon the labour of peasants to smaller conjugally based families among the growing classes of artisans and tradesmen. The relative mobility afforded by these new economic opportunities also contributed to changes regarding the primary sources of familial identity. Lineage and extended kinship were largely displaced by a more restricted, three-generational nexus of spouse, parents, offspring, and siblings as the principal factors defining a family. This trend was exacerbated by the devastation wrought by periodic outbreaks of plague that not only created a labour shortage, but also wiped out entire family lines. It is not surprising, then, that

---

[69] The offending party may also be required to pay alimony and child support.
[70] Ibid. 36–41.

marriage came to be regarded more as a contract between two consenting parties than as an alliance or economic exchange between two families. Aristocratic households resisted this trend, presumably to keep property and other financial resources within a family line. Thus aristocratic families tended to maintain what may be described as stem-based associations, whereas peasant, and later artisan, families were conjugally based. Whether the size and structure of these latter households reflect the preferences of their members, or mark pragmatic responses to social and economic circumstances preventing them from establishing stem-based families, is difficult to determine. What is important to note is that canon law, particularly in respect to the impediment of consanguinity and prohibition of divorce, often militated against aristocratic interests. Moreover, many women gained a limited degree of economic security through corresponding changes in civil law, granting them greater inheritance and commercial rights.

It should not be assumed, however, that the medieval church was simply granting greater freedom to individuals to choose their mates and form their families. Rather, canon law governing marriage embodied exogamous principles that bore distinct implications for social and political ordering. The peace and concord of civil society is promoted through marital and familial bonds formed among previously unaffiliated individuals and communities. Thus the family is drawn outward towards larger spheres of human association rather than pulled inward toward a narrow network of kin-based affiliations and alliances. This orientation encourages a wide range of social interactions and economic relationships expressed through a variety of institutions comprising civil society, while discouraging a defensive posturing by a few large, extended families to preserve their socio-economic dominance. Marriage and family are thereby affirmed as the basic components of social and political ordering, but unlike prior pagan accounts emphasizing the *familia* and *oikos* as the fundamental constituent elements of society, marital and familial bonds are the seedbed that nourishes the unfolding life of a society.[71]

Second, the tension between marriage and singleness bequeathed by previous generations of Christians was not so much resolved

---

[71] See e.g. Augustine, *City of God* 15. 16.

by medieval theologians as it was manifested in new institutional settings. Although regard for the family had been strengthened, particularly as reflected in the heightened sacramental status of marriage, singleness remained the superior vocation, especially for church leaders. Married priests elevated to the episcopacy, for instance, were expected to treat their wives as sisters. Moreover, the establishment of monastic orders provided an imposing institutional network that played a significant role in both church and state. The monastery emerged as the principal reservoir replenishing the church's hierarchy, governmental bureaucracies, and university faculties. The single way of life became itself a significant factor in the affairs of civil society, assuming temporal roles previously restricted to married heads of households. Consequently, the urgency of its eschatological witness was blunted, for singleness was now counterposed to a social and political order that was, at least ostensibly, Christian. Where once monks fled to the desert to bear witness against cities hostile to the faith, the monastery now often stood at the centre of new towns and villages, serving as a magnet for trade and commerce. Monastic orders also became increasingly the beneficiaries of large bequests of land, thereby becoming competitors with aristocratic families over manorial control of rural areas.

Nowhere was the power of this new role more vividly displayed than in the fact that the monastery had come to control the fabric of the medieval family. A cadre of single men provided a theological understanding of marriage that was codified in canon law and placed under the church's exclusive jurisdiction. So comfortable had the relationship between the once highly disparate ways of marriage and singleness presumably become that, with little apparent irony, Mary could simultaneously be upheld as the ideal virgin and with Joseph as the ideal parents and married couple. What differentiated marriage and singleness was no longer differing witnesses, for both pointed, albeit in different modes, toward a common destiny in Christ. Rather, singleness afforded the opportunity to serve God with a pure and single-hearted devotion that could not be achieved within the confines of marriage and family. Freed from the distractions of running a household, celibates could devote their time to ordering (or more likely explicating the theological and philosophical principles underlying the social and political structures of this ordering) the affairs of church, state, and civil society. In short, men with no stake in procreation or private wealth could attain the necessary distance to govern a Christian society in a faithful and disinterested manner. This does not suggest that this governance was free of corruption, or reflected unanimity in how it should be pursued. A more active role in temporal ordering entailed inevitable compromise. Even the requirement for priestly celibacy, for instance, was not enforced uniformly until the Council of Trent. Ironically, the same council that marks the apex of this medieval relationship between marriage and singleness was convened at the very time this synthesis was facing its severest challenge.

Reformation and Puritan themes

While the Council deliberated in Trent, marriage and family were already undergoing extensive reform throughout much of northern Europe. The Reformers produced a voluminous literature on marriage because the Catholic Church's jurisdiction exemplified, they believed, a particularly egregious usurpation of political authority, lodged properly in the secular, rather than ecclesial, sphere. In short, the social ordering of the earthly household was more the concern of the civil magistrate than the priest or minister. The more salient features of this Protestant claim can be seen by examining briefly the legal and social reforms inspired by Martin Luther and John Calvin.[72]

Lutheran reforms

According to Luther, marriage is both a duty and a remedy for sin.[73] As John Witte has observed: 'The duty of marriage stems from God's

[72] The following summary is indebted to Witte's discussion in *From Sacrament to Contract*, 42–129. See also his account of marriage as commonwealth in the Anglican tradition, ibid. 130–93.

[73] Luther's principal works on marriage and family include: 'A Sermon on the Estate of Marriage' (Luther's *Works*, xliv. 7–14), 'The Persons Related by Consanguinity and Affinity who are Forbidden to Marry According to the Scriptures,

command that man and woman unite, beget children, and raise them as God's servants. The remedy of marriage is a gift that God provides to allay the sexual lust and incontinence born of the fall into sin.'[74] Consequently, all persons have a presumptive obligation to marry, both for the sake of their own welfare and the good of society. The chief theological claim underlying this duty is that marriage is an order of God's creation, providing the basis of the family as one of the principal institutions or estates, alongside church and state, comprising civil society. The household is thereby a prerequisite for all other forms of human association. It must be emphasized, however, that for Luther marriage and family are not created by civil society or the church, but have an inherent integrity ordained by God which both church and state must respect, protect, and promote.

Luther's theological account of marriage as social estate, however, entailed a rejection of its sacramental status, and repudiation of singleness as a superior vocation. Since marriage is an order of creation it cannot be a sacrament. Invoking the imagery of two kingdoms, Luther confined marriage and family to the earthly or natural order of creation, denying that they played any redemptive role within the spiritual kingdom. Although marriage is ultimately subject to God's authority as creator, it is properly mediated through civil, rather than canon, law. Moreover, singleness is not a superior vocation, because parenthood is a gift bestowed by God, of equal or greater value than the rare gift of continence. There is no biblical or theological warrant for making celibacy a requirement for the church's ministry, and given the priesthood of all believers, married heads of households are equally competent to oversee the affairs of both church and state. Luther's denunciation is so scathing that

---

Leviticus 18' (xlv. 7–9), 'The Estate of Marriage' (xlv. 17–49), 'That Parents Should Neither Compel nor Hinder the Marriage of their Children and That Children Should Not Become Engaged Without Their Parents' Consent' (xlv. 385–93), 'A Sermon on Keeping Children in School' (xlv. 213–58), and 'On Marriage Matters' (xlv. 265–320). See also Paul Althaus, *The Ethics of Martin Luther* (1972), 83–100. For Luther's critique of monasticism and singleness, see 'The Judgment of Martin Luther on Monastic Vows' (*Works*, xliv. 251–400), and 'An Answer to Several Questions on Monastic Vows' (xlvi. 145–54).

[74] Witte, *From Sacrament to Contract*, 49.

he implies that singleness (except for minors, elderly widows and widowers, and rare cases of disability) is inherently unnatural and antisocial.[75] The subsequent closing of monasteries effectively dismantled the pervasive economic and political influence of monastic orders within Protestant territories.

Luther's teaching also necessitated a shift in jurisdiction over marriage from the church to the magistrate. This move resulted in more attenuated categories of impediments to marriage in civil law. Although Luther urged that only those impediments specifically sanctioned by scripture should be enforced, his wishes were largely ignored. Rather, legal reforms tended to define the limits of consanguinity less restrictively, but many of the physical and personal impediments promulgated in canon law were maintained. In addition, legal impediments protecting consent were often strengthened, while spiritual impediments were discarded altogether.[76] The most liberal reforms, however, involved divorce and remarriage. Divorce now marked the dissolution of a marriage, instead of separating a couple sharing 'bed and board'. Divorced individuals were usually permitted to remarry, and the causes for divorce were expanded beyond the biblical ground of adultery. The rationale for this more lenient view was partly pragmatic and partly theological. On the one hand, although lifelong marriage remained the ideal to be upheld by church and state, the sinful citizens of a fallen world often failed to obey the moral law. To preserve the peace of civil society, divorce and remarriage must be permitted in order to prevent even more grievous behaviour and misconduct. On the other hand, divorce was permissible because it had been instituted by Moses and affirmed by Christ, and God had revealed throughout history an expanded range of causes beyond adultery.[77] Although the church exerted less oversight, ministers were expected to provide the magistrate with spiritual advice and counsel in enacting, interpreting, and enforcing civil laws governing marriage and family.

---

[75] See Luther, 'The Judgment of Martin Luther on Monastic Vows'.
[76] For a summary of these reforms, see Witte, *From Sacrament to Contract*, 61–5.
[77] For an overview of early Lutheran reforms on divorce and remarriage, see ibid. 65–70.

Calvinist reforms

Whereas Luther had grounded marriage and family as natural institutions, Calvin emphasized covenant as its chief foundational feature.[78] The covenant between God and the elect provided a model for derivative covenants among various forms of human association. Marriage was not a private contract between two individuals, but a public and integral component of the overlapping covenants comprising civil society. The extent of this visible role can be seen in Calvin's portrayal of the roles that various parties must play in forming a marital covenant. In addition to the couple, parents, peers (witnesses), the minister, and magistrate must all be present to form a valid marriage. Moreover, these parties did not perform cursory roles in a wedding ceremony, but, in Witte's words, 'represented different dimensions of God's involvement in the marriage covenant, and they were thus essential to the legitimacy of the marriage itself. To omit any such party in the formation of the marriage was, in effect, to omit God from the marriage covenant.'[79] These social strands reinforced divine and natural laws that enabled a married couple to accomplish the threefold purpose of marriage, namely, mutual love and support, the procreation and rearing of children, and protection from sin. A more extensive list of impediments to marriage was maintained under Reformed, as opposed to Lutheran, regimes, especially in cases of physical impairment or defect. Although there was a strong presumption regarding the permanent nature of the marital covenant as taught in scripture, annulment and divorce were permitted. Annulments were granted if impediments had unknowingly or unwittingly been violated. Divorce was limited to cases of adultery or abandonment, with the prolonged absence of the offending spouse being virtually defined as presumed adultery.

Even though the marital covenant was formally under the jurisdiction of civil law, the church played an active role in its formulation and enforcement. The church could investigate and admonish quarrelsome or separated couples, and bans on participating in the Lord's Supper or excommunication were often assigned in conjunction

[78] There is a pronounced shift in emphasis in Calvin's mature understanding of marriage and family as reflected in a variety of biblical commentaries, sermons, and correspondence; ibid. 94.

[79] Ibid. 95–6.

with criminal or civil penalties in cases involving violations of marital statutes. Moreover, Geneva's consistory under Calvin heard an extensive range of cases involving disputed betrothals and marriages, sexual offences, and annulment and divorce pleadings. Its verdicts or rulings were routinely accepted and enforced by the magistrate.[80]

Although Calvin's covenantal foundation for marriage and family suggests some important themes for Christian social and political thought, his untimely death prevented him from developing these implications in a systematic manner. This task was undertaken by subsequent generations of Reformed theologians, particularly the Puritans. The Puritans produced an extensive and detailed literature on the family which drew heavily upon, while also refining, Calvin's work. We may catch the gist of these accounts by focusing on the work of a representative theologian.

Richard Baxter

An exemplary piece of Puritan literature on the family is Richard Baxter's *A Christian Directory*. According to Baxter, three principal traits characterize the family:

1. It is a *society* that belongs to God who is the 'Owner and Ruler' of families 'upon his title of creation' and 'by his right of redemption'.[81]

2. The family is an *instrument* used by God to govern the world, because 'he is not only Lord and Ruler of persons, but families; all societies being his'.[82]

3. A Christian household is a *community* sanctified by God to achieve 'the public and universal good which he has ordained'.[83] With God as its head, the family is ordered as a community of saints within a 'baptismal covenant'.[84] The structure of this covenanted community entails three sets of relationships, as set forth in the New Testament, between husband and wife, parents and children,

---

[80] There is a pronounced shift in emphasis in Calvin's mature understanding of marriage and family as reflected in a variety of biblical commentaries, sermons, and correspondence; ibid. 113–26.

[81] Richard Baxter, *A Christian Directory*, part 2 (1830), 56.

[82] Ibid. 57.   [83] Ibid. 55.   [84] Ibid. 60.

and master and servants. The man exercises his authority as household 'governor', reflecting Christ's love at the core of an orderly, and therefore limited, sovereignty in the family sphere.[85]

It is worth quoting Baxter at length regarding the proper assertion of this authority:

Your authority over your wife, is but such as is necessary to the order of your family, the safe and prudent management of your affairs, and your comfortable cohabitation. The power of love and complicated interest must do more than magisterial commands. Your authority over your children is much greater; but yet only such as conjunct with love, is needful to their good education and felicity. Your authority over your servants is to be measured by your contract with them (in these countries where there are no slaves) in order to your service, and the honour of God.[86]

Since all authority is granted by God, household governance also promotes obedience to divine law and the common good; a 'well-governed family' is the bedrock of a properly ordered church and commonwealth.[87]

Baxter describes familial roles and duties in meticulous detail. Husbands and wives are to share an 'entire conjugal love',[88] for they are 'as one flesh',[89] and 'must take delight in the love, and company, and converse of the other'.[90] Because of their union they have a mutual obligation to tend to each other's physical and spiritual health, a shared responsibility to govern their household, and a duty 'to help each other in works of charity and hospitality'.[91] Furthermore, marriage is a covenant ordained by God in which men and women are joined in the totality of their being.[92] It is only within this covenant that procreation should be pursued, and parents assume a grave

---

[85] Ibid. 90.   [86] Ibid. 91.

[87] Ibid. 96–105, on the 'Special Motives to persuade Men to the holy Governing of their Families'. Baxter also asserts that 'the holy government of families, is a considerable part of God's own government' (197). He allows, however, an element of self-interest: 'Be a good husband to your wife, and a good father to your children, and a good master to your servants, and let love have dominion in all your government, that your inferiors may easily find, that it is in their interest to obey you. For interest and self-love are the natural rulers of the world' (94).

[88] Ibid. 117.   [89] Ibid. 133.   [90] Ibid. 122.   [91] Ibid. 136–9.

[92] Baxter counsels realism regarding expectations spouses should have of each other: 'Resolve . . . to bear with one another as sinful, frail, and imperfect persons, and not as angels, or as blameless and perfect'; ibid. 125.

responsibility. Parental love is exhibited by instilling in children holiness 'as the most amicable and desirable life', directing them toward a worthwhile calling that has 'public usefulness for church or state'.[93] This is the most demanding duty, for children 'bear the image and nature' of their parents, and are born as rebellious sinners who must be disciplined and brought to a knowledge of Christ.[94] In return, Baxter admonishes children that since 'nature hath made you unfit to govern yourselves, so God hath mercifully provided governors for you'.[95] In return, children must obey their parents, treating them with gratitude, patience, and respect, reminding them that 'your parents have many faults themselves, yet you must love them as your parents still'.[96]

Baxter also wrote at length regarding the relationship between master and servant. According to Edmund S. Morgan, a servant in the seventeenth century 'meant anyone who worked for another in whatever capacity, in industry, commerce, or agriculture, as well as in what we now call domestic economy'.[97] Servants included individuals paid a wage, indentured or covenanted persons paying off a debt, and prisoners or prisoners of war. In addition, servants were regarded as members of the household, and masters were responsible for their welfare and overseeing their conduct.[98] Baxter instructs masters that servants are 'brethren and fellow-servants' who must be treated with 'tenderness and love', commanding 'nothing that is against the laws of God, or the good of their souls'.[99] Masters are obligated to pay servants

---

[93] Baxter counsels realism regarding expectations spouses should have of each other: 'Resolve ... to bear with one another as sinful, frail, and imperfect persons, and not as angels, or as blameless and perfect', 175–90.

[94] Ibid. 118. Baxter's admonition is sobering: 'Understand and lament the corrupted and miserable state of your children, which they have derived from you, and thankfully accept the offers of a Saviour for yourselves and them, and absolutely resign, and dedicate them to God in Christ in sacred covenant by their baptism. And to this end understand the command of God for entering your children solemnly into covenant with him, and the covenant mercies to them thereupon' (ibid. 175–6).

[95] Ibid. 192.   [96] Ibid. 191.

[97] Edmund S. Morgan, *The Puritan Family* (1980), 109.

[98] Morgan adds that servitude 'was not simply a device by which one class of men got work out of another class. It was also a school, where vocational training was combined with discipline in good manners and guidance in religion, a school of which all servants were the pupils and to which many respectable and godly men sent their children' (ibid. 132).

[99] Baxter, *Christian Directory*, 209.

a just wage, provide adequate food and shelter, and not assign any tasks that are beyond their ability to perform or which endanger their health or salvation. Servants are enjoined to obey their masters, performing their duties to the best of their abilities, and do their work to the glory of God. Servants in turn should choose their masters wisely, attaching themselves to pious households, and avoid fellow-servants who gossip or habitually complain.

There are three pertinent observations regarding Baxter's account of the family: first, the family does not exist to serve the self-interests of its individual members. A properly governed household bears witness to a *social order based on mutual and sacrificial love.* This is a central element in Baxter's argument, and it is again worth quoting him at length:

It is the pernicious subversion of all societies, and so of the world, that selfish, ungodly persons enter into all relations with a desire to serve themselves there and fish out all that gratifieth the flesh, but without any sense of the *duty of their relation.* They bethink them what honour, or profit or pleasure their relation will afford them, but not what *God or man require or expect from them.* All their thought is, what they shall have, but not what *they shall be, and do.*[100]

The family is naturally oriented towards pulling its members out beyond their respective self-interests, thereby equipping them to *embrace larger spheres of human association.* Spouses assist each other in charitable works and hospitality, children are prepared for useful vocations, servants and masters treat each other fairly for the sake of the household and civil society. Baxter, however, is not asserting an Aristotelian argument that the family is the foundation of the *polis.* Rather, he is explicating the family as a providential witness that also intimates an eschatological fellowship. Husbands and wives, parents and children, masters and servants, are also sisters and brothers in Christ.

Second, a family should be an *open and outward-looking community.* Beginning with marriage, the familial covenant envelopes a growing circle of children and servants, prefiguring their oneness in Christ. If there is an element of self-interest in performing one's familial roles, it is integrally linked to one's ultimate fulfilment in

---

[100] Ibid. 116–17 (emphasis added).

and fellowship with Christ. Consequently, the family points beyond itself to a time when, in O'Donovan's words: 'Humanity in the presence of God will know a community in which the fidelity of love which marriage makes possible will be extended beyond the limits of marriage.'[101]

Third, the family *resists turning in upon itself.* This is seen in the extensive attention Baxter devotes to household servants. They are not merely auxiliaries advancing a family's economic interests, but play a normative role in domestic governance. A household does not exist solely in terms of a shared or common bloodline, but includes fellowship with strangers. Moderns may object that contemporary economic structures render such a model untenable, yet it nonetheless suggests that a family is incomplete if insulated from larger social networks. It would be inconceivable to Baxter to write a *Christian Directory* on the family based exclusively on spouses, parents, and children, for the family is not ordained by God to provide a secluded enclave from the world, but to be a sign of the world's ordering toward its destiny of universal fellowship in Christ.

Although Baxter retains a tension between the family's providential witness and the eschatological end it intimates, he fails to clarify what role the church plays in accomplishing this task. On the one hand, he contends: 'Family teaching must give way to ministerial teaching, as families are subordinate to churches.'[102] On the other hand, he asserts that 'a Christian family is a church', but qualifies the assertion by claiming that it is not the family *per se*, but the worship and fellowship of its members that makes it a church.[103] What Baxter apparently had in mind is a relationship between the church and the family not unlike that found in the household codes of the New Testament. The providential roles of spouse, parent, child, master,

---

[101] Oliver O'Donovan, *Resurrection and Moral Order* (1986), 70.

[102] Baxter, *Christian Directory*, 63.

[103] 'All churches ought to pray to God and praise him: a Christian family is a church: therefore &c. The major is past doubt, the minor I prove from the nature of a church in general, which is a society of Christians combined for the better worshipping and serving of God. I say not that a family, formally as a family, is a church; but every family of Christians ought moreover, by such a combination to be a church: yea as Christians they are so combined, seeing Christianity teeth them to serve God conjunctly together in their relations' (ibid. 75). He proceeds to criticize 'Beza, Grotius, and many others acknowledging it to be meant of a family or domestic

and servant are subordinate to the eschatological roles of sisters and brothers in Christ. Yet, unlike the New Testament model, the emphasis is almost entirely providential, because Baxter neither assumes nor assigns any vocational significance to singleness. The institutions of family, church, and state provide the only channels for following one's calling.[104] A single person is simply someone who is currently not married. Both the family and the church had to simultaneously bear a providential *and* eschatological witness, resulting in the family reflecting strong images of ecclesial fellowship, while the church took on a striking familial character.

The lack of a clear line separating the family and the church created a peculiar difficulty in respect to procreation. Since all children share a 'natural corruption',[105] they are born as sinners, saved only by God's mercy and grace. Saints are not born but are adopted by Christ into his household, so that procreation has no redemptive significance.[106] Baxter, however, blunts his argument by asserting: 'A holy and well-governed family, doth tend to make a holy posterity, and so to propagate the fear of God from generation to generation.'[107] Children of 'godly seed'[108] seemingly do not suffer as extensively the effects of original sin as those begotten by 'ungodly parents'.[109] In short, the offspring of saints are more likely to be among the elect. This appeal

church, according to Tertullian, "ubi tres licet laici ibi Ecclesia," yet I say not that such a family-church is of the same species with a particular organized church of many families. But it could not (so much as analogically) be called a church if they might not and must not pray together, and praise God together; for these therefore it fully concludeth' (ibid. 75–6).

[104] It is important to note that church and state are comprised of households rather than individual believers or citizens: e.g. in colonial Massachusetts and Connecticut single persons were, by statute, assigned to established households (see Morgan, *Puritan Family,* 144–6).

[105] Baxter, *Christian Directory,* 90.

[106] Thus Baxter's emphasis on a parental duty to instruct children in a saving knowledge of their election: 'Consider how great power the education of children hath upon all their following lives; except nature and grace, there is nothing usually doth prevail so much with them' (ibid. 109). Moreover, the benefits of parental instruction are 'undeniable', for 'God appointeth parents diligently to teach their children the doctrine of his holy Word, before they come to public ministry: parents' teaching is the first teaching: and parents' teaching is for this end, as well as public teaching, even to beget faith and love, and holiness: and God appointeth no means to be used by us, on which we may not expect his blessing' (ibid. 109–10).

[107] Ibid. 99.   [108] Ibid. 30.   [109] Ibid. 109.

to 'godly seed', as an indicator of election, raises a number of troubling questions. If the household of faith is comprised primarily of saints born of godly seed, does this not suggest that the family and the church are both redemptive institutions, and thereby correlative agencies rather than the former being subordinate to the latter? If procreation is a means of propagating the faith, should godly families insulate themselves from the ill effects of ungodly strangers? What are the consequences of the family bearing an eschatological witness, or the church orienting its mission toward a providential end? Is the family a church, and is the church a family? We may identify some of the more important theological and moral implications of these questions by examining selected works of three nineteenth-century theologians.

NINETEENTH-CENTURY REARGUARD MANOEUVRES

Pertinent literature by Friedrich Schleiermacher, F. D. Maurice, and Horace Bushnell has been selected because it exhibits both continuity *and* sharp departures from themes addressed by Baxter in respect to marriage and family. Although some initial criticism and constructive interpretation of their respective accounts are offered in this chapter in conjunction with a more extensive analysis in Chapter 4, it is important to note at this juncture the varying degrees to which each author maintains this continuity or departure on such themes as the relationship between church and family, how households are related to strangers, and the complete absence of how familial roles and relationships might be ordered in conjunction with vocational singleness.

Friedrich Schleiermacher

The publication of Schleiermacher's *The Christian Household: A Sermonic Treatise* (1820)[110] marks his mature reflection on marriage and

---

[110] A series of nine sermons was originally delivered in 1818. A 2nd edition of the treatise was released in 1826.

family, as well as a rejection of his earlier, romantic sentiments.[111] Rather than placing a value upon marriage and family as a means of satisfying subjective desires, he portrays the Christian household as the essential foundation upon which the spiritual life of the church *and* the political ordering of civil society are based. The structure of the treatise is revealing in that two chapters are devoted to marriage, three to childrearing, two to domestic servants, and one chapter each to hospitality and charity.

According to Schleiermacher, the vitality of both the ecclesial and civil communities depend on marriage as the most basic natural institution established and sanctified by God. It is within devout families that piety is grounded and extended to larger groups of people. Consequently, marriage is the essential foundation of social and political ordering. As Schleiermacher makes clear, the significance of marriage cannot be underestimated: 'All other human relationships develop from this sacred covenant. The Christian household derives from it, and Christian communities are comprised of such households. On this sacred covenant rests the propagation of the human race and with it also the propagation of the power of the divine Word from one generation to the next.'[112] It is through marriage that humans learn to participate in larger social relationships that can never be separated from Christ as the Lord of creation, and it is within marriage that its apparent inequality 'dissolve ... into consummate equality' which presumably permeates civil society since marriage is the 'original root of all social life'.[113]

In developing this claim, Schleiermacher asserts that the ultimate equality of marriage is derived from its covenantal quality in which its 'earthly' and 'heavenly' dimensions are made one. The one-flesh unity of marriage captures this earthly dimension, reflecting the need for at least a modicum of cooperation between women and men in attending to their respective physical needs, as well as ensuring survival of the species from one generation to the next. This natural unity, however, does not on its own lead to an ultimate equality.

---

[111] See D. Seidel, 'Editor's Introduction', in Friedrich Schleiermacher, *The Christian Household* (1991), pp. xii–xxiii.

[112] Schleiermacher, *Christian Household*, 2.

[113] Ibid. 3–4.

Although marriage fulfils natural goods, a Christian marriage must strive for a higher, spiritual union, enabling the mutual development of both spouses. The heavenly dimension of self-sacrifice, as reflected in Christ's sacrifice on behalf of the church, is required if marriage is to achieve 'its higher goal ... to sanctify the other and to allow oneself to be sanctified in turn'. Without this self-sacrificial dimension, household concord cannot be achieved, and marriage becomes a fruitless enterprise, since to 'be a twosome then would not improve on being single!'[114] Yet Schleiermacher is quick to add that such a spiritual marriage cannot neglect its earthly necessities. The heavenly dimension cannot exist in isolation from the earthly, and the early church deluded itself in its preference for continent singleness, vainly believing that Christians should 'withdraw as much as possible from the world' in order 'to shun its joys and burdens, its sorrows and concerns'.[115] To the contrary, Christian households are strengthened and enhanced through their earthly pursuits,[116] for it is through these pursuits that 'every Christian home takes part in the greater household of civil society'. In short, Christians remain dependent upon marriage in fulfilling their earthly callings.

Although a wife and husband share an equality in Christ, it is not reflected in the ordering of the earthly household or civil society. The husband remains the head of his wife even though their union is based on a free covenant of mutual fidelity. Schleiermacher defends this apparent discrepancy by appealing to an order imposed by God upon both the church and creation in which the man has been assigned the role governing the *external* affairs of earthly institutions, such as the church and the family. Put succinctly, this

---

[114] Schleiermacher, *Christian Household*, 6–7.   [115] Ibid. 9.

[116] Specifically, Schleiermacher contends: 'The same delusion is also renewed if someone thinks that the covenant of love is not sanctified but profaned through a life of manifold activity in the world, that it is not thereby enriched but is robbed of a great part of the joys intended for it. This is a dangerous error! It is so because even the deepest love can only ready people for good and cleanse them from evil to the extent that they strive to fulfil their calling and do not avoid even a small portion of their destiny; and two human beings united by God can be sufficient for each other only insofar as an active life furnishes tests and temptations for each, against which they are to shield themselves in mutual support, only insofar as the lookout of both is sharpened so that they will be able to search the depths of the heart and to see into what is hidden there' (ibid. 9–10).

divine order, wherein the wife is subject to her husband and the husband is the head of the wife, continues undisturbed—and we would certainly not disturb it without penalty—because only in the Christian community and in the civil community can a Christian marriage take place as long as in both communities the man alone, to whom God has assigned the binding word and the external deed, is entitled to represent the household. There the wife, in contrast, is not entitled to involve herself directly in those greater affairs without penalty.[117]

In concentrating her attention on the internal ordering of the household, the wife frees her husband to order its external relations with other institutions comprising civil society. The result of this division of labour is that the 'seeming inequality' of this divine order 'dissolves itself into the most glorious equality'.[118]

In explicating this process, Schleiermacher invokes two theological images. First, marriage, to a limited extent, reflects the internal life of the godhead. A man leaving his parents to marry and establish a new household is not unlike the Son leaving the Father to establish an earthly kingdom. The inequality of the relationship between Christ and the church is actually premised upon an underlying eschatological equality, even though it is not reflected in the functional roles of the church's hierarchical ordering. Likewise the household's temporal hierarchical ordering does not negate its underlying equality in Christ.[119]

Second, as the church is Christ's body on earth, so too is the wife the body of a marriage. As Christ, as the head of the church, seeks a harmonious life with his earthly body, so too does the husband, as the head of his wife, seek a life of concord with the body of his household. Both instances prefigure an eschatological unity and equality, but it is especially within the earthly household that a wife and husband develop a depth of common life that transcends their respective and asymmetrical roles.

Thus, although, on the one hand, the wife is indeed subject to her husband and must be so, nevertheless, on the other hand, she will be increasingly liberated through the one whom she loves after the image of Christ. If the man is in fact the head, but only insofar as he cleaves to the wife in an unbreakable faithfulness and with innermost love, then any seeming

---

[117] Ibid. 14.   [118] Ibid. 14.   [119] Ibid. 15–17.

inequality, in which one is dominant and the other subordinate, will disappear within the lovelier, more elevated feeling of a complete commonality of life.[120]

Married couples attaining such a spiritual unity provide the 'cornerstone of the community of the Redeemer',[121] for Christ 'will always be there where two are united in his name'.[122] Consequently, the household is the spiritual foundation of both the church and civil society.

This foundational status, however, does not imply that the household is civil society writ small, or that civil society is a family writ large. An underlying spiritual bond is manifested in varying ways within the familial, ecclesial, social, and political spheres. This practical differentiation is seen in Schleiermacher's exposition on divorce.[123] Although the church rightfully propounds a doctrine of lifelong marriage, it has no right to impose this conviction through civil law. The only cause of divorce is a 'hardness of heart' that rejects God's will regarding a divine ordering of human associations. It is God who joins people together in households, and in turn joins households together into nations. Divorce magnifies a spiritual weakness that ignores this divine prerogative, prompting Schleiermacher to ask rhetorically, 'if someone should arbitrarily separate one's whole life from the life of one's people, must there not be a lack of feeling in the person's heart for the worth of this connection as it was ordained by God?'[124] Since stable households promote a well-ordered society, divorce is tantamount to rebelling against the creator's ordained order. Civil authority permits divorce for the sake of preserving the peace of civil society, but this permission should nonetheless produce a sense of shame within the larger (and overlapping) civil and ecclesial-communities. As Schleiermacher contends, although Moses was the founder of both civil and religious communities, it was only in his former capacity that he permitted divorce. Likewise, it is civil authority (albeit Christian) rather than the (Protestant) church that permits divorce.[125] Civil authority may accommodate hard-hearted

---

[120] Schleiermacher, 17–18.   [121] Ibid. 18.   [122] Ibid. 19.

[123] Ibid. 20–35.   [124] Ibid. 23.

[125] Ibid. 32. It is interesting to note that, although Christians should obey civil laws permitting divorced people to remarry, Christians are under no obligation to commend remarriage (ibid. 32–3).

individuals without countering the premise that the 'good health of the church and of civil society' is based on the normative expectation of lifelong marriage.[126]

According to Schleiermacher, households built upon the foundation of Christian marriage are 'destined to be nurseries for the coming generation'. In fulfilling this destiny, parents are charged with the principal responsibilities of preparing their offspring to undertake earthly work and awaken in them a longing for God.[127] These responsibilities are exhibited through parental discipline, love, and inculcating in children a sense of genuine obedience. Discipline is *not* synonymous with punishment, because the latter 'is a consequence of disobedience, while discipline presupposes obedience'.[128] Although there is a punitive dimension to parental discipline, its principal objective is to impart useful information to children, and help them to master practical skills. Schleiermacher is quick to add, however, that such practical knowledge and skill is insufficient without the love and knowledge of God in whose service children will apply their skills when they become adults.[129] Thus parents prefigure Christ's love that children can easily understand and later appropriate in more sophisticated ways. It is the totality of the parent–child relationship that bears witness to God who is love, and as parents work for the sanctification of their children they too become sanctified.[130]

Parental discipline, motivated and tempered by parental love, becomes the basis of genuine obedience because it can be attained only through love rather than fear.[131] Inculcating such obedience is the chief feature of Schleiermacher's account of parenthood, because in learning obedience children become adults who promote the common good of both the ecclesial and civil communities. Indeed, learning to truly honour one's parents is the lynchpin for passing on a love for God and promoting godly social and political ordering from one generation to the next.

Thus within the Christian community one generation that is pleasing to God will follow in the footsteps of another, in that each will develop in the

---

[126] Ibid. 34.

[127] Ibid. 36. This task, however, is not confined to parents. Rather, they perform these duties in cooperation with the church and civil society (ibid. 36–7).

[128] Ibid. 57.   [129] Ibid. 60–2.   [130] Ibid. 71–4.   [131] Ibid. 78–80.

same manner, through the respect of children toward their parents, the seed of reverence toward some higher common will, and both will be united in the devout love for the One who is revealed through every law that is written in our hearts.[132]

Moreover, parental love and discipline culminating in obedience is progressive and cumulative, for children 'improve over what their parents have been, so that in its own time each rising generation will surpass the one that has educated it'.[133] Honouring one's parents has an eschatological urgency, for it is only through such progressive improvement that the kingdom of God can be built.

Given the urgency of this intergenerational relationship, it is important to note that Christian households do not practise the virtue of obedience to preserve themselves as private enclaves. Rather, practising such obedience within a familial context shapes the household as the foundation of a larger social and political life. The household's foundational status is further enhanced in Schleiermacher's treatment of domestic servants.[134] Pragmatically, domestic servants enable the efficient management of a household's internal affairs, while also supplementing and solidifying the man's ordering of the household's external relationships. Thus Schleiermacher instructs servants to provide good service and resist being discontent, while enjoining masters to be fair and just while avoiding displays of power over their servants.[135]

At a deeper level, however, the relationship between masters and servants models the basic principles of a Christian social and political order. Although servants and masters share a fundamental equality in Christ, this fact does not alter the necessity of their hierarchical relationship for the sake of the household. In this respect, the relationship between master and servant provides one more link in Schleiermacher's chain of obedience: as wives are obedient to their husbands and children to their parents, so too are servants obedient to their masters. The very structure of the household inculcates and reinforces a chief civic virtue, namely, that obedience to a higher political authority is required in order to protect and preserve the peace of civil society. Moreover, in providing good and obedient

---

132 Schleiermacher, 89.   133 Ibid.
134 Ibid. 91–122.   135 Ibid. 108.

service, servants find a spiritual liberation from the temporal confines of their servitude, thereby enabling them to better serve Christ, who is their ultimate master.[136] Indeed, Schleiermacher asserts that the master–servant relationship is emblematic of the 'whole relationship of human beings toward God. Thus, we may also rightly consider the situation of servants in domestic life and treat it as a symbol of that general relationship between human beings and God.'[137]

A household structured along this pattern of obedience is drawn out towards larger spheres of human association, for its hierarchical relationships are based upon, and ultimately dissolve into, a radical equality in Christ. Schleiermacher admits that the freedom which comes through perfect obedience is rarely accomplished by sinful people, so the household is also a place where divine grace is experienced with a unique intensity. This experience should have a reverberating effect throughout civil society because 'feeling the abundance of divine grace, the Christian household should be ready to extend this grace to others, so that God will be glorified'.[138] It is through obedient practices rooted in love and concern for the common welfare of the household that a pattern of habitual conduct is nurtured, one that Schleiermacher identifies as 'hospitality, which people practice mutually in both closer and wider circles'.[139] Most importantly, it is through hospitable households that Christian charity is extended throughout civil society.[140]

To a much a greater extent than the other nineteenth-century theologians examined below, Schleiermacher preserves the household structure as explicated in the household codes. This is especially the case in that he continues to argue that domestic servants are members of a household. A *Christian* household is not simply a collection of individuals bound together through marital and familial bonds, but is also ordered in relationship to strangers. Thus it is not surprising that Schleiermacher also asserts the public nature of the household, for it must provide a firm foundation for the orderly continuation of civil society over time. The private virtues of the household, then, are virtually indistinguishable from the public

---

[136] Ibid. 111–12.   [137] Ibid. 121–2.   [138] Ibid. 124.
[139] Ibid. See pp. 126–39 for Schleiermacher's explication of hospitality.
[140] Ibid. 140–60.

virtues required for a well-ordered society and political regime—a loving obedience originating in the home permeates all of civil society.

Yet to what extent a Christian household succeeds or fails in performing this foundational role cannot be determined within Schleiermacher's programme. The only criterion for making such an assessment is that the household should inculcate a loving obedience in its members, but there is virtually no discussion of what moral content constitutes this obedience. Nor is there any suggestion of contrasting institutions or relationships against which the strengths and limitations of the household, in respect to social and political ordering, might be judged. This is seen in the absence of any discussion concerning the relationship between the church and the family. Although Baxter had blurred the distinction between the two, he nonetheless insisted that ecclesial authority was superior to that of the household. Presumably the church could judge whether or not the ordering of obedience within the household was in accordance with Christian convictions. Schleiermacher, however, removes the boundaries altogether. He insists that the home, the church, and civil authority work together to achieve a common obedience rooted in love. He can talk about a Christian household, and a Christian social and political order, but he cannot portray the church as bearing witness to a transcending and transforming end of household, social, and political ordering. Consequently, the equality into which present hierarchical relationships dissolve remains highly ambiguous.

It is particularly telling in this regard that Schleiermacher has nothing to say about the relationship between the family and singleness. Following Luther, it appears incomprehensible to Schleiermacher that Christians would refrain from marrying and establishing families. Indeed, it would reflect a stubborn refusal to participate in the foundation of a godly social and political order. Consequently, there is no vocation embodying the church's eschatological witness over and against the providential witness of the household. There is little inkling that the household is being drawn towards its transformation in Christ in which its hierarchical roles and relationships will be displaced by sisterhood and brotherhood. This does not mean, however, that eschatology is entirely absent in Schleiermacher's account of the Christian household, but it is displaced onto children. The household, along with the social and political order it supports, will simply improve over time as each generation progresses beyond its predecessor. Consequently, Schleiermacher can baldly assert, with no sense of irony or discontinuity with previous strands of Christian thought, that children provide the only hope for overcoming death and establishing the kingdom of God on earth. 'How else...are we to look to the future if not in our children, for they are the closest ones to us on whom we are able to confer a better order of things as an inheritance.'[141] It is, after all, flesh and blood that will inherit the kingdom of heaven.

Since Schleiermacher offers no eschatological vision regarding the end of household ordering, as well as the social and political order it underwrites, he also has no need to describe what the eventual outcome of the progressive work of generations of Christian households might look like. That task was undertaken by two subsequent nineteenth-century theologians.

F. D. Maurice

One consequence of an ambiguous relationship between the family and the church is that familial relationships are construed as the foundation *and* end of social and political ordering. The church proliferates itself as the *universal family of God*. This tendency is seen in Maurice's *Social Morality*, in which he propounds an account of social ordering encompassing the interrelated dimensions of 'domestic life', 'civilization', and 'human society'.[142] He claims that, although these categories have inspired separate forms of philosophical enquiry, they are nonetheless incorporated within the larger 'sphere of Social Morality'.[143] Maurice is attempting to forge a synthetic social ethic that preserves a significant role for the family in relation to civil society and the state. The principal foci of his inquiry are families, nations, and universal society. The historical development of these associations does not mark a cumulative sequence in which a

---

[141] Ibid. 50.   [142] See F. D. Maurice, *Social Morality* (1869), 10.
[143] Ibid. 10–11.

former stage is subsumed by the latter, but are 'coexistent': the 'Family is not lost in the Nation, nor the Nation in Human Society'.[144]

Maurice begins his account of domestic morality[145] with the factual observation that individuals are born into societies, meaning that every person is biologically related to at least two other persons. Consequently, given familial relationships provide the foundation and contours of human identity. Denying this fact results in a destructive egotism, because an individual places himself at the hub of his moral universe instead of in relation to others upon whom he is dependent. Specifically, Maurice asserts: 'I cannot be the centre of the circle in which I find myself, be it as small as it may. I refer myself to another. There is a root below me. There is an Author of my existence.'[146] He also sees no alternative foundation for social morality, insisting 'that a son cannot be without a father, or a father without a son. To dissolve the relation into its elements is to remake the world.'[147] Maurice, however, draws a distinction between parental authority and dominion, the former commanding obedience, the latter imposing subjection. Nor can the significance of this distinction be underestimated, for a proper respect for authority, as learnt in the family, provides the foundation of social and political order. Rome is used as both a positive and negative example: 'To the paternal *authority* Rome owed its strength and freedom. The claim of paternal dominion resulted in Imperial Tyranny.'[148]

Maurice shifts his attention to the relationship between husband and wife, admitting that the order of his presentation breaks with the custom of placing the 'conjugal relation . . . of choice' prior to the 'filial relation of necessity'.[149] He defends this strategy on the basis that the affinity between parent and child precedes all other relationships, emphasizing the given, rather than voluntary, structures of human associations. Marriage is a natural relationship of fundamental trust that a man and a woman enter as incomplete persons, but in their mutual dependence make each other whole. He again draws a distinction between authority and dominion in which the former is 'the dependence of each upon the other; not of the weak upon the strong more than of the strong upon the weak'.[150] The trust engendered in a

[144] See F. D. Maurice, *Social Morality* (1869), 19.
[145] Ibid. 24–119.   [146] Ibid. 25.   [147] Ibid. 26.
[148] Ibid. 45 (emphasis original).   [149] Ibid. 48.   [150] Ibid. 50.

couple's mutual dependence is in turn extended outward towards the family, friends, and nation.

Maurice rejects any form of household servitude as a perversion of paternal authority. A man owning slaves may come to believe that he also owns his wife and children; property displaces trust as the household's foundation.[151] Nor does he permit the employment of servants, because normative relationships characterizing a family are displaced by a degrading contract of economic exchange.[152] What he wishes to commend, however, 'is not a repudiation of service... but a much profounder reverence for it; not an assertion that all have a right to rule, but rather a conviction that everyone is bound to serve'.[153] Since the moral task of the family is to prepare its members to live under the authority of mutual dependence and service, household servants only deflect the educative example of familial relationships.

The cornerstone of domestic morality is the relationship between brothers and sisters. Fraternity is the essence of society, constituting not only its 'well-being' but 'its very being'.[154] The 'ethos of consanguinity' provides the foundation of social morality. Recognizing a common origin in at least one parent can, in principle, be expanded to include others within 'a certain habit or manner'.[155] Unlike filial, parental, and spousal relationships, fraternity is naturally inclined towards equality, promoting fellowship while ameliorating an artificial impetus toward destructive competition. The family provides the normative bedrock of a fraternal social order, for despite the evils its members inflict on each other, the family nevertheless encapsulates the values of mutual loyalty and sacrificial obligation. Brothers and sisters are committed to each other not because of their shared interests, but by their affinity.

Maurice builds on this fraternal ethos in developing a national morality.[156] He begins again with the factual observation that, as humans are born into families, so too are they born into nations. Although civil society is comprised of individuals, they cannot develop as such without larger familial and national frameworks.[157] The family and the nation, as the principal factors shaping individual

---

[151] Ibid. 88–9.   [152] Ibid. 94–5.
[153] Ibid. 96.   [154] Ibid. 67.   [155] Ibid. 71–4.
[156] Ibid. 121–245.   [157] Ibid. 121–32.

and corporate identities, provide the basis of a civil morality. Law and government, then, are aspects of a social force that 'unfolds and deepens'[158] the family, institutionalizing a bond of obligation between individuals and the nation. More importantly, familial and national identities are bulwarks against imperial pretensions. Maurice again contrasts authority with dominion: a society based on familial and national affinities is governed by law, whereas empires assert a possessive dominion. A society honouring its familial and national identities resists an impulse toward false and destructive imperial pretensions. Thus, a 'nation cannot stand upon fictions. An Empire may demand them as necessary supports.'[159]

The final part of *Social Morality* explicates a universal ethic.[160] Although every person is born into a family and a nation, there is a yearning for a greater sphere of association. This proclivity is expressed in one of two ways: it may follow the authority of law promoting a 'universal family',[161] or it may assert the dominion of a 'universal empire'.[162] In contrasting these two options, Maurice likens the latter to Rome while equating the former with the church. The church's formative event is Pentecost, where a unifying spirit descends on the people, empowering them to 'confess their Father in Christ. They are brothers.'[163] The church takes on a national quality in its spiritual unity. Through the sacraments, Christ's nation, established on the sacrificial act of its founder, is reconciled with the nations of the world. Christ's 'Universal Sacrifice which is commemorated by the Eucharist' discloses the 'deepest basis of Human Morality, the meeting-point of a fellowship between the Father of all and the children of men'.[164] In obeying the Father, Christ sets a pattern of life to be emulated in human associations, namely, that since Christ is the brother of all people, everyone shares a universal fraternity. The church is a holy nation, heralding 'a foundation or underground for that *ethos* which we found to be demanded of all relationships of the family'.[165] The yearning for a more expansive sphere of association, originating in familial and national affinities, is satisfied in Christ's nation and universal family, prompting Maurice

---

[158] See F. D. Maurice, *Social Morality* (1869), 145.   [159] Ibid. 224.
[160] Ibid. 246–483.   [161] Ibid. 266–93.   [162] Ibid. 246–65.
[163] Ibid. 272.   [164] Ibid. 274.
[165] Ibid. 289 (emphasis original in Greek characters).

to ponder: 'Believing in a God who has constituted families, who has constituted Nations, we may ask whether there is any Universal Human Constitution which is in harmony with these; for which these may prepare us.'[166]

Maurice answers his question by examining several possibilities. He repudiates the options of the church enjoying a collaborative, but subservient, relationship with a universal empire,[167] or the church supplanting and dominating an empire.[168] He also objects to the Reformation's individualism,[169] seventeenth- and eighteenth-century efforts to impose artificial principles of social ordering,[170] and modern attempts to assert positivist structures.[171] Each of these options is rejected because it promotes, either wittingly or unwittingly, the formation of a universal empire, perverting the human longing for greater affinity into inhumane domination. The one reliable source for a universal morality is universal fraternity, for it alone fosters this longing for a larger sphere of human association. Moreover, it is the church, *as universal family*, that satisfies this longing. Although the church has often failed to live up to this ideal, its sacrificial ethos nevertheless provides a suitable context where the ethic of the Sermon on the Mount may serve as a blueprint for social and political ordering.[172] Christ's teaching reveals God's will for humans to become a universal family, and they may draw on their particular familial and national identities as resources for proceeding onward as brothers and sisters in Christ's family, and as citizens of the nation bearing his name.

---

[166] Ibid. 293.

[167] Ibid., lecture 15: 'The Universal Family Subject to the Universal Empire (Constantinople)', 294–315.

[168] Ibid., lecture 16: 'The Universal Family a Latin Family (Rome)', 316–42.

[169] Ibid., lecture 17: 'The Universal and Individual Morality in Conflict', 343–73.

[170] Ibid., lecture 18: 'Attempts to Deduce the Principles of Human Morality from Observations on Human Nature', 374–408.

[171] Ibid., lecture 19: 'The Modern Conception of Humanity', 409–32.

[172] Maurice argues: 'Because I can find no other which is adequate to our emergencies, I go back to the principle of a Universal Family which was announced eighteen centuries ago, and which has been subject to so many contractions and mutilations in subsequent periods. I accept the principle in that primitive form which has been preserved among the people of Christendom, whatever may have been the opinions of its different doctors' (ibid. 434).

Although Maurice's social morality marks a serious attempt to counteract the individualism underlying prevalent social and political thinking of his time, his programme fails because the church or universal community he envisions is not a family writ large. The source of this failure is seen in his awkward effort to interject a cumbersome Christology. He portrays familial and national identities as natural, coextensive, and divinely established affinities. What has frustrated their further development is the lack of an effective means for satisfying a longing for a greater sphere of human association. Christ provides this means through his church, for through his sacrifice humans are empowered to call God their father, and one another sister and brother.

What is not clear is *why* Christ's sacrifice should lead to the founding of a universal family. Maurice is correct in arguing that Christ confirms the principle that enduring social bonds can only be sustained when based on the sacrificial quality of human affinity. But he fails to acknowledge that Christ does not simply satisfy a longing for greater affinity; he also judges and redeems it, requiring a reorientation of what is desired. Christ is not merely a preacher proclaiming the fatherhood of God and brotherhood of man, but the saviour of the world, challenging the partial claims of familial and national loyalties. For Maurice, Christ does not transform human society but coaxes it along in a progressive direction.

Moreover, Maurice eliminates the tension between the family as providential witness and church as eschatological community, portraying them instead as points along a common spectrum of human affinity. In doing so, he undercuts his argument that it is through particular families that a universal sphere of human association is pursued. If universal fraternity is the end of familial ordering, it is not apparent why spousal, parental, and filial roles retain any special, as opposed to functional, significance. The centripetal nature of familial bonds constrain a longing for a more expansive affinity unless there is a countervailing centrifugal force that *both affirms and judges* the inherent limits of familial loyalty. Contrary to Maurice, the family is not naturally inclined towards a universal fraternity that is satisfied by the church as the universal family. Rather, the church bears an eschatological witness to a reordering of human life in which familial relationships shall be transformed.

Maurice's argument would be more convincing had he stopped with the church as a nation of sacrificial service, drawing families out towards greater spheres of human association. The ordering of the family would then bear witness to the *telos* of this larger affinity, incorporating, while also transcending, its limited character. Yet in taking the next step of casting the church as universal family, its particular counterpart is left with nothing to bear witness to other than itself as a collection of individuals who, through accident of birth, share a close proximity in learning the social skills of universal fraternity. In removing the tension between providence and eschatology, the church magnifies the family instead of representing its impending reordering. It is telling that Maurice has little to say about singleness, other than to castigate celibacy as an enemy of the family, and presumably the universal fraternity it inspires,[173] for if the family bears no distinctive providential witness then nor does singleness embody any eschatological significance.

The most troubling aspect of Maurice's account of the family, however, is the disappearance of strangers. Since all humans are ultimately members of a universal family there are, strictly speaking, no strangers but only sisters and brothers. Thus the inequality of the master–servant relationship is rejected in favour of fraternal equality, and unlike earlier Christians, he is unwilling to maintain an inequality of household roles that become reoriented towards equality in Christ. Although Maurice wants to preserve the value of service, it is unclear how it is promoted within the family in the absence of genuine strangers. He implies that service can be learnt by family members being servants to one another, but such a scheme blunts his argument. Familial roles and relationships must be set aside for members of a household to become servants and strangers to each other. Yet this role-playing not only ignores the particularity of the familial bonds Maurice wishes to preserve, but is also incompatible with the fraternity he wants to promote within a universal family.

---

[173] Ibid. 320–2. In his lecture on the church's temptation to become a universal empire, Maurice asserts that 'even if Celibacy had not become the universal law of the Latin priesthood, it must have shaken to its roots the feeling of connexion between the Universal Family and the particular Family and have reacted most injuriously to the former' (ibid. 322).

It is a puzzling arrangement unless particular families are merely rehearsals for living in a universal family, a conclusion Maurice is unwilling to entertain.

In failing to uphold a tension between the family and the church, Maurice can neither maintain their distinct identities, nor explicate their coextensive identities. The family must somehow preserve its identity, *vis-à-vis* strangers, through the inequality of its inherent roles, while the church is characterized by a radical equality in which there are no strangers. Yet the roles and relationships within these two spheres cannot be easily shifted from one to the other. For Maurice, the family and the church are redundant societies, shaping the character of their overlapping members within relatively small or large settings, their principal difference being one of scale. But if these two modes of human association can be distilled to a universal fraternity, then neither the particularity of the familial household nor the universality of the household of faith can be sustained. This is seen in a loss of symmetry between the Lord's table and the household table, for both are reduced to nearly identical meals. The Eucharist loses its eschatological exclusivity, becoming a time of spiritual renewal for members of a universal fraternity, while the household meal is a time of fellowship of the same persons on a more modest scale. Tellingly, there are no strangers to exclude from the former or extend hospitality to in the latter. By portraying the *telos* of *both* the family and the church along the lines of familial affinity, Maurice confuses the timely belonging afforded by the family with belonging in the fullness of time anticipated by the church, distorting eschatological sisterhood and brotherhood in Christ into a mode of temporal social ordering. Consequently, he also fails to acknowledge that strangers and singleness also disclose the end of familial and ecclesial ordering in a creation being drawn towards its destiny in Christ.

Horace Bushnell

If Maurice's portrayal of the *church as universal family* represents one extreme reaction to an ambiguous relationship between the family and the church, then the other extreme can be seen in accounts of the *family as the church.* Seizing upon the notions of 'godly seed' and 'godly parents', procreation and childrearing take on salvific significance. It is through the family that faith is passed on and nurtured.

According to Bushnell, the family should provide an environment in which a *'child is to grow up a Christian, and never know himself as being otherwise'.*[174] Rejecting the doctrine that children are born into sin and convert later in life, he contends that from birth they are open to God's grace and may be taught to love 'what is good'.[175] His argument is based on the belief that humans are neither inherently sinful nor virtuous,[176] but have a 'malleable will'.[177] The institution best equipped for directing a child's will towards God is the family, because parents and children share 'something like a law of organic connection as regards character', so the 'faith of the one will be propagated in the other'.[178] Since an acquired sanctification can be passed on to offspring, it is vital that children be reared in pious families in order that the progressive and cumulative effects of Christian virtue are reinforced and magnified over time, for Bushnell assumes that 'it is well understood that qualities received by training and *not* in themselves natural, do also pass by transmission'.[179] Consequently, it is not 'reasonable to doubt that where there is a long line of godly fathers and mothers, kept up in regular succession for many generations, religious temperament may at length be produced, that is more in the power of conscience, less wayward as regards principles of integrity, and more pliant to the Christian motives'.[180]

---

[174] Horace Bushnell, *Christian Nurture* (1960), 4 (emphasis original).

[175] Ibid. 5–6.

[176] Although Bushnell argues that humans have an innate capacity for resisting evil (ibid. 9–10), he does not see any evidence that they are by nature good. 'The natural pravity of man is plainly asserted in the Scriptures, and if it were not, the familiar laws of physiology would require us to believe what amount to the same thing' (ibid. 15). Thus Christian nurture is not a programme 'to form the child to virtue, by simply educing or drawing out what is in him'. Rather, children are born into a world bent towards sin, so the formation of virtue requires countering inimical physical and cultural forces already in place. 'The child . . . may as well begin life under a law of heredity damage, as to plunge himself into evil by his impulse of curiosity, or the instinct of knowledge, as from any noxious quality in his mold derived from descent. For it is not sin in any sense which imparts blame, but only some prejudice to the perfect harmony of his mold, some kind of pravity or obliquity, which inclines him to evil' (ibid. 15–16).

[177] Ibid. 203–11.   [178] Ibid. 18.   [179] Ibid. 81 (emphasis original).

[180] Ibid. 81–2.

The family plays the chief role in bringing the gospel to fruition because faith 'never thoroughly penetrates life, till it becomes domestic'.[181] Since parents pass on their faith to children, the 'house itself is a converting ordinance'.[182] Moreover, the family plays *the* crucial role in breaking the transmission of sin from one generation to the next, for through its organic unity the family's 'regenerative purpose' is reoriented as an instrument of grace instead of a 'vehicle only of depravity'.[183] The household is a 'seal of faith' through which the Holy Spirit 'collects families into a common organism, and then sanctifying the laws of organic unity in families, extends its quickening power to the generation following, so as to include the future and make it one with the past'.[184] Under the guidance of their parents, children are incorporated into a realm of grace, and trained for virtuous lives rather than prepared for conversion. The church assists the work of the Holy Spirit by playing a supportive, if not subordinate, role to the family. Parents are the principal evangelists[185] because their nurture personifies God's providential care.[186] Thus the family is a 'little primary bishopric under the father',[187] and his authority is that of a vice-regent bearing God's 'natural and moral image', so the home is 'a kind of household religion, that may widen out into the measures of God's ideal majesty and empire'.[188]

Baptism is the most important act the church performs in supporting families. According to Bushnell, refusing to baptize infants is tantamount to denying the family's organic unity. It is families, not individuals, which comprise God's kingdom. A child of Christian parents has a birthright to be included in the church that baptism validates.[189] More importantly, baptism confirms the organic, and thereby redemptive, unity of parents and children. The 'Christian parent has, in his character, a germ which has power, presumptively, to produce its like in his children', so in baptism a child is seen in his parents and counted 'a believer and a Christian'.[190] Baptism is *the* foremost evangelistic tool, because parental piety is reproduced in

---

[181] F. D. Maurice, 50.   [182] Ibid. 62.   [183] Ibid. 91–2.
[184] Ibid. 94.   [185] Ibid. 211–12.
[186] Ibid. 221–2. Consequently, the church should train its members to be good parents since incompetent parenting is likened to sin (ibid. 216–17).
[187] Ibid. 269.   [188] Ibid. 271–2.   [189] Ibid. 141–5.   [190] Ibid. 30.

offspring. Thus the church is not comprised of 'Christians with families' but 'Christian families'.[191]

The anticipated outcome of this household ordering is explicated in a chapter on 'The Out-Populating Power of the Christian Stock'. Bushnell contends that God created the first man and woman that 'he might have a godly seed', and established reproductive laws that 'piety itself shall finally over-populate the world'.[192] Although God's reign is extended through both conversion and procreation, the former has been underscored to the detriment of the latter. A quantitative *and* qualitative growth of a Christian population should be emphasized, for transmitting grace from one generation to the next exerts a faithful dominion over creation. Appealing to the selective breeding of livestock, Bushnell asserts that since acquired traits are passed on to subsequent generations, 'civilization is, in great part, an inbred civility'.[193] Likewise, a Christian lineage produces an 'inbred piety'.[194] Through a 'kind of ante-natal and post-natal nurture combined, the new-born generations will be started into Christian piety, and the world itself over-populated and taken possession by a truly sanctified stock'.[195] Procreation and childrearing are the principal instruments of the world's salvation, because God must permeate every aspect of a fallen creation. If, as Christian tradition claims, heredity is a means of transmitting sin, then it must also be a means of receiving grace. The church is called by God to support its families because in making 'her sons a talented and powerful race', it is doing nothing less than fulfilling its mandate to build a holy nation.[196] Consequently, the church's hope, as well as creation's destiny, lies in the propagation of godly seed, through which God 'will reclaim and resanctify the great principle of reproductive order and life'.[197]

Like Maurice, Bushnell countered what he perceived to be a destructive individualism by emphasizing the family's organic unity. But he reverses Maurice's strategy by refashioning the family in the image of the church. Christian households do not enable the church to become the universal family, but are the instruments through which the church fulfils its mission. There is a pronounced soteriological accent in Bushnell's account, but it is associated with

---

[191] Ibid. 120. [192] Ibid. 165. [193] Ibid. 171–2. [194] Ibid. 172–3.
[195] Ibid. 173. [196] Ibid. 179–85. [197] Ibid. 183–4.

the Holy Spirit rather than Christ's sacrificial act. The Spirit guides the propagation of godly seed towards its fruition of a holy nation. This strategy is apparent in his prognosis for breaking the transmission of sin. According to the Bible and the 'laws of physiology', vicious and virtuous parents beget their own kind, and given the world's proclivity towards sin, the former have come to outnumber the latter. The solution is to reverse this cycle by nurturing an inbred piety, and properly ordered families are best suited to accomplish this goal. Drawing upon Lamarckian principles, Bushnell believes that traits can be acquired, enhanced, and passed on to subsequent generations. Children not only receive their parents' physical characteristics, but also their virtue that is reinforced by pious parental care, resulting in a progressively robust Christian stock. The reproduction and cumulative improvement of godly seed play central roles in humankind's redemption.

The price for placing this burden on the family is dear, for in fixating on the nature of its organic unity Bushnell disfigures its teleological unfolding. The family's *telos* is no longer transcendent, drawing it out of itself towards larger spheres of human association, but is contained within itself. There is no necessary tension between the family and the church, because the latter is a confederation of Christian families instead of an eschatological community of Christians with families. The church and the family share an identical rather than complementary witness: one need look no further than the earthly household to see humankind's destiny. The new creation entails no transformation of familial affinity into a fellowship of sisters and brothers in Christ, but is the perfection of a reproductive order. And in building the kingdom on a foundation of godly seed, parents are the primary evangelists, and their offspring the harbingers of God's new age.

This theological distortion is seen in Bushnell's emphasis on infant baptism.[198] It is unthinkable that the church would deny the organic unity of the family by withholding this sacrament from newborns. Birth and baptism are two aspects of a single act, for those born of godly seed are already members of the church. Yet eliminating a theological distinction between the two also distorts the parent–

---

[198] Two chapters of *Christian Nurture* are devoted to this topic, as well as extensive portions of other chapters.

child relationship. Children are no longer gifts God entrusts to the care of parents, but outcomes of a pious will to generate a Christian stock. The organic unity of parent and child has displaced the one-flesh unity of marriage as both the foundation of the family, and sign of God's providential care. Since baptism does not signify the receipt of children as gifts that are consigned back again to the care of God, then nor can it acknowledge that the earthly household is tempered, and ultimately replaced, by eschatological fellowship.

This attempt to annul the tension between providence and eschatology is further seen in Bushnell's treatment of singleness and strangers. Given his doctrine of salvation through procreation, it is difficult to imagine what witness singleness could be called to bear. It is at best an enigma, and at worse a stubborn refusal to participate in God's redemptive plan. Like Maurice, Bushnell has also eliminated strangers from playing any role in household ordering. Unlike Maurice he does not accomplish this by incorporating them into a universal family. Rather, strangers are threats to the organic unity of the family, and he counsels parents to prevent their children from having extended contact with unbelieving families because of their inevitably corrosive influence.[199] This is seen in the absence of the Eucharist in Bushnell's account of the relationship between the family and the church. In eliminating the tension between them, their respective tables bear witness to a common end instead of complementary purposes. The Eucharist is no longer a foretaste of eschatological fellowship, and more tellingly, the household meal is not used to extend familial hospitality to strangers. In short, godly and ungodly seed do not mix, and in propagating God's kingdom strangers shall eventually be 'out populated' by superior Christian stock.

In order to utilize the historical strands surveyed in this chapter in a constructive manner, a more critical appraisal is needed.[200] Before this more extensive task is undertaken, however, we need to take two prior steps regarding the role of the family in modern liberal social and political thought, as well as subsequent responses by contemporary Christian theologians. It is towards taking the first of these steps that we turn our attention in the next chapter.

---

[199] Ibid. 99–101.   [200] See Ch. 4.

2

Modern Liberalism and its Critics

The previous chapter surveyed some of the principal historical patterns that emerged in Christian social and political thought in respect to marriage and family, disclosing both a number of continuities and discontinuities. The most influential disjuncture, at least in terms of setting the context for contemporary theological discussions, occurred with the Reformers and Puritans. With the rejection of vocational singleness and the blurring of the lines separating the church and the family, the household emerges as a bastion of privacy, rather than an institution mediating and linking its members with broader spheres of human association. Subsequent theological reflection, particularly as reflected in the works of Schleiermacher, Maurice, and Bushnell, exacerbated these tensions. For each of these theologians the household and the church must simultaneously bear a providential *and* eschatological witness, rather than embodying respective witnesses that are contrasting yet complementary. It is noteworthy, in this respect, that except for Schleiermacher the absence of domestic servants from the Christian household served to confine the family as a private enclave, only indirectly related through its members to other social spheres comprising civil community. Although the normative ordering of a Christian household did not necessitate the presence of servants, no substitute category was recommended for how a family's relationship with strangers might be mediated.

These nineteenth-century theological accounts of the family did not occur in an intellectual vacuum, and should be assessed against the background of what may be called modern liberalism as the dominant social and political theory. What does this shorthand phrase designate? 'Modern' refers to a historical epoch beginning in the late eighteenth century—roughly coincident with the demise of Christendom—and extending to the present day.[1] 'Liberalism' denotes a range of convictions and principles asserting the primacy of freedom and autonomy, enabling individuals to pursue their respective visions of the good. As Robert Song contends, although there are a number of sharp disagreements among liberal theorists, there is nonetheless a 'pattern of characteristic family resemblances', including 'a voluntarist conception of the human subject; a constructivist meta-ethics; an abstract, universalist, and individualist mode of thought; and a broadly progressivist philosophy of history'.[2] Liberalism is the principal modern political ideology, because it shares certain affinities with the Enlightenment regarding the nature of human agency and rationality, the basis of value, direction of history, and the uses of power, property, and the state.[3] These affinities, however, receive varying expressions and emphases among liberal theorists. Constitutional liberalism, for example, stresses the inherent character of individual rights independent of civil society, which are mediated and protected through a social contract enforced by the state.[4] By way of contrast, *laissez-faire* liberalism emphasizes free trade and exchange, minimal government, and individual rights,[5] whereas welfare or revisionist liberals argue on behalf of economic redistribution, welfare, and civil rights for minorities.[6] Consequently, the critical overview of modern liberalism undertaken in this chapter presupposes a loosely knit collection of these principal claims, rather than a tightly woven series of philosophical arguments.

THE EMERGING CONTEXT OF MODERN LIBERALISM

Modern liberalism does not appear *ex nihilo* at the end of the eighteenth century, but marks a transformation of precepts that had been

---

[1] O'Donovan contends that Christendom is an 'era in which the truth of Christianity was taken to be the truth of secular politics', an interval demarcated symbolically by the Edict of Milan in 313 and the First Amendment of the US Constitution in 1791 (*The Desire of the Nations* (1996), 195).

[2] Robert Song, *Christianity and Liberal Society* (1997), 9.   [3] Ibid. 11.

[4] Ibid. 37. Locke and Kant are examples of constitutional liberal theorists.

[5] Ibid. 38. Nozick is an example of a *laissez-faire* liberal.

[6] Ibid. 38–9. Rawls is an example of a revisionist liberal.

developed over the previous two centuries. An extensive investigation of this development is beyond the scope of this chapter, but some revealing signposts can be identified in representative theorists. Moreover, focusing this survey on the declining role of the family in modern liberal social and political theory sheds further light on a corresponding decline in modern Christian social and political thought.

Early liberalism

Early liberalism grounded social and political ordering in the law of nature as established by God. Hugo Grotius, for example, maintained that nature has endowed humans with reason and society, and in their absence human life is unsustainable. The efficacy of the law of nature does not depend on human will or consent; rather individuals are obligated to do what is right as dictated by the requirements of reason, and the constraints of their social nature.[7] For Grotius, civil society entails a series of voluntary acts conducted by humans for their mutual protection and benefit, whose institution and lawful governance are approved by God.[8] It must be stressed, however, that political governance is not a subjective assertion of the corporate human will, but is pursued in accordance with the dictates of reason, and the inherent nature of civil society as a 'kind of body which consists of separate elements' but, having one 'name' or 'spirit', enables 'the full and perfect common participation of civil society'. The artificial body of the political state is 'plainly' analogous to a natural body.[9] Political ordering encompasses a right to form compacts grounded in, and

---

[7] 'Natural law is the Dictate of Right Reason, indicating that any act, from its agreement or disagreement with the rational [and social] nature [of man] has in it a moral turpitude or a moral necessity; and consequently that such an act is forbidden or commanded by God, the author of nature' (Grotius, *On the Rights of War and Peace* (1853 edn), 2. 1. 10(1)). In addition, Grotius asserts that the laws of the New Testament are the same as the law of nature or do not contradict it (ibid. 1. 2. 6–7).

[8] 'But it is to be noted that Civil Society is the result, not of Divine precept, but of the experience of the weakness of separate families to protect themselves; and is thus called by Peter an *ordinance of man*, though it is also an ordinance of God, because He approves it. And God, approving a human law, must be conceived approving it as human, and in a human manner' (ibid. 1. 4. 6(3), emphasis original).

[9] Ibid. 2. 9. 3(1).

constrained by, natural law. This is especially reflected in Grotius's account of the ownership and alienation of property in which contracts are establish to set an equitable basis of exchange.[10] Consequently, a properly ordered regime directs the human will in accordance with the right ordering of humankind's social nature.

Johannes Althusius asserts a social human nature more emphatically, insisting that communication or 'symbiotics' lies at the heart of what it means to be a creature, created in the image and likeness of God. No individual is endowed by nature to be self-sufficient.[11] Rather, humans are endowed with a natural capacity that drives them towards fellowship and communion.[12] Although the basis of this affiliation is mutual agreement, the accompanying rights and duties disclose 'that the commonwealth, or civil society, exists by nature, and that man is by nature a civil animal who strives eagerly for association'.[13] This striving permeates every aspect of human life, for although Althusius divides associations into 'simple and private'[14] and 'mixed and public',[15] this separation is not a gulf separating two domains, but marks complementary poles. The right of association is exercised throughout the various levels of civil society in accordance with the nature of each particular association. There is an organic quality to social and political ordering in which individuals live symbiotically within a series of integrally related associations.

These general principles of social and political ordering are reflected in, as well as derived from, Grotius's and Althusius's respective accounts of marriage and family. For Grotius, familial affinity engenders the social human nature from which civil and political institutions garner their rationale.[16] The family is founded upon marriage, the 'most natural form of partnership',[17] wherein husbands and wives educate

[10] Ibid. 2. 7. 3–10.

[11] 'Clearly, man by nature is a gregarious animal born for cultivating society with other men, not by nature living alone as wild beasts do, nor wandering about as birds' (Althusius, *The Politics* (1964), 17).

[12] Ibid. 18. It should not be assumed, however, that this natural drive inevitably leads to concord. The tasks of social ordering can also result in acts of violence and other injustices.   [13] Ibid. 20.

[14] Simple and private associations include families and *collegia* (ibid. 22–33).

[15] Mixed and public associations include cities, provinces, and commonwealths (ibid. 34–73).

[16] See Grotius, *Rights of War*, 'Preliminary Remarks' (6–7).

[17] Ibid. 2. 5. 8 and 8–16.

their offspring in ways anticipating civil conduct. Children are taught to promote the common good of the family, 'for it is equitable that a part should follow the analogy of the whole'.[18] Such education is best achieved through exercising a natural paternal authority, for as the father is the head of his household, so too does the sovereign govern his nation.[19] This status, however, does not authorize arbitrary assertions of paternal or political power. Rather, their rule must conform to the natural right of their respective offices, reflecting what the law of nature requires of them in performing their duties to promote the common good of the family or nation. This means, for example, that children are not property that can be bought or sold,[20] nor may a father relinquish his paternal right voluntarily, although he may assign it to a substitute if he is unable to exercise his authority properly.[21] Social and political ordering, as afforded by the family or commonwealth respectively, consists of discharging a natural right which conforms to the dictates of the offices, delimiting how a parent or sovereign is to govern in a manner promoting the welfare of those under their authority.

Althusius emphasizes a more seminal role for the family. Human life and lives are formed within a series of overlapping symbiotic associations. The respective rights of these associations are determined by their inherent natures and structures. The family is a simple and private association based upon the natural institution of marriage, and is the primary association from which all others constituting civil society are derived, because of the mutual affection and assistance it affords. The family is 'rightly called the most intense society, friendship, relationship, and union, the seedbed of every other symbiotic association'.[22] Families consist of conjugal and kinship associations, the former encompassing a covenant between wife and husband, the latter entailing the education of children.[23] What is perhaps Althusius's most perceptive contribution to social and political thought is his insistence that the family is a political rather than economic institution, for no other private or public association can be ordered properly in its absence. Consequently, household governance

---

[18] See Grotius, *Rights of War*, 'Preliminary Remarks' 2. 5. 3.   [19] Ibid. 2. 5. 23.
[20] Although a 'father may put his son in pledge, and if necessary, even sell him, where there is no other means of providing for him' (ibid. 2. 5. 5).
[21] Ibid. 2. 5. 26.   [22] See Althusius, *Politics*, 23.   [23] Ibid. 24–6.

is foundational to just social and political ordering: well-ordered families are a prerequisite for preserving a right social and political order, because '*all* symbiotic association is essentially, authentically, and generically political. But not *every* symbiotic association is public.'[24] Rather, private associations, such as families, 'are the seedbeds of public association',[25] and as such are political in nature.

There are two prominent points regarding this inquiry into early liberalism that should be noted:

1. Authority devolves from the nature of a particular office as opposed to originating in the individual or corporate will. Paternal authority, for example, is derived from a peculiar right pertaining to the nature of paternity. A father is not asserting his subjective rights in respect of childrearing, but assumes certain duties and privileges in virtue of his paternal role. Thus the family discloses a structure of social and political ordering exercised *under the authority and right of the law of nature.*

2. Social and political ordering encompasses private and public associations, but their distinctive qualities demarcate integral boundaries. The family is related to but also differentiated from other forms of social and political association. The family, for instance, is a private association linked to public associations, because both are political in nature. Their respective patterns of governance should not be confused, however, for a family cannot be governed as a commonwealth, nor can a commonwealth be governed as a family, given the differing natures of their association. A well-ordered society entails a *right ordering of private and public associations to each other.* Consequently, early liberalism linked the family directly to social and political ordering through the principles of the *law of nature* and a *natural right of association.*

Contractarian revision

The contractarians initiated a substantial revision of these foundational principles. Humans are not drawn by nature into civil society,

---

[24] Ibid. 27 (emphasis added).   [25] Ibid. 27.

but form it to overcome a state of nature that is inimical or indifferent to their welfare. Social and political ordering is not an outgrowth of a natural inclination, but a response to an inadequate natural endowment. This caricature is especially pronounced in Thomas Hobbes, who portrays the state of nature as a realm of perpetual strife.[26] If humans are to avoid perpetual warfare, they must form commonwealths governed by reason rather than subjected to the capricious and destructive elements of their natural proclivities. This task requires individuals to surrender their natural freedom to a sovereign, who in turn redistributes it as political rights and duties.[27] Humans must carve out for themselves a peaceful niche in the midst of a hostile natural environment. A central element of Hobbes's account is a fundamental dichotomy between history and nature: history is the exclusive domain of purposeful human action in which social and political ordering is constructed and imposed for the sake of keeping a threatening state of nature at bay.

Although John Locke does not portray the state of nature in as bleak terms, he is nonetheless confident that it is not inclined towards promoting human welfare.[28] The same natural forces that sustain life also inflict suffering and death. Moreover, since nature does not endow individuals equally, the weak are at the mercy of the strong, further exacerbating a condition of misery.[29] The only recourse is to use reason in consenting to self-imposed but mutually beneficial limitations, entailing, similarly to Hobbes, surrendering natural freedoms that are redistributed as political rights. The foundation of social and political ordering is contractual, for the social contract exists to prevent humans from regressing to an anarchic state of nature;[30] natural inequality is replaced with social and political equality expressed through citizens exercising their rights.[31] Locke shares with Hobbes the conviction that

---

[26] See Hobbes, *Leviathan* (1996 edn), 1. 13.   [27] Ibid. 1. 14.

[28] See Locke, *Two Treatises of Government* (1967 edn), 2. 2.

[29] Ibid. 2. 3.

[30] This is especially the case regarding the protection of property. Ibid. 2. 9.

[31] Commenting on Locke, George Grant has observed: 'All members of society are equal in the possession of these rights, because whatever other differences there may be between human beings, these differences are minor compared to the equality of our fundamental position: to be rational is to be directed by the dominating desire for comfortable preservation' (*English-Speaking Justice* (1985), 18).

meaningful human existence is grounded in history (as opposed to nature), but he is more suspicious of centralized political power, fearing that natural inequalities will be exchanged for artificial disparities.[32] Consequently, he fashions a notion of fundamental rights that cannot be transgressed or surrendered, especially in respect to private property;[33] a society forged within a history separated from nature is further divided into distinct private and public realms. Although individuals consent to restrictions on their natural liberty for the sake of a peaceful social and political order, there remains an unassailable domain of inalienable human rights.

The contractarians effectively expunged the early liberal perception of humans as inherently social creatures, and thereby civil society as a reflection of human nature. Rather, civil society is an artificial construct, marking an attempt to overcome both nature and human nature in fashioning a more humane world. Reason and the will are the pivotal forces in constructing a rational social and political order. Civil rights are not grounded in a natural right, but in the consent of the parties to a social contract. Missing too is an organic image of civil society, for the private and public domains are not poles demarcating a spectrum of human associations, but divisible realms of human activity. The contractarians displaced the law of nature with the *laws of contractual consent*, and the right of natural association with the *rights of voluntary affiliation*. Since the public realm reflects the consent of the people to the social contract, the sovereign constitutes and asserts their general will. Authority is reduced to assigning roles and tasks to implement the will of the contracting parties. A similar pattern holds true in the associations comprising the private domain. Since there is no inherent nature to particular institutions or offices (such as are found in the family), the persons performing these roles assume functional responsibilities in fulfilling the terms of a contract. The social and political ordering enabled by such contracts encapsulates peaceful regimes of law, but it is a law originating in the consent of the parties overcoming a natural state of affairs instead of conforming to the law of nature.

[32] See Locke, *Two Treatises*, 2. 11–13. This suspicion is also present in his criticism of Filmer's account of monarchy in the first treatise.

[33] Ibid. 2. 7, esp. § 87.

In addition, to ensure that the social contract does not replicate the state of nature's arbitrary distribution of power, procedural safeguards are needed, further widening the gulf separating the private and public domains. Ideally, the public domain consists of alienable rights that are assigned and surrendered in accordance with the general will of the people, whereas the private realm encompasses inalienable rights that are exercised freely by the persons possessing them. The contractarians placed the family exclusively within the private realm where, as Althusius feared, it was reduced to an economic institution for accumulating and exchanging property. The domestic household was thereby rendered a superficial consideration in the social and political theory of the contractarians, and was addressed only to the extent that it either assisted or impeded the implementation of the social contract.

This meant, however, that contractarians could not account for the continuing necessity of the family, or some equivalent substitute, within the terms of their theoretical frameworks. Marriage was explicable as a contract between consenting adults, but how were offspring to be understood within the parameters of this relationship? Clearly children cannot consent to the parents that rear them, yet given the need of civil society to perpetuate itself, the social and political ordering of procreation and childrearing could not be ignored. Promiscuous reproduction would prove anarchic, and parents seemed to be in the best position to provide childcare. The proffered resolution was to preserve families as a necessary vestige of the state of nature, while containing them so as not to contaminate the larger political community. Hobbes portrayed the family as a 'little monarchy' unrelated to governing the commonwealth,[34] while Locke appealed to a divine ordinance enjoining parents to care for their children, but it was a relationship from which no larger political implications could be drawn.[35] These 'solutions', however, amplified rather than eased the predicament, for civil society remained dependent on the state of nature it was trying to escape. Somehow a natural parental right should be exercised in a manner that prepared children to enter a contractual social and political order but, as the contractarians argued, the household and civil society are based on antagonistic principles: the former is

---

[34] See Hobbes, *Leviathan*, 2. 20.
[35] See Locke, *Two Treatises*, 2. 6; cf. Robert Filmer, *Patriarcha* (1991 edn).

founded on natural parental authority, while the latter is derived from free and rational consent. Moreover, the transition from the private to public sphere appeared inexplicable, so the perpetuation of civil society remained fixed on an unreliable groundwork. Consequently, the contractarians failed to provide a constructive foundation of social and political ordering, for their programme was founded upon a critical prognosis of the state of nature. Although nature had been displaced as the basis of civil society, no compelling substitute was offered to fill the resulting void.

The Kantian revision

It was Immanuel Kant who tried to fill this void by shifting the rationale for social and political ordering away from avoiding the state of nature to asserting the power of the rational human will over nature. According to Kant, social and political construction is an act of free human will.[36] Unrestrained freedom, however, promotes anarchy and warfare, because individuals are inclined to assert themselves against each other, nor does an irrational will enable the construction of a peaceful civil society. Rather, law based on reason is required to constrain freedom, directing it in an orderly manner towards the realization of a civil society and political state reflecting the rational and universal will of the people.[37] The practical implication of this universal will is the social contract in which the people freely consent to lawful constraints upon their freedom, for nature has endowed humankind with a capacity for reason to be used in forging a history of its own self-mastery.

Fashioning such a history is a complex undertaking, because humans are simultaneously inclined to live as isolated individuals *and* in societies or communities.[38] These divergent inclinations are not debilitating,

---

[36] Noting a similarity with Hobbes, Reiss asserts that, according to Kant, politics 'belongs to that sphere of human experience in which man's will can be corrected by another will, for like Hobbes, Kant reduces all action to the will' ('Introduction', in Kant, *Political Writings* (1991 edn), 21).

[37] As Reiss argues: 'What is ... needed is a will that binds every one equally, i.e., a collectively universal will that alone can give security to each and all' (ibid. 29).

[38] This is a condition that Kant describes as 'the *unsocial sociability* of men' in which a 'tendency to come together in society, couples, however, with a continual resistance

however, for nature uses them to achieve its 'highest purpose',[39] namely, the progressive development of latent human talents. For Kant, nature is synonymous with providence,[40] so the conflict stimulated by a society that humans 'cannot *bear* yet cannot *bear to leave*'[41] directs them towards their own fulfilment.[42] It is due to nature, 'fostering social incompatibility, enviously competitive vanity, and insatiable desires for possession or even power'[43] that humans are stirred to subject their conduct to the dictates of reason. Since 'man wishes concord, but nature, knowing better what is good for his species, wishes discord',[44] humans are goaded into developing their reason. Civil society is composed of individuals in a state of conflicting desires that can only be channelled in a constructive direction through the wilful ordering of their rational self-constraint. In short, the ghost of the state of nature haunts humankind, spurring a lawful ordering of its social life as a moral and political practice of self-mastery.

Such social and political ordering can only be accomplished by autonomous individuals, otherwise their capacity for reason remains underdeveloped. There is a corresponding law of freedom that should be willed universally by rational people, and reflected in the structures of social and political institutions. In maximizing their autonomy, humans are emancipated from unwarranted interference and coercion, resulting in peaceful civil societies and political regimes which all rational people desire. Yet, as noted above, this desirable concord is not

which constantly threatens to break this society up. This propensity is obviously rooted in human nature. Man has an inclination to *live in society*, since he feels in this state more like a man, that is, he feels able to develop his natural capacities. But he also has a great tendency to *live as an individual*, to isolate himself, since he encounters in himself the unsocial characteristic of wanting to direct everything in accordance with his own ideas' ('Idea for a Universal History', ibid. 44; emphasis original).

[39] Kant, Political Writings 45–6. Elsewhere, Kant contends that man 'is the true *end of nature*, and that nothing which lives on earth can compete with him in this respect' ('The Contest of Ideas', ibid. 226; emphasis original).

[40] See Kant, 'Perpetual Peace', ibid. 108–9.

[41] Kant, 'Idea for a Universal History', ibid. 44 (emphasis original).

[42] Ibid. 45–6.

[43] Ibid. 45. Thus Kant's emphasis on law rather than nature for achieving civil and international peace, and his criticism of Grotius and Pufendorf for using the law of nature to justify aggression (see 'Perpetual Peace', ibid., 103–4).

[44] Kant, 'Idea for a Universal History', ibid. 45. Elsewhere Kant asserts: 'The mechanical process of nature visibly exhibits the purposive plan of producing among men, even against their will and indeed by means of their discord' ('Perpetual Peace', ibid. 108).

the discord imposed by nature. In reconciling this discrepancy, individuals must freely submit themselves to self-imposed and universally legislated constraints upon their freedom. In this respect, Kant establishes a constructive base for a liberal account of social and political ordering, in that nature provides a providential and eschatological impetus for asserting the primacy of the human will. The contending inclinations of human nature unleash a progressive historical process, ending in the perfection of civil society that humans have willed themselves to construct and inhabit; they transform their own nature through the power of their reason and rational will.[45] Humans may imagine, and hence will, a destiny in which they emerge 'from the guardianship of nature to the state of freedom'.[46]

It may appear that Kant has worked his way back circuitously to the foundational principles of early liberalism. As in Grotius, rights are founded upon the bedrock of law, and similar to Althusius, reason stimulates a natural inclination towards sociability. This appearance is misleading, however, for Kant does not attempt to place an early liberal account of social and political ordering upon a firmer theoretical foundation, but negates its underlying principles. The rational will does not evoke a history enabling the perfection of human nature, but a constructed history designed to reshape nature in the image of the human will. Nature is stripped of its normative status, and reduced to raw material that humans may use in forging their history. The practical import of Kant's programme is seen in his presumption that natural inequalities are not merely unfortunate but irrational, and should be redressed through political rights enabling individuals to pursue a universally willed good. The means of exercising these rights is the social contract, entailing self-imposed constraints upon personal freedom. This implies that freedom is synonymous with autonomy, for it is only autonomous persons who may submit themselves freely to such restrictions. Moreover, his account of freedom requires a form of social and political ordering protecting the primacy of rights, 'because any limitations on *external* freedom stand in the way of the exercise of our autonomy'.[47] Hence Grotius is turned upside down, for rights are

---

[45] See Kant, 'The Contest of Faculties', ibid. 184–5.

[46] Kant, 'Conjectures on the Beginning of Human History', ibid. 226.

[47] Grant, *English-Speaking Justice*, 27 (emphasis added).

not based on a law of nature, but are wilfully asserted in constructing a rational social and political life.

Implementing the social contract requires a wider separation of the private and public realms than was envisioned by the contractarians. If the social contract is to reflect genuine consent, then the practical means of executing its terms cannot impose a particular morality upon the contracting parties. Kant divides morality from reason, assigning the former to the private domain and the latter to the public realm. Nor should there be any formal overlap, for peaceful social and political ordering is achieved through procedural mechanisms which are morally neutral, thereby protecting the autonomy of individuals.[48] Such a scheme ensures that social and political institutions assist individuals in correcting natural inequalities, further implying that civil society exists for the purpose of enabling humans to assert their rational will over an irrational nature. A limited political state, promoting a morally neutral public life, is both a practical accommodation and normative commitment to a mastery of nature, and transformation of human nature. Any organic imagery of civil society is swept aside, for the line drawn by Locke between the private and public realms becomes for Kant a wide chasm. Contrary to Althusius, individuals do not discover their freedom within imposed structures of natural associations, but in asserting their autonomy through self-imposed restraints. The private realm must thereby be protected from external interference, while the public domain must ensure that individual autonomy is not violated. Consequently, civil society does not entail an integral ordering of given affinities, but the rational negotiation of contracts among autonomous individuals.

Kant's emphasis on contractual relationships allows him to reduce the family to a rational performance of marital and parental duties that accord with the general will of the people. Since most private associations incorporate unequal relationships, the welfare of the weaker parties depend on the goodwill of the stronger. Procedural safeguards are required to promote such beneficence for, in the eyes of civil law,

---

[48] Criticizing Kant, Grant argues: 'Properly understood, morality is autonomous action, the making of our own moral laws. Indeed any action is not moral unless it is freely legislated by the individual. Therefore the state is transgressing its proper limits when it attempts to impose on us our moral duties' (ibid. 28).

'as the pronouncement of the general will',[49] they are equal since every person possess inalienable birthrights within the larger social contract.[50] The same pattern holds true for the familial association. The wife depends on the goodwill of her husband, and children depend on the goodwill of their parents. Yet as members of a larger commonwealth they are equally free, acquiring political rights in virtue of that membership which limits the prerogatives of husbands and parents. Indeed, Kant implies that national affinity is equivalent, if not superior, to familial association since both occur through birth.

The human beings who make up a nation can, as natives of the country be represented as analogous to descendants from a common ancestry (*congeniti*) even if this is not in fact the case. But in an intellectual sense or for the purpose of right, they can be thought of as offspring of a common mother (the republic), constituting, as it were, a single family (*gens natio*) whose members (the citizens) are all equal by birth.[51]

Civil society has a right to ensure that spousal and parental goodwill accords with the general will, and may enforce the appropriate discharge of their respective duties. Parents, for instance, are obligated to prepare their children to exercise their freedom, equality, and independence within a society of free, equal, and independent citizens.[52]

In subjecting childrearing to the general will, Kant rescues the family from the state of nature by delimiting parental prerogatives through legal obligations and constraints. Parents are the agents of civil society and the state in preparing new generations of citizens, thus their authority is derived from the general will rather than any inherent qualities pertaining to the parental office. In dismantling this final vestige of the state of nature, the only remaining dimension of procreation and childrearing that is not potentially subject to public regulation is sexual intercourse, which, within the bounds of lawful marriage, may be pursued without any external restrictions.[53] In respect to the social and political ordering of the family, the boundary separating the private and public domains

[49] See Kant, 'On the Relationship of Theory to Practice in Political Right', ibid. 75.
[50] Ibid. 75–7. Certain rights are inalienable because their surrender would deprive individuals of the right to enter into contracts, thereby invalidating the prior contract that allows them to surrender alienable rights.
[51] Kant, *The Metaphysics of Morals* (1996 edn), 'The Theory of Right', 2. 2. 53.
[52] Ibid. 2. 1. 46–8.   [53] Ibid. 3. 24–7.

becomes a flexible apparatus that may be shifted in accordance with the general will. Kant, in short, marks a further revision of liberal social and political theory that had been introduced by the contractarians. The laws of contractual consent become the *legislated will*, while the rights of voluntary association are transformed into the *rights of citizenship*. Subtly, the burden of the interdependent relationship between civil society and the state is shifted, with the former becoming dependent upon the latter rather than vice versa. Moreover, since both civil society and the state are artefacts reflecting the general will, there is no inherent nature or structure of the familial association that determines what it means to be a spouse, parent, or child. Instead, these roles manifest a rational performance of duties ultimately benefiting the parties involved directly, as well as civil society and the state indirectly. There are no parental or familial rights that must be safeguarded by civil law, but members of families are protected by, and may assert, their civil rights as citizens. The privacy of the family is thereby further reduced to economic and interpersonal activities satisfying the physical and affective needs of its members.

LATE LIBERAL VOICES

Kant may be used to conveniently locate the origin of modern liberalism,[54] for his work has shaped many subsequent developments in liberal social and political theory.[55] This influence can be seen by examining the works of two contemporary liberal theorists.

John Rawls

Rawls is one of the most influential political theorists of late liberalism, endeavouring to place the broad principles of the social contract

---

[54] According to MacIntyre, Kant is the most prominent figure in transforming liberalism into a distinct moral tradition (see *Whose Justice? Which Rationality?* (1988), 326–48).

[55] For overviews of Kant's influence on the development of modern liberal social and political theory, see Ronald Beiner and William James Booth (eds), *Kant and Political Philosophy* (1993); Patrick Riley, *Kant's Political Philosophy* (1983); and Hans Saner, *Kant's Political Thought* (1973).

within a Kantian framework.[56] Although an extensive examination of his work is beyond the scope of this chapter, focusing on the more salient features of his account of justice as fairness will serve to illustrate the general tenets of late liberal social and political theory.[57]

According to Rawls, a well-ordered society is based on a distribution of rights and duties promoting a fair distribution of social and economic advantages. This goal is achieved when individuals consent freely to rational principles enabling a pursuit of their respective interests.[58] A just society cannot be based on either nature or history, for justice cannot be rendered when shackled by either natural or historical accidents. Hence the need for the hypothetical 'original position'[59] in which individuals deliberate behind a 'veil of ignorance'[60] on how a society based on the dictates of reason should be constructed. Rational people will not choose to be encumbered by natural or social inequalities, and will therefore envision a society devoted to mitigating these limitations.

The practical import of this theoretical account of justice is that it intensifies a fundamental dichotomy between the private and public domains that had been introduced by the contractarian and Kantian revisions. For Rawls, free and rational individuals are by definition autonomous persons, because they are in a position to legislate self-imposed constraints, promoting a fair pursuit of their respective interests.[61] The private realm is where individuals are at liberty to hold whatever moral convictions and form whatever associations or communities they may choose, while the public domain enables a fair exercising of rights protecting the autonomy of persons pursuing their interests. These rights are political, economic, and individualistic in character, because the 'distribution of wealth and income, and the hierarchies of authority must be consistent with both the liberties

---

[56] See John Rawls, *A Theory of Justice* (1972), p. viii. Kant plays a more nuanced role in Rawls's later book, *Political Liberalism* (1996).

[57] For a theological critique of late liberal social and political theory, especially as it pertains to Rawls, see Song, *Christianity and Liberal Society*, 85–127.

[58] See Rawls, *Theory of Justice*, 3–17.

[59] Ibid. 17–22, 118–36. See also Rawls, *Political Liberalism*, 304–10.

[60] See Rawls, *Theory of Justice*, 136–42.

[61] In *Political Liberalism*, Rawls draws a distinction between political and moral autonomy (see pp. 72–81).

of equal citizenship and equality of opportunity'.[62] The political ordering of social institutions assists individuals in holding their personal convictions and forming voluntary associations, while ensuring that others are not prevented or unfairly impeded from doing the same. Nothing other than a procedural[63] or 'free standing'[64] account of the public sphere can result from the original position, because no reasonable society would impose a normative vision of the good without violating the liberty of persons holding contending visions. Social and political ordering is necessarily procedural in character, for it is the only fair mechanism for inspiring the free consent and universal will of reasonable people.[65]

The public domain is not as morally vacuous as it may first appear, for Rawls establishes his procedural account of justice on two normative convictions. First, he presumes that moral discernment consists of hypothetical deliberation, cut off from any natural or historical contexts. Autonomy, liberty, and fairness are invoked as self-evident standards of social and political ordering. Second, freestanding public mechanisms are not value-neutral, but incorporate an overlapping consensus of moral beliefs held by private citizens and voluntary associations comprising a pluralist society.[66] Within the bounds of procedural discourse contending claims may be reconciled, although the normative reasons for arriving at such an overlapping consensus may differ. As Rawls admits, this means that 'a liberal view removes from the political agenda the most divisive issues, serious contention about which must undermine the bases of social cooperation'.[67] Moreover, there is an eschatological imperative underlying these normative convictions, namely, that the will should displace nature and history in determining humankind's destiny. And the practical means of asserting the will is technology, especially in ensuring that future generations receive the best possible genetic inheritance.[68]

---

[62] Rawls, *Theory of Justice*, 61; see also pp. 60–5.   [63] Ibid. 83–90.

[64] See Rawls, *Political Liberalism*, 140–4.

[65] Rawls asserts: 'The original position may be viewed ... as a procedural interpretation of Kant's conception of autonomy and the categorical imperative' (*Theory of Justice*, 256; see also 251–7).

[66] See Rawls, *Political Liberalism*, 133–72. Cf. Trigg's critique in *Rationality and Religion* (1998), 8–28.

[67] Rawls, *Political Liberalism*, 157.   [68] See Rawls, *Theory of Justice*, 107–8.

Since a well-ordered society consists of free, equal, and autonomous persons,[69] Rawls observes that the 'monogamous family' often institutionalizes social and economic inequality,[70] erecting barriers to fair opportunity.[71] Although the family may incorporate some positive values, its possible abolition, in the name of social justice, must nevertheless be entertained.[72] Some type of familial association is appropriate, provided it assists children in maturing into free and autonomous adults.[73] Given the psycho-social needs of children, parents may assert a limited and provisional authority tempered by the principle of fairness. This proviso is required to ensure that children develop an adequate foundation for their subsequent independence. Parents instil in their offspring moral attitudes, and since the chief familial values are 'obedience, humility, and fidelity',[74] they must be supplemented by egalitarian values, based on reason rather than parental authority and natural sentiment. Consequently, the family plays a minor role in the social ordering of childrearing, while other institutions assume primary responsibilities for the health, education, and welfare of children. Parents are reduced to meeting the basic needs of their children and promoting their self-esteem which serves as the cornerstone of a well-ordered society.[75] The family is merely one human association among many where children learn how to pursue their interests and exercise their rights.[76]

[69] These qualities entail the absence of external constraints that prevent persons from pursuing their reasonable interests. Ibid. 201–5, 513–20; see also Rawls, *Political Liberalism*, 77–81.

[70] See Rawls, *Theory of Justice*, 7.   [71] Ibid. 301.

[72] 'It seems that even when fair opportunity...is satisfied, the family will lead to unequal chances between individuals. Is the family to be abolished then? Taken by itself and given a certain primacy, the idea of equal opportunity inclines in this direction' (ibid. 511; cf. Rawls, *Political Liberalism*, pp. xxx–xxxi).

[73] 'Now I shall assume that the basic structure of a well-ordered society includes the family in some form, and therefore that children are at first subject to the legitimate authority of their parents. Of course, in a broader inquiry the institution of the family might be questioned, and other arrangements might indeed prove to be preferable' (Rawls, *Theory of Justice*, 462–3).

[74] Ibid. 466.   [75] Ibid. 463–4; see also Rawls, *Political Liberalism*, 173–211.

[76] See Rawls, *Theory of Justice*, 467–72. Rawls also contends that the 'nature of the family', as well as its 'legally recognized forms of property' and 'organization of the economy', belong to the basic structure of civil society (see *Political Liberalism*, 257–9). Consequently, if parental authority retards the personal development of children there is no reason why it should 'govern our lives' (See *Theory of Justice*, 514–15.)

Rawls represents the capstone of a series of revisions in liberal social and political theory. What Grotius propounded as the law of nature and what became for contractarians the laws of consent, in turn refined by Kant into the legislated will, is transformed by late liberalism into the *mastery of nature*. Likewise, Althusius's right of association is metamorphosed into a right to form voluntary associations and rights of citizenship, culminating in the *rights of persons*. Late liberal social and political theory marks a reversal of its own origins, for rather than imposing a social and political order attempting to safeguard nature while evoking out from it a history, it subsumes both within an assertive individual and corporate will. Consequently, there is no social human nature that law must honour, but rather law exists to assist persons in mastering their own nature and history. Nor is there any natural structure of human associations from which humans derive their personhood, but instead persons assert their rights against the external and malleable constraints of human associations.

Susan Moller Okin

According to Susan Moller Okin, the principal weakness of late liberal social and political theory is that it continues to maintain a deep divide between private, domestic life and public, political life. This division effectively excludes women from the civil and political spheres, because only men can easily move back and forth across the divide. The fact that most liberal theorists ignore the family or dismiss it as a largely irrelevant consideration reflects a strong bias against women. The cost of this omission is dear, because the unjust division of labour between the sexes 'is inflicting increasingly serious damage on children as well as women, and it is also destroying the family's potential to be a crucial first school where children develop a sense of fairness'.[77] Moreover, as long as this omission continues, the damage inflicted upon women and children will be perpetuated if not amplified, for unless there is 'justice within the family, women will not be able to gain equality in politics, at work, or in any other sphere'.[78]

[77] Susan Moller Okin, *Justice, Gender, and the Family* (1989), p. vii.
[78] Ibid. 4.

Okin, however, is not sanguine about any of late liberalism's competing social and political theories. She contends that libertarianism is based on absurd principles, and that tradition-based and communitarian alternatives are incoherent, male-centric, and misogynist.[79] If a just social and political order for women and children is to be established, there is no realistic alternative to liberalism, and despite Rawls's failure to adequately address gender issues, his doctrine of justice as fairness offers the most promising route for radically reforming the family. A 'consistent and wholehearted application' of his doctrine will 'challenge fundamentally the gender system of our society'.[80] The principal problem with the contemporary family is that it is buried deeply within the private sphere, and is therefore not subject to public scrutiny and regulation. This placement is categorically incorrect, because the family, as an involuntary association, is properly a political, rather than social, institution. Specifically, the familial is political, for power—the paradigmatic political category—is central to family life, and the domestic sphere is a creation of political decisions. Moreover, it is within the family that we become gendered selves, and where basic divisions of labour are learnt.[81] Given these crucial formative tasks, it is imperative that women and children are rescued from their domestic captivity. Yet how can late liberal households be brought into the political domain?

It is at this juncture that Okin commends the tenet of justice as fairness as a useful instrument of feminist critique.[82] In particular, the 'significance of Rawls's central, brilliant idea, the original position, is that it forces one to question and consider traditions, customs, and institutions from all points of view, and ensures that the principles of justice will be acceptable to everyone, regardless of what position "he" ends up in'.[83] Since gender is the principal consideration at stake, analysing the justice of familial structures and relationships must be conducted behind this veil of ignorance. People thus deliberating would surely insist that women and men interact, and girls and boys be reared in households that honour their equality. In the absence of

---

[79] See her critiques of Nozick (ibid. 76–88), MacIntyre (ibid. 42–62), and Walzer (ibid. 62–8, 111–17).

[80] Ibid. 89–90.   [81] Ibid. 124–33.   [82] Ibid. 101–9.   [83] Ibid. 101.

such equalitarian homes, injustice will continue to permeate society through sexist behaviours and divisions of labour. All individuals must benefit from a pattern of psychological and moral development that 'is in all essentials identical'. Consequently, children must be equally 'mothered and fathered', for the goal is to develop 'a more complete *human* personality than has hitherto been possible'.[84] Given this potential, it is incumbent upon the state to promote a radical restructuring of the family. This is *the* premier task of late liberal social and political theory, for contemporary families, more often than not, hinder child development, especially in respect of instilling a sense of justice, given their inherently unequal structures.

What is the primary characteristic of Okin's radically restructured family? In a word, it is genderless. This is the essential prerequisite, for a 'just future' is 'one without gender'.[85] Gender roles must be eliminated, because they impede the actualization of democratic ideals through their inherent inequality. The family is therefore a pivotal political institution for realizing democracy's true potential, since it is the principal institution that, for good or ill, reproduces civil society. The only pressing issue at stake is whether it will produce a future of justice or injustice. The primary benefit of a genderless family is that, in being fairer to women, a widespread commitment to equal opportunity and equity will also be promoted. In order to achieve this ambitious goal, Okin proposes a twofold strategy of moving simultaneously away from gender while protecting the vulnerable. The first vital step is to effectively separate childbearing from childrearing, so that the latter is not necessarily associated with women. So long as women are burdened with primary responsibility for childrearing, they will be denied the opportunity for full participation in the public realm. In order to effectively separate childbearing from childrearing, Okin contends that the workplace should be required by law to be genuinely gender-neutral. Such neutrality, however, would require employers to accommodate the familial needs of employees, particularly women. 'Pregnancy and childbirth, to whatever varying extent they require leave from work, should be regarded as temporarily disabling conditions like any others, and employers should

[84] See her critiques of Nozick (Moller Okin, *Justice, Gender, and the Family,* 76–88), MacIntyre (ibid. 42–62), and Walzer. 107 (emphasis original).
[85] Ibid. 171–2.

be mandated to provide leave for all such conditions.'[86] More sweep-
ingly, leave should also be granted to care for ageing parents, and
employers should be required to provide on-site daycare.

Although transforming the workplace marks an important step
towards a genderless society, care must be taken to protect the
vulnerable in making the transition. Okin's principal concern is
that some women, either by choice or necessity, will remain tied to
gendered marriages and families. In these cases, laws should be
enacted which prevent one spouse from becoming economically
dependent on the other. 'Such dependence can be avoided if both
partners have *equal legal entitlement* to all earnings coming into the
household.'[87] The easiest way to implement this policy would be to
require employers to issue pay cheques equally divided to both
partners. This does not mean that the wage-earner is paying the
partner for rendering domestic services and childcare. Rather, it
recognizes the 'fact that the wage-earning spouse is no more supporting the homemaking and child-rearing spouse than the latter is
supporting the former; the form of support each offers the family is
simply different'.[88] In short, it would be households, not individual
workers, who would sell their labour in the market.

Although protecting the vulnerable is an important dimension of
public policy, it should not distract attention from the larger goal of
creating a genderless society. Constructing egalitarian families and
workplaces will have reverberating consequences for all other social
and political institutions, culminating in a standard of justice that is
thoroughly humanistic. Okin is confident that a radical transformation of families is the lynchpin for achieving this lofty goal, especially
in respect of raising new generations freed from the shackles of their
gendered captivity. This is why households cannot be neglected in late
liberal social and political thought, for it is in childhood that basic
democratic values are shaped, and the 'disappearance of gender will
make the family a much better place for children to develop a sense of
justice'.[89] As women and men share parenting responsibilities equally,

---

[86] Ibid. 176. Okin offers the following qualification to her assertion: 'Of course,
pregnancy and childbirth are far *more* than simply "disabling conditions," but they
should be treated as such for leave purposes, in part because their disabling effects
vary from one woman to the next' (ibid.).

[87] Ibid. 180–1 (emphasis original).   [88] Ibid. 181.   [89] Ibid. 185.

both they and children will benefit from an enhanced sense of inter-dependence and capacity for empathy. The positive consequence of genderless parental care will not only be children with greater self-esteem and capacity for individual development, but more import-antly they will be nurtured as citizens dedicated to equality and justice.

Okin may be said to take Rawls's account of justice a step further than he is willing to go. She does not abolish the family, but accom-plishes the same effect by subsuming it into the political sphere, thereby rendering it invisible. This move is accomplished by separat-ing childbearing from childrearing, thereby charging government with the task of regulating childcare. This does not mean that the state has become the parent of its citizens, but ensuring that children are reared correctly requires extensive economic and educational reforms that make civil society more directly dependent upon the state. This extensive encroachment of the public domain into the private is required if gender is to be eradicated in order that justice might be rendered fairly and impartially. In this respect, there is no familial nature that government should protect and promote. Rather, the family, like all other social and political institutions, is a wilful and artificial construct, subject to periodic alteration as needed. More broadly, for Okin, *nature* is not something to be mastered, but a *concept to be deconstructed.* More importantly, this dismantling culminates in the construction of *genderless persons who are now free to exercise their rights in a genuinely humanistic and just manner.*

LATE LIBERAL CRITICS

Although Rawls and Okin contend that the trajectories of late liberal social and political thought lead logically to the family's abolition or radical transformation, their respective claims are not incontestable. It can be argued, for instance, that the family plays a crucial role in forming requisite liberal social values and political virtues. Contrary to Okin, however, justice does not require a radical reconstruction of familial roles and relationships along egalitarian lines. Rather, what is needed is to defend particular familial traditions from unwarranted political intervention. It is within these protected locales that democratic convictions and practices are best nurtured, precisely because they are sequestered from public scrutiny and regulation. In short, the modern bourgeois family is the institution best positioned to develop the sense of freedom and autonomy envisioned by late liberal social and political theory. Rawls and Okin are assaulting the very foundation of the justice they are purportedly championing and are thereby, perhaps unwittingly, opening the floodgates to moral nihilism and political anarchy. If freedom *and* justice are to prevail, the family must be strengthened instead of weakened. The remainder of this chapter examines two variant defences of the bourgeois family.

Brigitte Berger and Peter Berger

According to Brigitte and Peter Berger, the family has become a problem within late modern societies. The origin of this problem can be traced back to the Enlightenment's rebellion against tradition and authority. In casting off these structures, the family had to be reformed in line with liberal contractarian principles. Such reform, however, required that any organic understanding of the family also had to be jettisoned. The family was not a natural affiliation, but an intergenerational affiliation of individuals. The principal result of this reform, which took on a particular urgency in the nineteenth century, was the creation of the bourgeois family in Europe and North America. The ideal structure of this family incorporated 'a married couple and their minor children, living together in their own home, forming an intimate and protective environment, providing nurture and care to the individuals concerned'.[90] The principal values of the bourgeois family include a strong work ethic, delayed gratification, and personal responsibility. These values in turn reinforce an autonomous individualism, congruent with emerging liberal mores and convictions. Following Talcott Parsons, the development of these values are in response to the twin processes of secularization and modernization. The practical consequence of coping with these processes is that the family changed from a unit of production to that of

[90] Brigitte Berger and Peter L. Berger, *The War over the Family* (1983), 59.

consumption, effectively diminishing the value of household labour because it is not productive. Moreover, accommodating modernizing and secularizing trends means that the socialization of children is no longer confined primarily to the family, but is shared with other social institutions such as schools and social service agencies. The practical effect is to reduce the familial household to a private enclave of intimacy, affection, and, most importantly, consumption.

Although the bourgeois family was initially successful in accommodating rapid social and economic change, it was nonetheless ill-equipped to sustain itself in the face of the relentless forces of secularization and modernization. These forces encapsulated the liberal values of freedom and autonomy which the bourgeois family prevented individuals from fully realizing, given the inherently hierarchical relationships between spouses, and parents and children. Rather than being the nursery of civic virtues and values, the family was an impediment to be neutralized in creating liberal, egalitarian societies. Families were, after all, nothing more than collections of individuals sharing common interests and pursuits, from which no normative implications should be drawn, especially in regard to marriage and parenthood. Consequently, the family became the object of the withering critique, and vitriolic scorn of the various liberation movements and liberal political policies of the latter part of the twentieth century. Since this relic of male and class privilege is now in its death throes, the principal social and political problem to be solved is how to enable a wide variety of structures and relationships which may be described as familial in character to flourish. Or more prosaically: how to go about dismantling *the* family in favour of *families*.

The Bergers insist that the problem with this problem is that it is pure fiction. Portraying the family as a problem that needs to be fixed reflects a combination of revisionist history and flawed social science, driven by simplistic and anti-democratic ideological commitments. The family has not become problematic because of any so-called historical process; rather, this is a quandary fabricated by belligerent ideologues and self-interested bureaucrats. Contrary to the prevailing thesis that the bourgeois family is a provisional response to changing social, political, and economic circumstances, they contend that it served as the foundational source in the formation of modern, liberal democracy. It is the privacy afforded by this particular familial structure that enables the political rights and liberties enjoyed by citizens of democratic regimes. To attack the family, therefore, is tantamount to assaulting the lifeline of individual freedom and autonomy, prompting the Bergers to rise to its defence, for they 'believe in the basic legitimacy of the bourgeois family, historically as well as today, both in terms of morality and in terms of the requirements of a free polity'.[91]

The Bergers face three prominent enemies in waging their defensive campaign. They label the first group as the *critical camp*, a loose confederation of radical reformers dominated by feminists.[92] Their primary goal is to combine political equality with personal self-assertion, expressed practically as freedom from the bourgeois family. Consequently, the critical camp is often perceived as being anti-family and hostile to children, especially given its highly visible support of unrestricted access to contraception and abortion as an inviolable political right.

The *neo-traditionalist camp* is a reactionary movement against the radical reformers.[93] Comprised of religious and social conservatives, the movement was stirred up initially by liberalized abortion laws, and the 'new morality' legitimating sexual promiscuity and adultery. These issues, however, merely reflected a broader assault against the natural or organic structure of the family. Legislation embodying traditional values must therefore be enacted to protect and strengthen the family, and by extension civil society, from the menacing critics.

Finally, the *professional camp* is comprised of experts drawn largely from the fields of law and the social sciences.[94] Less ideologically motivated than the other two camps, it is nonetheless a highly self-interested movement. Drawing upon its expertise, it defines the problems afflicting the family defined in a manner that can only be remedied through professional intervention. There is a prevailing assumption, for example, that families are not organic units, but networks of individuals with unique needs. Other institutions, such as schools and social service agencies, are in a better position than the family to meet these needs.

---

[91] Berger and Berger, *The War over the Family*, p. vii.

[92] Ibid. 24–8. The authors also include a wide variety of other groups in this camp, such as swinging singles, gay activists, anti-natalists, and pacifists (see ibid. 134–5).

[93] Ibid. 28–32.   [94] Ibid. 32–6.

The Bergers reject all three camps for a variety of reasons. The critics are decadent anarchists whose self-indulgence is eroding the moral foundation of social ordering, while the neo-traditionalists are mired in a nostalgic longing to recover an ideal family that never existed. The professionals have compiled largely inaccurate data, thereby exacerbating rather than solving the problems they have defined. Moreover, the Bergers contend that the vast majority of people do not ally themselves with any of the camps, and find their respective claims and counter-claims baffling and irrelevant to the real needs of families. Consequently, they attempt to capture this middle ground through a reasonable defence of the bourgeois family. This defence is based on two criteria.[95] First, it must adopt a mediating and non-doctrinaire approach. Recognizing the highly pluralistic character of late modern societies, the authors do not appeal to any religious or ideological convictions in making their case. This move effectively mutes the shrill rhetoric of both the critics and neo-traditionalists.[96] The second criterion is that history and the social sciences must be taken into any contemporary account of marriage and family. History is needed to ground theoretical constructs of the family, thereby preventing unwarranted and irrelevant abstractions, and social scientific research is required to base public policies on empirical data instead of ideological assumptions.

Armed with these criteria, the Bergers defend the nuclear family as a '*precondition*, rather than a *consequence*, of modernization'.[97] The family's nuclear nature is not a modern invention, but has remained constant over time. The presence of household servants and apprentices in previous eras 'tended to obfuscate the nuclearity of the family structure'.[98] The nuclear structure grew more apparent as the family became a unit of consumption rather than production. This transition was a crucial step in promoting the growth of liberal democratic societies, for the 'bourgeois family has been the matrix... of a variety of values, norms, and "definition of reality." Put differently, the bourgeois family has engendered specific structures

---

[95] Berger and Berger, *The War and the Family*, 139–40.

[96] In order to make this move, the Bergers also insist that the highly contentious issue of abortion be removed as a weapon in this war over the family (ibid. 203–4).

[97] Ibid. 87 (emphasis original).   [98] Ibid. See also p. 95.

of human consciousness.'[99] These structures, which embodied the primary values of self-control and autonomy, were extended to other social institutions, and since bourgeois virtues derived from these values could be practised by anyone, they emphasized an inherent proclivity towards democracy. The nuclear family, in short, was the engine driving the transformation of Western civilization from protected enclaves of aristocratic privilege into free societies.

The Bergers believe that the structure of human consciousness embodied in the nuclear family is worth defending against the assaults that have weakened it, and by extension the free societies it helped create. Their belief is based on social scientific data, demonstrating that, contrary to the ideological claims of the critics and many members of the professional camp, other social institutions cannot adequately perform the crucial tasks of socialization. It is within the nuclear family that democratic values are best learnt and perpetuated. To attack the family, then, is tantamount to waging war against liberal democracy, and conversely defending the family is synonymous with protecting a worthy quest for human dignity and happiness. Consequently, the critics', and in some instances the professionals', attack on the family is either misinformed or incorporates a political agenda that is anti-capitalist and anti-democratic. This does not mean, however, that the Bergers align themselves with the neo-traditionalists, for that political agenda is too narrowly based on religious convictions that are no longer shared by pluralistic societies. Rather, what is needed is a normative *and* minimalist familial structure that allows for cultural variation and expression.

The Bergers' analysis regarding the relationship between the family and democracy discloses the centrepiece of their defence.[100] They contend that, since the nuclear family provides the best setting in which autonomous persons may develop, it is the '*empirical foundation of political democracy*'.[101] In making this claim, they place themselves in a philosophical tradition originating in Aristotle and extending through Locke, Hegel, and De Tocqueville, as opposed to an anti-family trajectory marked by Plato, Rousseau, and Marx. Following Aristotle, the Bergers contend that if children cannot learn to love their parents and siblings they will only love themselves. Such selfishness would be

[99] Ibid. 106.   [100] Ibid. 169–85.   [101] Ibid. 172 (emphasis original).

disastrous for subsequent social and political ordering. 'The family permits an individual to develop love and security—and most important, the capacity to trust others. Such trust is the prerequisite for any larger social bonds.'[102] If individuals cannot, or are not permitted to forge strong familial bonds, they will in turn be hard-pressed as citizens to develop social and political loyalties. The bourgeois family, then, 'is essential for the survival of a democratic polity'.[103]

More expansively, 'every human society is a moral community', and without a strong sense of shared values it will 'disintegrate'.[104] If no moral consensus exists, coercion becomes the only effective mechanism for maintaining social and political order, but such extensive coercion is incompatible with democracy. Moreover, other social and political institutions replace the family in forming and inculcating democratic values that effectively resist such recourse to coercion. 'No amount of legislation and court decisions can produce in the individual such basic moral ideas as the inviolability of human rights, the willing assent to legal norms, or the notion that contractual agreements must be respected.'[105] These institutions can only reinforce values formed in families, and political regimes attempting to become the creators of such values also tend to become totalitarian, a tendency, the authors note, shared by many critics of the family.[106] In the absence of any religious consensus, the family stands as the only reliable bulwark against these totalitarian tendencies, and is, therefore, an indispensable institution for preserving democratic values, and resisting the imperious pretensions of the late modern state.

The Bergers believe their defence of the family reflects the sentiments of the vast middle ground between the extremes of the critics and neo-traditionalists, and that social scientific data supports the family's indispensable role, thereby reorienting the influence of the professional camp. With these assumptions in mind, they suggest five broadly conceived policy recommendations for supporting the foundational status of the family in a democratic society.[107] First, the family should be restored as a private sphere, and protected

---

[102] In order to make this move, the Bergers also insist that the highly contentious issue of abortion be removed as a weapon in this war over the family', Berger and Berger, *The War and the Family,* 174.
[103] Ibid. 175.   [104] Ibid. 175–6.   [105] Ibid. 176.
[106] Ibid. 178–9.   [107] Ibid. 195–216.

from unwarranted political intrusions. Second, pluralism should be respected by enabling families to care for their members rather than relieving them of this responsibility. Third, autonomy should be empowered through the issuance of vouchers for various social services, especially education. Fourth, parental rights must be restored and defended. Finally, policies should recognize the varying communal structures in which particular families are embedded.

The Bergers' defence of the family may be said to be liberal, given its emphasis on autonomy and democratic values. Yet unlike late liberals, such as Rawls and Okin, they appeal to earlier contractarian rather than Kantian principles. The family is not an outgrowth of cooperative individuals pursuing their respective interests, but a natural affiliation underlying larger social and political associations. In this respect, parents are not Kant's agents of civil society and therefore subject to public regulation, but private custodians of the moral foundations of social and political order. Consequently, no amount of deliberation behind a veil of ignorance can displace the family's crucial role in maintaining a democratic polity, and hence, their insistence on the normative and particular structure of the bourgeois family. In appealing to Aristotle and Locke, the Bergers offer an alternative liberal variant to late liberalism as represented by Rawls and Okin. The associations comprising civil society are admittedly social constructs, but they are delineated by the given attributes and limits of familial affinity rather than created *ex nihilo*. It is the very privacy of the family that enables a robust public life. Justice is not achieved but impeded by unwarranted political interventions into this vital private sphere. A free civil society and democratic polity is, therefore, a *natural outgrowth of the bourgeois family*. They refuse, however, to appeal to any religious convictions in making this normative claim, thereby distancing themselves from neo-traditionalists. Rather, they appeal to the empirical data of history and social science to provide the necessary moral grounding as opposed to ignorant deliberation. The particular familial structures resulting from this admittedly minimalist moral foundation will be highly variable, but the Bergers are confident that, given the nature of the familial association, democratic values will nonetheless be inculcated, so long as families can be protected from unwarranted intrusions.

Christopher Lasch

A cursory reading of Christopher Lasch's *Haven in a Heartless World* may give the impression that it is a complementary text to the Bergers' work summarized above, perhaps even providing grist for their analysis.[108] Although they address similar issues, Lasch's critique undermines the moral grounding of the bourgeois family. History and social science do not disclose a natural familial association as the seedbed of democratic values. The Bergers believe that, since the professional camp has been sufficiently purged of false ideological assumptions, they can be allies in restoring the family by capturing the so-called middle ground. Their belief is misplaced, however, because the late modern nuclear family they wish to defend is not natural, but an artefact constructed by the professional camp whose aid they are soliciting. They assume that the problem at hand is to cleanse this group of its radical ideological assumptions in order that their social scientific methodologies may be properly applied as value-neutral enquiry. What they fail to recognize is that these very methodologies incorporate ideological presuppositions that are inherently illiberal, and now serve as a surrogate religious foundation of late modernity. The family is not so much besieged by other social institutions from which it has become alienated, but the seeds of its own internal destruction have already been planted and germinated. Whatever remnant of the bourgeois family may still exist, it is little more than an empty shell. The Bergers are waging a war that has already been lost.

Lasch makes this claim by undertaking a historical examination of the construction of the late modern family. He agrees that the bourgeois family was a driving force in the formation of liberal democracies and capitalist economies, but it was also a casualty. In response to these changing political and economic structures, the bourgeois family emphasized work, prudence, and domestic tranquillity by adopting the market-driven values of competition, individualism, postponed gratification, rational foresight, and accumulation of material goods. In adopting these values, a 'radical separation between work and leisure

[108] *Haven in a Heartless World* was originally published, six years before *The War over the Family*.

and between public life and private life' was taken for granted.[109] The price of this separation, however, was to transform the family into a secluded and insular enclave. 'As business, politics, and diplomacy grow more savage and warlike, men seek a haven in private life, in personal relations, above all in the family—the last refuge of love and decency.'[110] Family members on their own, however, are incompetent to build such a haven, and must turn to various experts to learn the requisite skills. A cadre of professionals—trained in social work, psychology, or law— are needed to teach individuals how to be competent spouses, parents, and homemakers. A happy marriage requires the mastery of interpersonal skills and sexual techniques. Parenthood is transformed into a parenting process, designed to promote the healthy psychological development of children. And parallel to the husband's career outside the home, the wife must also learn the 'careers' of 'motherhood and housewifery' based on the 'domestic science' of 'home economics'.[111] The family as haven was reconstructed as the outcome of various techniques, rather than a setting in which normative familial roles are performed.

The net result of this reconstruction was to make the family utterly dependent upon professional expertise. This is especially the case in respect to parenthood, for by first declaring 'parents incompetent to raise their offspring without professional help, social pathologists "gave back" the knowledge they had appropriated—gave it back in a mystifying fashion that rendered parents more helpless than ever, more abject in their dependence on expert opinion'.[112] The primary consequence of this dependency was to remake the family as a problem to be solved, for as a 'unity of interacting personalities'[113] the respective interests of wives and husbands, and children and parents were pitted against each other. This conflict became particularly pronounced in the latter half of the twentieth century, as evidenced by the so-called youth rebellion and women's liberation movement. The familial haven was actually a simmering caldron of

---

[109] See Lasch, *Haven*, 6–7.   [110] Ibid., p. xvix.

[111] Ibid. 10. The burden has been especially heavy on women in this professional reconstruction of the family, for a woman was not only expected to be an efficient household economist, but also a 'sexual partner, companion, playmate, and therapist' (ibid. 10–11).

[112] Ibid. 18.   [113] Ibid. 31–2.

discontent, requiring professional diagnosis and prescription to keep it under control.

Lasch devotes the bulk of his book to a detailed analysis of how this control is exercised. Summarizing two strands of his analysis, which are particularly pertinent to this inquiry, may serve to explicate the salient features of his argument. The first strand involves *economic control.* One way to manage the conflicting interests of family members is to increase household consumption of goods and services. Increased consumption presumably satisfies the respective interests of family members, thereby easing their inherent conflict. It is through consuming that interacting persons express their individuality. In this respect, the bourgeois family can be described as the engine that drove the initial development of early modern capitalist economies. In late modern capitalist economies the family is no longer a driving engine, but a passive receptacle of commodities. More tellingly, the economic imagery of autonomous consumers was internalized by the family in respect to its own sense of values and purpose; the walls delineating the family haven are illusory. 'The spirit of economic rationality had become so pervasive in modern society that it invaded even the family, the last stronghold of precapitalist modes of thought and feeling.'[114] The burden of this encroachment was especially heavy upon men in their roles as husbands and fathers. To secure the necessary capital for greater consumption they were increasingly absent from their family's daily life. This absence had a deleterious affect on the man's marital role as intimate lover and companion, as well as his paternal role. The market-driven logic of the bourgeois family worked against its own survival, for ever-increasing consumption required greater absence, which in turn exacerbated latent dysfunctional behaviours leading to marital and parental failure. The strength of this trend is seen in the steady increase of small families and childless marriages throughout the twentieth century. Since children were financial liabilities, they became optional by-products of marital relationships.

The second strand of Lasch's analysis may be characterized as *therapeutic control.* By the mid-twentieth century intellectual,

---

[114] Lasch, *Haven,* 36.

professional, and political elites agreed that something had to be done about the terrible state of the family. The problem was not merely the alarming divorce rate, and spread of juvenile delinquency; rather, the family had become a barrier to individual fulfilment, thereby exerting a cancerous effect upon the wellbeing of civil society. One plank of the remedy was a series of policies that displaced responsibility for the health, education, and welfare of children from families to other institutions, where socialization could be overseen by professionals instead of amateurish parents. More drastic measures were needed, however, to cure the family's inherent pathologies that were producing 'authoritarian personalities', the very antithesis of what was needed in a democratic society.[115] In short, the family had to be democratized for the sake of 'social hygiene'.[116] Consequently, the family became an illness to be cured, and members of the professional class came to see themselves as 'doctors to a sick society'.[117] In waging this hygenic war, the social sciences claimed a moral mantel once held by religion and philosophy. The principal goal was 'to spread the new gospel of relativism, tolerance, personal growth, and psychic maturity'.[118] In order to achieve this goal the antiquated notions of good and evil, ' "right and wrong", "guilt and sin"', had to be replaced 'with the new morality of "human relations" '.[119] Friendship replaced love and commitment as the underlying rationale for marital and familial relationships, but it is a flexible relation subject to frequent alteration. Nowhere was this malleable principle applied with more gusto than in the area of sexuality. Adultery and divorce, for instance, were not necessarily inappropriate, for they could actually enable the personal growth of the respective partners. And parents should have neither the authority nor the right to dictate the sexual behaviour of their adolescent children since effective contraception made experimentation readily available, and relatively safe, in this crucial area of personal development. In effect, in order to rid the family of its pathology it had to be reduced to one small group among many within the ideological matrix of 'nonbinding commitments'.[120]

---

[115] Ibid. 85–96.   [116] Ibid. 96.   [117] Ibid. 97–110, 150–7.
[118] Ibid. 97.   [119] Ibid. 102–3.   [120] Ibid. 134–41.

According to Lasch, the convergence of these controlling strategies had devastating consequences for social and political ordering. Since family members are 'autonomous agents', their unique needs reduce their relationships to a nexus of interpersonal interactions. Yet given the family's 'misguided obsession with order and stability', it effectively 'imprisons people in predetermining roles which inhibit personal growth'.[121] The family cannot thereby serve as a foundation of social and political ordering, but only reflects broader social and political conflicts. 'Conditions in the family thus mirror conditions in society as a whole, which have created an ever-present sense of menace and reduced social life to a state of warfare, often carried out under the guise of friendly cooperation.'[122] Individuals fit to be citizens of a democratic society were developed not because of but despite the enslaving confines of their families. The new cult of public hygiene, in league with governmental bureaucracies, has undertaken this liberation with a zeal to create a society that is not only radically egalitarian, but also thoroughly therapeutic.[123] The principal result of these twin emphases is the 'dissolution of authority', which 'brings not freedom but new forms of domination'.[124] When the moral authority of the family is no longer respected, the will is asserted through psychological manipulation or violence. Political ordering in particular is stripped to management or public relations, and power is, therefore, its own justification.

Contrary to the Bergers, there is simply no bourgeois family left to be defended. Although the old structures are seemingly still intact, its previous religious core cannot be replaced by the philosophical principles they champion. Nor does this imply that the contemporary family is an empty husk waiting to be filled. Rather, the family is an artefact and patient of the religion of public health. The Bergers are mistaken in their belief that the war over the family is a conflict between religious and profane forces that can be mediated on their middle ground. No such middle ground exists, for the war is being waged by contending religious armies, and the professional camp they claim has been neutered in this conflict is in fact a leading partisan in the struggle against traditional bourgeois values and

---

[121] Lasch, *Haven*, 151.   [122] Ibid. 157.
[123] Ibid. 171–4.   [124] Ibid. 183–4.

virtues. Lasch is aware that this struggle is necessarily religious, for it is only religion that can ultimately establish some type of moral authority. Consequently, the issue is not whether the family can or should recover its lost authority, but rather what kind of religion will establish the moral foundation of human associations broadly conceived as *familial* in character, and what implications this moral authority might have for social and political ordering. The only certainty is that any human association claiming to be a family in any normative sense must necessarily remain a besieged institution if late liberal society continues its illiberal evolution. Lasch offers no hint whether the war over the family is still worth contesting or has already been effectively settled, and provides no counsel whether Christianity should ally itself with bourgeois or public health combatants, or attempt to remain neutral. It is towards addressing these muted issues that I turn my attention in the next chapter.

3

Late Liberalism and Contemporary Christian Thought

According to many late liberal theorists, the family is a social institution in dire need of radical reform and political regulation. Rawls,
for instance, can muster no normative rationale for the family in a
well-ordered society. Its only value is its potential for promoting the
self-esteem of children, a task he readily admits could be undertaken
more effectively by other institutions. Okin builds upon this premise,
insisting that the state should enact legislation and regulations which
ensure the just and egalitarian ordering of households. The values
inherent in the family are inimical to liberal democratic society, and
their influence must be expunged or severely restricted. This attack on
the family has been chronicled and criticized by such writers as the
Bergers and Lasch. Contrary to the claim that families are pathological
breeding grounds of anti-democratic values, the Bergers contend that
the nuclear family embodies the foundational bourgeois morality of
liberal democracy. Defending the family is synonymous with protecting
freedom and liberty. Lasch is more ambivalent about the relationship
between the family and democracy, but he is alarmed by the untoward
social and political consequences of the family's deteriorating moral
authority. He is also less sanguine about mounting a successful defence
of the family, for he sees the attack as part of a religious, rather than
social and political, struggle, and he refuses, or is unable, to offer any
advice for how this culture war should be conducted.

One need not accept Lasch's speculative prognosis to recognize that
contemporary Christian thinking on the family must take into account
that it has become the object of heated moral debate. The purpose of this
chapter is to survey a representative range of Christian positions that

purportedly attempt to engage this volatile social and political context in an overtly theological manner. The first two approaches may be characterized, respectively, as *reformulation* and *resistance*. The former believes that a Christian understanding of the family must be radically reformulated in light of rapid social change; what is at stake is the adaptability and continuing relevancy of Christian faith. In contrast, the latter contends that the traditional family must be strengthened as a bulwark to resist late modernity's moral and social chaos; the issue at hand is the preservation of and fidelity to historic Christian doctrine. A third stance is that of *critical adaptation*. This approach selectively reinterprets *and* defends traditional doctrinal teaching on the family in response to late liberal social and political thought, as exemplified in three proposals that may be characterized, respectively, as *critical familism*, *church as first family*, and *household management*.

REFORMULATION

One possible theological response to late liberal social and political thought is to reformulate a Christian understanding of family in the light of dominant liberal values and presuppositions. Such revision is needed if the church is to make significant contributions to the social and political ordering of the family, and failing to do so would result in its curt dismissal as an antiquated and irrelevant institution. A promising route for reformulating a pertinent model of the family is to link core late liberal principles with appropriate theological convictions. The principle of individual autonomy, for example, is seemingly compatible with Christian notions of love and freedom. Humans, for instance, have an inherent capacity to love God and neighbour. A relationship with the neighbour, however, must be formed freely and willingly if it is to be a genuinely loving one. These relationships are formed by individuals who, in the freedom of their love, regard each other as equals who contribute to each other's welfare. Neighbour love is thereby characterized by mutuality and reciprocity. Consequently, late liberalism's commitment to autonomy and equality offers a fitting social setting in which loving relationships may be formed, and something akin to Rawls's portrayal of 'justice as fairness' secures a complementary political framework in which the core theological convictions of love and freedom are enacted.

More importantly, if loving relationships with neighbours are to be genuinely mutual and reciprocal, then adequate attention must be directed towards an individual's self-regard. This emphasis does not represent a transparent attempt to rationalize hedonism or narcissism with theological rhetoric, but is based on the assumption that self-love is not incompatible with or unrelated to neighbour love.[1] A love of neighbour is not inherently sacrificial, but should promote mutual self-fulfilment. Indeed, individuals cannot be said to be truly participating in a mutual and reciprocal relationship if they have not sufficiently developed certain qualities which can be offered freely to others. Appropriate self-love is therefore a prerequisite for neighbour love. In this respect, sin may be understood as psycho-social conditions that prevent individuals from pursuing self-fulfilment, and being liberated from these conditions may be said to be redemptive. We cannot love our neighbours freely until we love ourselves fully. Rawls's contention that self-esteem plays a pivotal role in a well-ordered society is again compatible with this theological conviction.

These emphases on self-fulfilment, mutuality, and reciprocity have received considerable attention in the spate of contemporary theological treatises praising the human body in general, and sexuality in particular.[2] It is as embodied creatures that we love ourselves and our neighbours. Moreover, being embodied means that we are also sexual beings. It is as women and men that we relate to each other, so there is a sexual component to every human relationship. An individual's self-fulfilment is dependent upon a series of both other-sex and same-sex relationships. Denying an individual the opportunity to develop the full range of these relationships is tantamount to prohibiting the possibility of maximizing her self-fulfilment. More importantly, these relationships are embedded in moral and

---

[1] See Gene Outka, *Agape* (1976), 55–74.

[2] See e.g. Christine E. Gudorf, *Body, Sex, and Pleasure* (1994). It should also be noted that not all theological discourse on embodiment supports these divisions, as exemplified in the encyclicals of John Paul II.

social traditions that are expressed through gender roles. These roles, however, are social constructs, rather than normative categories, and should not receive any political support or privilege. Indeed, traditional gender roles often impede the psycho-social development of individuals. Since these roles are malleable constructs, political ordering should permit a wide range of experimentation in order to deconstruct and reconstruct the sexual relationships that enable individuals to construct their respective identities as sexual beings. Consequently, social mores and legal codes which discriminate against homosexual, bisexual, and promiscuous lifestyles, for example, are unjust, because they are based on artificial distinctions that favour a so-called normative heterosexuality. In this respect, Okin's goal of establishing a genderless society is compatible with a theological emphasis on embodiment.

There are two implications that can be drawn from this theological emphasis on embodiment that are particularly germane to this inquiry. First, sexual behaviour is separated from procreation. This is not a novel development since same-sex relationships have always precluded the possibility of procreation, and birth control has a long history.[3] What has changed is that sexual experimentation, largely liberated from the prospect of unwanted offspring, is becoming an object of social approbation rather than stigma, and, co-laterally, being granted the status of a political right. Marriage, then, is a matter of personal taste, and should not be either a socially or politically privileged institution for ordering sexual behaviour or procreation. It follows that, secondly, marriage is effectively separated from family. Although some, if not many, individuals may choose to have children within the context of a marital relationship, there is no compelling reason why this pattern should be favoured over other alternatives. Since marriage enjoys no inherently superior moral status, other childrearing alternatives, such as single-parent, same-sex, or communal arrangements, should not be prohibited, unless harm, especially in the case of children, can be clearly demonstrated. Indeed, a highly diverse range of families should be encouraged to promote the self-development and fulfilment of parents and children.

[3] See Michel Foucault, *The History of Sexuality* (1985) and John T. Noonan, *Contraception* (1986).

From a theological perspective, these two divisions should not be mourned, but celebrated, for they facilitate the redemptive liberation of humans from oppressive gender roles and repressed sexual expression. The work of James B. Nelson may serve as a leading representative of this celebrative stance. His central contention is that the church must overcome two pervasive dualisms that warp its moral teaching.[4] On the one hand, a spiritualistic dualism separates an inferior body from the superior soul, while on the other hand, a patriarchal dualism subordinates inferior women to superior men. These dualisms incorporate the worse features of early Christian theology, Platonic philosophy, and Hebrew custom which were, in turn, perpetuated and reinforced by Augustine, Thomas Aquinas, and the Reformers. The principal consequence of this theological tradition is the creation of social and political orders comprised of individuals alienated from their bodies and feelings. This sad legacy must be expunged if the church is to help late modern societies escape the debilitating dichotomies that stem from this alienation. Nelson is not reticent in reducing the source of this alienation to human sexuality, for no social or political issue can be understood and solved in absence from this underlying sexual component.

The strategy for overcoming this alienation is to affirm embodiment as *the* defining characteristic of human beings, a trait that is sexual in nature. Nelson uses the 'notion of sexuality as something far more inclusive than specifically genital sex acts and their erotic accompaniments'.[5] Rather, sexuality is 'our self-understanding and way of being in the world', expressing 'God's intention that we find our authentic humanness in relationship'.[6] All human relationships are thereby sexual by definition, including the relationship with God. Consequently, the church is a 'sexual community'[7] seeking its 'sexual salvation'.[8] Salvation consists of healing and overcoming alienation. Humans are saved as sexual beings, and their hope therefore resides in the 'resurrection of the sexual body'.[9] The resurrection of the body is a powerful symbol of self-discovery as sexual beings, a process of self-acceptance prevented by the church's spiritual and patriarchal

---

[4] See James B. Nelson, *Embodiment* (1978), 37–69.
[5] Ibid. 17.   [6] Ibid. 17–18.   [7] Ibid. 14–16.
[8] Ibid. 70–4.   [9] Ibid 70.

dualisms. Coextensively, the incarnation affirms human sexuality, since Jesus was a sexual being. Together, incarnation and resurrection invite humans to embrace the flesh that God affirms, promoting in turn the values of self-acceptance, sensuousness, and freedom that lead inevitably to androgyny. According to Nelson, every person is by nature androgynous. This claim reflects the 'fact' that homosexual and heterosexual dimensions are present in each individual.[10] A fully developed psychological bisexuality is salvific and sacramental, because it inspires an empathy among females and males that liberates them from the bondage of their dualistic alienation. A growing acceptance of androgyny promotes greater unity with other persons and with God. Consequently, androgyny provides a natural and moral base for more egalitarian forms of social and political ordering.[11]

The more striking implications of such ordering are seen most vividly in Nelson's discussions of marital fidelity and same-sex unions. According to Nelson, adultery and infidelity are not synonymous terms. Adultery is sexual intercourse with a person who is not one's spouse, whereas infidelity marks the 'rupture of the bonds of faithfulness, honesty, trust, and commitment'.[12] Fidelity is commitment to a marital relationship over time, yet congruent with 'marital fidelity and supportive of it can be certain secondary relationships of some emotional and sensual depth, possibly including genital intercourse'.[13] Although the Bible and the teaching of Jesus seemingly forbid adultery, 'it is unrealistic and unfair to expect that one person can always meet the partner's companionate needs—needs which are legitimate and not merely individualistic, hedonistic, or egocentric'.[14] Interpersonal intimacy with others does not necessarily exclude the possibility of sexual intimacy as well, for friendship among sexual beings must *always* be open to the possibility of sexual interaction. Spouses, after all, are not hermits who happen to be living together. In addition, secondary relationships can strengthen a marriage. Only immature persons will not be open to the possibility of sexual intimacy with another person other than one's spouse, because each partner is concerned about the growth and fulfilment of the other. Extramarital affairs are therefore justified if the 'sexual sharing realistically

---

[10] Ibid. 78–9.   [11] For specific implications and proposals, ibid. 261–71.
[12] Ibid. 143.   [13] Ibid. 144.   [14] Ibid. 146.

promises to enhance and not damage the capacity for interpersonal fidelity and personal wholeness'.[15] This is compatible with a Christian understanding of marriage, because Jesus condemned an adultery of the heart, not the genitals. Nelson admits that his proposal challenges so-called traditional Christian moral teaching on marriage and the family, but he insists there is nothing inherently normative about monogamy or the nuclear family, and that the church should embrace a wide range of committed relationships and childrearing arrangements.

It is within the context of this expansive acceptance that Nelson addresses the issue of homosexuality in general, and same-sex union in particular. He contends that there is no sweeping condemnation of homosexuality in the Bible, and biblical passages which appear to be condemnatory can be dismissed because they are culturally conditioned and historically relative. Since biblical teaching offers no clear moral guidance—other than Jesus' invitation to seek 'wholeness and communion'[16]—the church is also free to discard or correct its traditional theological opinions in light of new scientific evidence and social circumstances. Natural law arguments that condemn homosexual acts, for example, because there is no reproductive potential, fail to recognize that human nature is a social construct rather than a given norm, and overpopulation has rendered the Bible's procreative mandate irrelevant. In addition, the assertion that only heterosexual relationships embody the *imago dei* is too narrow, and fails to recognize that every person has both heterosexual and homosexual dimensions. God's image and likeness is borne by androgynous individuals, and not by males and females joined in a one-flesh heterosexual union. It is only in the complete acceptance of same-sex relationships that God's 'humanizing intentions' are fulfilled, because such acceptance liberates everyone from oppressive sexual stereotypes.[17] Since gays and lesbians require relationships like everyone else, and since all relationships have an underlying sexual component, they should not be denied the freedom of sexual expression. Consequently, the church should simultaneously permit same-sex union for those desiring a lifelong relationship, and support the

---

[15] For specific implications and proposals, see Nelson, *Embodiment*, 151.
[16] Ibid. 181–2.   [17] Ibid. 197–8.

civil rights of homosexuals. 'When and if the church moves toward liturgical support of gay union, it should also press toward civil recognition.'[18]

Although Adrian Thatcher shares Nelson's presuppositions that all human relationships have a strong sexual component that unfortunately suffes the alienating effects of Christianity's dualistic traditions, he believes that late modernity offers an opportunity for a critical reaffirmation of Christian teaching on marriage and family rather than a curt dismissal. The quest for sexual fulfilment that Nelson commends as liberating can prove to be as equally enslaving in the absence of institutional structures that marriage and family provide, albeit in revised configurations. Consequently, his principal goal is to reclaim and affirm these institutions in the light of alarming increases in divorce, cohabitation, and child neglect, but to reclaim and to affirm in a manner that is palatable to a postmodern audience.

The foundation of Thatcher's reclamation project is a series of 'loyal', but critical, enquiries. As a theologian, he endeavours to be loyal to Christ, the Bible, tradition, and the church. But he must also be loyal to the experience of people who have been harmed by marriage, and the contemporary culture in which the church is presently located.[19] These loyalties inspire simultaneous 'internal' and 'external' dialogues.[20] The internal dialogue results in a particular Christian understanding of marriage as covenant and sacrament. As covenant, marriage is a public *'agreement between two people'* that is *'ratified by Jesus Christ'*. As sacrament, the partners of a marital covenant are *'equal recipients'* of Christ's love, and participate equally *'in the divine-human covenant between Christ and the Church'*.[21] The biblical notion of one-flesh union is an important symbol to reclaim, for its emphasis on marriage as a lifelong covenant of mutual fidelity and an openness to children. This symbol is important, because any theological account of marriage that takes embodiment seriously cannot casually sever the links between sexuality, covenant, and procreation. Consequently, unlike Nelson, Thatcher insists that adultery and infidelity are not two unrelated categories, but integrally related. Sexual intimacy with a person who is not one's spouse

---

[18] Ibid. 209.   [19] See Adrian Thatcher, *Marriage after Modernity* (1999), 12–25.
[20] Ibid. 31–66.   [21] Ibid. 87–95 (emphasis original).

violates the one-flesh character of the marital covenant. Moreover, the natural link between sexual intercourse and procreation should not be ignored. Although Thatcher is not opposed to contraception,[22] and admits that not all couples should become parents, he nonetheless insists that marriage is oriented towards procreation and childrearing. Again in contrast to Nelson, who rarely makes any mention of children, Thatcher contends that Christian discourse on marriage should begin with children.[23] Although marriage is in itself a complete institution, it nonetheless loses its moral intelligibility when separated from a larger familial context.

In the external dialogue, the church presents its reclaimed tradition of marriage, but it is a reclamation shorn of all sexist and patriarchal distortions, making it more acceptable to postmodern sensibilities. This dialogue partner remains highly sceptical of marriage, however, as witnessed by the growing popularity of cohabitation, and its exclusion of gays and lesbians. In response to cohabitation, Thatcher proposes that betrothal should be recovered and reinstituted as a vital component of marriage. He draws on the role it played in the Christian tradition until the eighteenth century, and wishes to recover and reinstitute it as a way of granting ecclesial and civil recognition of a couple's intent or promise to marry.[24] Thatcher argues that betrothal is morally superior to either cohabitation or trial marriage. Cohabitation is merely a private arrangement which is not subject to any public recognition or affirmation,[25] and trial marriages do not necessarily entail any explicit consent to a lifelong commitment.[26] As well as providing a preferable option to cohabitation or trial marriage, betrothal offers a couple a sanctioned time and institutional setting to determine whether they are being joined in the eyes of God,[27] and to protect the legal status of children born or conceived during the betrothed period.[28] In short, betrothal is needed to

---

[22] See Thatcher, *Marriage after Modernity*, 171–208.   [23] Ibid. 132–70.

[24] Ibid. 108–31.

[25] In this respect, Thatcher is critical of the Church of England permitting cohabitation in their report, *Something to Celebrate*; see ibid. 129–31.

[26] Thatcher takes Spong to task in this regard; ibid. 124–7. It should also be noted that the promise to marry which betrothal institutionalizes is not irrevocable; ibid. 127–8.

[27] Ibid. 267–8.   [28] Ibid. 171–2.

support marriage properly as an evolving process rather than the aftermath of a wedding.

In response to the exclusion of gays and lesbians, Thatcher proposes that the marital covenant should be extended to same-sex couples. He admits that, unlike betrothal, his proposal represents a radical reform rather than retrieval of the Christian tradition. This proposal appears to be incongruent with his insistence on maintaining the link between sexuality and procreation. Thatcher contends, however, that friendship is the foundation of all relational commitments, and is the principal force preserving marriage over time. There is, therefore, no compelling reason why this 'special kind of friendship'[29] cannot be extended to same-sex couples. Thatcher admits that, given its close association with procreation and childrearing, marriage can be regarded as a 'heterosexual institution'.[30] This restriction, however, is no longer definitive. As Christian history demonstrates, marriage is an adaptable institution, and can be altered in response to changing cultural circumstances. Children, for instance, can now be obtained through a variety of methods that do not require sexual intercourse, and as adoption and reproductive technology make clear, biology is not *the* defining characteristic of parenthood. Consequently, same-sex couples do not necessarily sever the link between the marital covenant and procreation, thereby enabling the church and civil society to extend the institution of marriage to gays and lesbians. Moreover, the friendship of same-sex unions provides a good model of egalitarian and post-patriarchal relationships that should be emulated by heterosexual couples. Since the friendship emanating from a covenanted same-sex couple is identical to the sacramental quality experienced by an equally committed heterosexual couple, there is no reason why the former should not be recognized and blessed as a marriage.

RESISTANCE

In contrast to accommodating Christian teaching and practice to late liberal tenets of moral, social, and political ordering in respect of

---

[29] Ibid. 217–22.   [30] Ibid. 297–9.

marriage and family, an alternative approach is to resist all such attempts by reasserting traditional dogma. Some of the principal features of this resistance can be captured by examining selected aspects of contemporary Catholic social teaching.

The promulgation of *Humanae Vitae* dashed expectations that Catholic prohibitions on contraception would be relaxed. Given the development of more reliable techniques, population concerns, and the reforms of Vatican II, many assumed that Paul VI would position the church's moral teaching in response to the growing need to regulate procreation. The encyclical, however, forbade all methods of artificial birth control, in many respects reinforcing strictures imposed by *Casti Connubii*. According to *Humanae Vitae*, humankind has reached a crucial historical moment with its ability to control its own propagation. This prospect raises the issue of 'whether, because people are more conscious today of their responsibilities, the time has come when the transmission of life should be regulated by their intelligence and will rather than through the specific rhythms of their own bodies'.[31] The moral response to this prospect must be based on natural law and divine revelation, for in following their precepts 'married people collaborate freely and responsibly with God the Creator'.[32]

Although the encyclical's brief reference to contraception captured the attention of both theologians and the media, it was largely focused on a theological explication of marriage and family. Unlike attempts to reformulate Christian doctrine in the light of changing cultural mores and values, the issue at stake is not sexual expression, but an ordering of sexual conduct in line with the integral goals of fidelity and procreation. Marriage is foundational to the encyclical's argument, because it provides the normative setting governing both sexual intimacy and the transmission of life. Especially in respect of the latter, the sacred union of a woman and a man provides the natural social environment for the birth and education of children. It is within marriage that moral issues regarding procreation should

---

[31] *Humanae Vitae* 5. 3, p. 224. All the encyclicals cited in what follows (apart from *Donum Vitae*) can be found in *The Papal Encyclicals*, ed. Claudia Carlen (1981), ii–v.
[32] Ibid. 5. 1, p. 223.

be addressed, for in it women and men perfect each other while 'cooperating with God in the generation and rearing of new lives'.[33]

Marriage satisfies many physical and emotional needs, but it is not an institution grounded exclusively in nature. A person has the ability to transcend natural needs, giving marriage a deeper character than mutual gratification. A wife and husband become one-flesh, which promotes each other's fulfilment. Moreover, conjugal love does not turn in upon itself, but prompts a couple to extend their marital fellowship to include children. Appealing to the Second Vatican Council, *Humane Vitae* stipulates: 'Marriage and conjugal love are by their nature ordained toward the procreation and education of children. Children are really the supreme gift of marriage and contribute in the highest degree to their parents' welfare.'[34]

The encyclical enjoins spouses to exhibit self-control, assessing relevant physical, economic, and psychological factors in determining the size of their families. In exercising this responsibility, they are not free to use any means available, but may only employ methods corresponding to God's will by following a natural course of spacing the interval between pregnancies. No act of sexual intercourse should be separated from its potential for transmitting life, because marriage is oriented toward fecundity. Marriage, then, is constituted by both its unitive and procreative significance, and violating either aspect impairs the couple's collaboration with God. The encyclical declares that the 'direct interruption of the generative process', once initiated, is 'absolutely excluded as a lawful means of regulating the number of children'.[35] In short, contraception perverts marriage, for 'it is a serious error to think that a whole married life of otherwise normal relations can justify sexual intercourse which is deliberately contraceptive and so intrinsically wrong.'[36]

Since it is wrong to use contraception to control fertility, it is also wrong to use artificial means to overcome infertility, a principle that was ensconced by the publication of *Donum Vitae* to provide instruction on 'biomedical techniques which make it possible to intervene in the initial phase of the life of a human being and in the very processes of procreation and their conformity with the principles

---

[33] Ibid. 5. 8, p. 225.   [34] Ibid. 5. 9, p. 225.
[35] Ibid. 5. 14, p. 226.   [36] Ibid. 227.

of Catholic morality'.[37] The Vatican's concern was not an aversion to reproductive medicine *per se*, but to ensure that its use respected the 'inalienable rights' of persons 'according to the design and will of God'.[38] Procreation should be pursued in ways acknowledging the spiritual and physical totality of embodied persons, honouring their fundamental right to life and inherent dignity. Specifically, reproductive technology should be evaluated by the moral standard of the 'life of the human being called into existence and the special nature of the transmission of human life in marriage'.[39]

Given these principles, *Donum Vitae* prohibits virtually all forms of assisted reproduction. The first set of prohibitions focus on the dignity of embryos,[40] while a second set concentrates on marriage as the normative foundation of procreation.[41] Since personhood begins at conception, proper respect must be shown embryos in their creation and subsequent development. Embryos, like all persons, have a right to life, and should not be destroyed if they are not needed or carry deleterious traits. Moreover, a new life should only be brought into being through means that respect a person's inherent dignity. Embryos should not be created for the purpose of improving the chances for a pregnancy, nor should disembodied techniques of conception be employed. On these grounds, *in vitro* fertilization (IVF), for instance, is wrong because it often involves the destruction of unneeded embryos, as well as employing a non-coital method of conception.

All methods of achieving conception, other than sexual intercourse between a wife and husband, are illicit since they violate the one-flesh unity of marriage. It is only within marriage that procreation should be pursued, for it upholds the dignity of both parents and offspring. Heterologous techniques are wrong, because they divest children of a biological relationship with their parents, as well as rupturing the social dimensions of parenthood. Homologous methods are also wrong for, although no donated gametes or surrogate wombs are used, the techniques employed disrupt the unitive meaning

---

[37] *Donum Vitae*, 'Foreword'. Available at: http://www.vatican.va/roman_curia/congregations/cfaith/documents/rc_con_cfaith_doc_19870222_respect-for-human-life_en.html

[38] Ibid., 'Introduction/2'.   [39] Ibid., 'Introduction/4'.   [40] Ibid. 1.
[41] Ibid. 2.

of marriage. Thus, artificial insemination, IVF, and surrogacy are proscribed. In addition, *Donum Vitae* admits that, although the desire for children is natural, marriage does not entitle an individual to become a parent, and infertile couples are urged to satisfy their desire through adoption or charitable work with disadvantaged children.

Donum Vitae builds upon *Humanae Vitae* in two respects. At one level, the former extends the argument of the latter regarding the natural ends and means of procreation: the natural process of transmitting life is sacrosanct, and its embodied structure should not be violated. At another level, *Donum Vitae* contends that assisted reproduction is wrong, because it disrupts the relation between the unitive and procreative aspects of marriage, thereby diminishing the dignity of spouses and offspring. This is especially the case with children who have the right to be born within marriage, and reared by parents to whom they are biologically related.[42] With this emphasis, *Donum Vitae* shifts the issue away from the purpose of sexual intercourse, and towards the normative relation between parents and children.

Taken together *Humanae Vitae* and *Donum Vitae* argue that the ordering of human fertility and infertility encompass issues of social and political ordering. Marriage is the normative institution in which this ordering is initiated and grounded. Yet marriage alone is an insufficient bridge to accomplish the necessary social and political tasks; it is the family, built upon the moral foundation of marriage, that must bear the weight. More importantly, in the absence of strong families these tasks cannot be accomplished in a proper manner. *Humanae Vitae*, for instance, exhorts public authorities to protect the family's integrity since it is the 'primary unit of the state', and they should 'not tolerate any legislation which would introduce into the family those practices which are opposed to the natural law of God'.[43] The state has a duty to promote the common good that is best achieved through upholding marriage and family, and since contraception harms these institutions it should be prohibited, or at least proscribed.

More expansively, *Donum Vitae* asserts that the 'good of the children and of parents contribute to the good of civil society',

---

[42] Ibid. 2A.   [43] *Humanae Vitae*, 5. 23, p. 229.

for the 'vitality and stability of society require that children come into the world within a family and that the family be firmly based on marriage'.⁴⁴ The 'inviolable right to life' is given its strongest protection in marriage and family, thereby constituting the basic 'elements of civil society and its order'. Consequently, reproductive medicine must be restricted and regulated, because conscience alone is insufficient for 'ensuring respect for personal right and public order'. Moreover, public policies must embody a rational relationship between civil and moral law, in recognition that civil rights are not granted by the state but 'pertain to human nature and are inherent in the person by virtue of the creative act from which the person took his or her origin'. Since civil society is built upon the family the state must uphold it by protecting the rights of children to be conceived, born, and reared within marriage.⁴⁵

In making these claims about the foundational status of marriage and family, *Humanae Vitae* and *Donum Vitae* also draw upon the tradition of modern encyclical social teaching. Leo XIII, for example, asserted that 'family life itself... is the cornerstone of all society and government', and is crucial 'to the right ordering and preservation of every State and kingdom'.⁴⁶ Pius XI built upon this teaching, insisting that the family is the 'germ of all social life', and warning that failing to protect it will 'result in poisoning and drying up the very sources of domestic and social life'.⁴⁷ Stable families engender political stability, because 'what families and individuals are, so also is the State, for a body is determined by its parts'.⁴⁸ Pius XII further delineated the state's role in upholding marriage and family, claiming it should 'control, aid and direct the private and individual activities of national life that they converge harmoniously towards the common good'.⁴⁹ Although the family is the 'essential cell of society', it is 'by nature anterior to the State',⁵⁰ and God has assigned these respective spheres distinct, yet complementary, roles in pursuing the common good. Political leaders are thereby urged to resist ideologies leading to the 'gradual abolition of rights peculiar to the family'.⁵¹ John XXIII

---

⁴⁴ See *Donum Vitae*, 2A.1.   ⁴⁵ Ibid. 3.
⁴⁶ *Quod Apostolici Muneris*, 2. 8, p. 14.   ⁴⁷ *Ubi Arcano Dei Consilo*, 3. 29, p. 231.
⁴⁸ *Casti Connubii*, 3. 37, p. 397.   ⁴⁹ *Summi Pontificatus*, 4. 59, p. 13.
⁵⁰ Ibid. 4. 61, p. 13.   ⁵¹ Ibid. 4. 63, p. 13.

commended the family as the microcosmic foundation to civil society, for there can be no genuine tranquillity in the absence of stable families. Moreover, there are dire consequences if the family is weakened: 'The Christian family is a sacred institution. If it totters, if the norms which the divine Redeemer laid down for it are rejected or ignored, then the very foundation of the state tremble; civil society stands betrayed and in peril.'[52] Paul VI further highlighted the social sources of human identity, contending that man 'is not really himself... except within the framework of society and the family plays the basic and most important role'.[53] The 'natural family, stable and monogamous—as fashioned by God and sanctified by Christianity—in which different generations live together, helping each other to acquire greater wisdom and to harmonize personal rights with social needs, is the basis of society'.[54]

In his apostolic exhortation, *Familiaris Consortio,* John Paul II systematically ties together the various emphases of the documents surveyed above, while also portraying the family as an evangelical witness complementing the witness of celibacy. The primary role of the family is to be a 'living reflection of and a real sharing in God's love for humanity and the love of Christ the Lord for the Church his bride'.[55] This role is now performed against a social and political background in which marriage and family are weakened by 'an autonomous power of self-affirmation... for one's own selfish well-being'.[56] Consequently, the family is called to witness to the power of sacrificial love, and is empowered by God to bear this witness by manifesting a divine love that is the source of every vocation. The marital vocation expresses not only God's love for humankind, but more poignantly Christ's love for the church. In their one-flesh unity a married couple becomes a salvific witness of mutual self-giving. Their one-flesh unity serves also as the foundation of the parental vocation, for marriage is oriented towards procreation and child-rearing. In their reciprocal and exclusive act of transmitting life, a couple cooperates with God in receiving the gift of children. Marital and parental love reflect God's love while also exhibiting a love for God, together providing the basis for familial love.

---

[52] *Ad Petri Cathedram*, 5. 51, p. 10.   [53] *Populorum Progressio*, 5. 36, p. 189.
[54] Ibid. 5. 36, p. 190.   [55] *Familiarus Consortio*, 3. 17, p. 33.
[56] Ibid. 1. 6, p. 13; see also 1. 4–10, pp. 8–18.

Marriage and family alone, however, cannot bear the weight of their witness, and require the complementary witness of vocational singleness. 'Virginity or celibacy for the sake of the Kingdom of God not only does not contradict the dignity of marriage but presupposes it and confirms it. Marriage and virginity or celibacy are two ways of expressing and living the one mystery of the covenant of God with his people.'[57] Singleness is a witness to the eschatological union of Christ with his church in anticipation of the new creation. In embodying this witness, singleness protects marriage from any disparagement, reminding the church that it is an institution ordained by God as part of a created order awaiting its consummation in Christ. Celibacy remains a superior vocation, however, because this rare *charism* enables a single-minded devotion to God's kingdom, but this work in turn assists the family in becoming what God intends it to be.

God intends the family to be an 'authentic community of persons' whose members are bound together by an 'unceasing inner dynamism' of love which is displayed initially in marriage that matures into the 'foundation and soul' of the family.[58] Conjugal communion is grounded in a natural relationship between woman and man, that is sanctified by God as a 'vocation and commandment' of mutual fidelity.[59] It is upon this sanctified foundation that the familial community is built. The natural bonds of 'flesh and blood' are nurtured by love into the 'deeper and richer bonds of the spirit', animating the structure of familial roles and relationships.[60] These roles and relationships instil the values of mutual respect and reciprocity, and are perfected through sacrificial love. The virtues of patience, forgiveness, reconciliation, and fidelity are practised most intensely in the family, and authentic familial fellowship cannot exist in their absence. Most importantly, the proper ordering of familial roles and relationships promotes the 'dignity and vocation' of all persons, thereby protecting the inherent rights of women, men, children, and the elderly.[61]

As a community, the family is called by God to perform the tasks of serving life, participating in the development of society, and sharing in the life and mission of the church. Spouses serve life

---

[57] *Familiarus Consortio*, 2. 16, pp. 28–9.
[58] Ibid. 3. 18, pp. 34–5.   [59] Ibid. 3. 20, pp. 37–9.
[60] Ibid. 3. 21, pp. 39–40.   [61] Ibid. 3. 22–7, pp. 42–52.

by cooperating with God 'in transmitting the gift of human life'. The essential task of the family is 'to actualize in history the original blessing of the Creator', namely, that through procreation the *imago dei* is passed on from generation to generation. Fecundity is the 'living testimony' of mutual self-giving.[62] The church assists the family in being this living testimony in two ways: first, the church 'stands for life' against the 'anti-life mentality' of the present age. The church steadfastly opposes contraception, abortion, and any reproductive technique that violates the family's conjugal core, preserving the 'full sense of mutual self-giving and human procreation in the context of true love'.[63] Second, the church is the teacher and mother of married couples. As teacher, the church proclaims the 'moral norm' guiding the 'responsible transmission of life'. In doing so, it draws upon a knowledge of human biology and natural birth regulation in providing an 'education in self-control', protecting the conjugal relationship 'from the perils of selfishness and aggressiveness'. A couple must be assisted in seeing their marriage 'as a sign of the unitive and fruitful love of Christ for his Church'. As mother, the church provides pastoral care for married couples who find this teaching difficult to follow, 'instilling conviction and offering practical help to those who wish to live out their parenthood in a truly responsible way.'[64]

In serving life, parents have the vocational right and duty to educate their children. Since the family is the primary school of personal and civic virtues, parents must impart to their offspring the 'values of kindness, constancy, goodness, service, disinterestedness, and self-sacrifice'.[65] Since the family is a school of 'social living', familial relationships should exemplify sacrificial mutuality and solicitude as opposed to individualistic, selfish, and materialistic attitudes. Through their mutual service, family members discover their personhood not through self-love, but in accepting the 'gift of self in love'.[66] Since the sacramentality of marriage bestows on parenthood its essential dignity, the education of children is a ministry of the church performed by parents on its behalf.

---

[62] Ibid. 3. 28, pp. 53–4.   [63] Ibid. 3. 30–2, pp. 55–62.
[64] Ibid. 3. 33–5, pp. 62–70.   [65] Ibid. 3. 36, pp. 70–1.
[66] Ibid. 3. 37, pp. 72–4.

The family participates in developing society by providing its social foundation. In serving life, the family 'is by nature and vocation open to other families and to society, and undertakes its social role'.[67] It fulfils this role, on the one hand, by reinforcing a sense of personal dignity, inculcating social values, and providing a bulwark against the depersonalizing trends of contemporary life. On the other hand, the family accomplishes its role by participating in social service projects, offering hospitality to those in need, and advocating appropriate legislation.[68] Since the family is the moral foundation of civil society, the state must order other social spheres in ways that support the family, and assist it in upholding the values of 'truth, freedom, justice, and love'.[69]

By participating in the life and mission of the church, the family is a community of love and fidelity, contributing to Christ's prophetic, priestly, and kingly ministries. This participation is marked by the family as a 'believing and evangelizing community', a 'community in dialogue with God', and a 'community at the service of man'.[70] The prophetic ministry is fulfilled by receiving and communicating the gospel. Parents proclaim the gospel to their children, and together evangelize other families. As the seedbed of vocational life, the family serves needy neighbours and supports missionary activities. Family members are sanctified in their dialogue with God, which in turn assists the sanctification of the church and world. Familial spirituality follows a pattern of creation, covenant, crucifixion, and resurrection, for it is within the family that life's joys and sorrows, as well as the realities of sin and grace, are experienced most intensely and woven into the fabric of daily living. Alongside the sacraments of marriage and baptism, the Eucharist enables the performance of the priestly role. In sharing the bread, family members 'become one body', disclosing the 'wider unity of the Church'.[71] In response to God's gift and commandment of love, the family is a community of service. The 'inner communion' of familial love is expanded to embrace every

---

[67] *Familiarus Consortio*, 3.42, p. 82.

[68] Ibid. 3. 43–4, pp. 82–5.

[69] Ibid. 3. 45–8, pp. 85–91. A charter of family rights codifying this principle of subsidiarity is included in 3. 46.

[70] Ibid. 3. 50, p. 94.　　　　[71] Ibid. 3. 55–62, pp. 102–14.

'brother and sister', especially the poor, weak, and disposed, whom Christ calls his followers to serve in his kingly ministry.[72] In helping the family fulfil these ministries, the church provides pastoral care and practical assistance, particularly in the areas of marriage preparation, education, and political advocacy.[73]

In his theological account of marriage and family, Germain Grisez defends and builds upon the Catholic social teaching summarized above.[74] A detailed summary of his work would prove redundant, but there are two emphases worth mentioning given their particular relevancy to this inquiry.

First, Grisez emphasizes marriage as an open-ended community. Marriage by 'its very nature is part of a larger whole', anticipating the emergence of a family. 'Because parenthood fulfills marriage, it shapes the spouses' interpersonal communion; and the way children come to be sets requirements for marriage as a whole, among them that it be an open-ended community.'[75] Humans are biologically complete individuals, except for the purpose of reproducing. In fulfilling this function, they complete each other, becoming a single organic unit. In this respect, children perfect marriage, forming a cooperative community in pursuit of its intrinsic common good.[76] This pursuit determines the community's structure and forms of cooperation, for although marriage cannot be reduced to parenthood, its orientation towards offspring shapes its inherent virtues and practices. Childrearing is not a task undertaken by parents, but a foundational element of the family as an open-ended community in which children are simultaneously derived from but also differentiated from their parents; there is both familiarity *and* difference. In this respect, the family mirrors larger cultural processes of development in which social differentiation is derived from shared or common characteristics.

Second, although marriage is oriented towards familial communion, a marriage is nonetheless an intrinsically good and complete relationship in the absence of children. This absence, however, does not alter marital virtues and practices which remain oriented towards its

---

[72] Ibid. 3. 63–4, pp. 114–18.   [73] Ibid. 4. 119–62.

[74] See Germain Grisez, *The Way of the Lord Jesus* (1993), ii. 553–752.

[75] Ibid. 569.

[76] Grisez specifies the elements of this common good, ibid. 555–69.

familial *telos*, and Grisez compares a childless couple to a crypt for a great church that was never built but retains its integrity as a place of worship.[77] Although it is natural for an infertile couple to desire offspring, they may not resort to assisted reproduction because it would violate the normative structure of marriage. Rather, he urges infertile couples to pursue this good desire through either adoption or charitable work with disadvantaged children.[78]

CRITICAL ADAPTATION

The literature surveyed in this section represent theological portrayals of marriage and family that are simultaneously cognizant of changing social mores and values, while at the same time maintaining the efficacy of traditional Christian moral teaching on marriage and family. This is not to suggest that these positions are merely proposals offering a compromise between the 'extreme' options summarized above. Rather, they are attempts to appropriate and expound selected traditional emphases in the light of contemporary social and political circumstances. In this respect, they may be characterized as interpretations that are critical of both the traditions they represent, and the late liberal context in which they are enacted.

Critical familism

Don Browning and his co-authors in *From Culture Wars to Common Ground* contend that the time is ripe to move beyond the acrimonious family values debate.[79] The plight of the late modern family is no longer an exclusively conservative issue, but has moved to the centre of the political landscape. Given substantial evidence of the detrimental effects of divorce and household instability on children,

---

[77] Grisez specifies the elements of this common good, 569.   [78] Ibid. 689–90.

[79] The following section is adapted from a book review of Browning *et al.*, *From Culture Wars to Common Ground* which appeared in *Studies in Christian Ethics*, 13/1 (2000).

there is a consensus on both the left and right that families are in crisis and need to be supported through various political initiatives. The way is now open to find a common ground.[80]

The authors' central claim is that religious traditions, and especially Christianity, have much to offer in building this consensus. The family they propound is egalitarian, requiring 'new religious and communal supports, and a new theory of authority'. Such a family is characterized by a married or committed couple, whose relationship is based on equal regard and mutual respect, and both having equal privileges and responsibilities in the public and private domains. Although they endorse an intact mother–father family as an ideal, families failing to embody it should nonetheless be supported. In lifting up this model, they advocate a 'new *critical familism* and a new *critical culture of marriage*', promoting the 'democratization' of the family.[81]

The principal factors contributing to the family crisis include rampant individualism, changing economic circumstances, dysfunctional behavioural patterns, and lingering patriarchy. To redress these issues, marriage and family should be based on a new understanding of the relationship between intimacy, work, value formation, and parenting which enables, rather than restricts, personal fulfilment. This dominant, and essentially positive, cultural emphasis on personal fulfilment is forcing a democratization of the family, founded upon the authority of mutuality and ethic of equal regard. In making their case, the authors explicate the basic lineaments of this authority and ethic 'surrounded by the Christian story'.[82]

Early Christians, for instance, challenged the patriarchy of the Graeco-Roman household with their belief in radical equality in Christ. Marital and familial love are particular expressions of a more general love of God and neighbour, indicating that Jesus' criticism of the family was aimed at tribal loyalties instead of its 'conjugal core'. Although the household codes of the New Testament reflect a conservative reaction against Jesus' and Paul's emphases on equality, the seeds of equal regard were nonetheless sown in a Christian understanding of the family.[83] The harvest is seen in Thomistic teaching, in tandem with evolutionary psychology, to

---

remedy what is described as the 'male problematic'. Men are always uncertain about their biological connection to offspring. Monogamy eases this anxiety, promoting greater male investment in childrearing. This Thomistic principle accords well with contemporary findings that parental care is largely motivated by a genetic relationship with children. These natural bonds alone, however, provide an insufficient foundation for the family, because they do not address the subjective needs of its individual members. Although Christian teaching on the one-flesh unity of marriage implies mutuality and equality, what is missing is a concept of 'inter-subjectivity' around which an egalitarian family may be structured.[84] To address this deficiency, the authors turn to a variety of contemporary feminist, therapeutic, activist, and economic 'voices'.

Feminists are correct to criticize patriarchal structures that prevent women from achieving their full potential. The family is often a barrier in attaining sexual equality, because family roles can institutionalize a fundamental inequality between women and men. This is particularly the case when women are expected to sacrifice their careers or creative interests for the sake of other family members. Echoing Okin, familial roles and relationships must be radically restructured, for women can only be liberated in a 'genderless society and gender-free family'.[85] This emphasis on self-regard over self-sacrifice, however, is often achieved at the expense of any constructive account of the family. Religious feminists, such as Lisa Sowle Cahill and Mary Stewart van Leeuwen, offer more nuanced alternatives by drawing 'critical connections between love, sexual pleasure, and bearing children that are grounded in a common humanity and common human experience'.[86] 'Womanist' critiques in particular are lifted up as illuminating how genuine self-love provides a basis for mutuality, in which family relationships are empowered by images of discipleship as opposed to sacrificial service.[87]

Therapeutic approaches play a limited, yet crucial, role in promoting critical familism. Critics of a so-called therapeutic culture, such as Lasch, go too far in dismissing the positive contributions of therapeutic techniques. Cultivating interpersonal communication and negotiating

---

[84] See Browning *et al.*, *From Culture Wars to Common Ground*, 101–28.
[85] Ibid. 162–8.   [86] Ibid. 181–5.   [87] Ibid. 185–8.

skills, for example, is not incompatible with an ethic of mutual regard, or promoting egalitarian relationships. Self-improvement need not be selfish when pursued within a social context based on mutuality and reciprocity. Emphasizing 'intersubjective dialogue' assists marriage and family to realize such 'premoral' goods as 'procreation, parental certainty, sexual exchange, and mutual helpfulness'.[88] Consequently, therapeutic techniques help individuals to develop the necessary skills for performing their roles within a 'critical marriage culture and critical familism'.[89]

Activist 'profamily' voices are commended for focusing on the problem of absent fathers rather than single mothers. The African-American community, with its stress on sexual equality, strong relationship with the church, and extended kinship networks, and the Catholic principle of subsidiarity are extolled as illuminating examples for drawing connections between selfhood, social ordering, and the moral significance of biological bonds. These movements are criticized, however, because they 'lack understanding of love as equal regard', lapsing 'easily into "soft" patriarchy', and the 'Christian right' is denounced for its slavish devotion to patriarchal structures based on a misreading of biblical texts.[90] To correct these tendencies, the authors assert that the Reformed doctrine of the orders of creation overlaps significantly with the principle of subsidiarity, providing a theological model for 'dialogue between Catholics and evangelicals' on a pattern of 'natural regularities' governing the social ordering of marriage and family.[91]

In assessing the economic voices, it is assumed that families are inevitably threatened with the decline of a robust civil society. Economic accounts, which often presume 'kin altruism' as the foundation of rational acts, can bolster the stability of families by addressing the male problematic: economic policies are needed that reinforce, rather than discount, a father's genetic investment in offspring. These economic theories, however, are often too reductionistic to provide an adequate foundation for the family as a social sphere. Given the late liberal commitment to atomistic individualism, children are often reduced to commodities, and it is citizenship, instead of familial bonds,

---

[88] Ibid. 197–202.   [89] Ibid. 202–18.
[90] Ibid. 222–42.   [91] Ibid. 242–3.

which provides the dominant category of human association. Consequently, economic theories must be overlaid with a thicker account of affiliation based on equal regard and mutuality.[92]

In their 'practical theology' of the family, the authors contend that Christian confessions are not 'arguable in public discourse'.[93] In response, they propose a framework informed by Thomistic thought, the principle of subsidiarity, and the orders of creation to translate confessional rhetoric into public discourse. The one-flesh unity of marriage, for instance, becomes a 'covenant of intersubjective dialogue', and monogamy, contrary to Nelson, is a superior expression of equal regard.[94] Mutuality between spouses is achieved by empathizing with each other's 'narrative identity', for marriage consists of acknowledging the 'ultimate worth' of these personal stories. It is upon the intersubjective dialogue between these identities that a familial covenant is built, for self-regard is a prerequisite of equal regard. It is in this context that sacrificial love is explicable, for it enables or restores mutual love, but is *never* an end in itself. Moreover, this relation between mutual and sacrificial love is revealed in both the triune God and *imago dei* which are, in turn, manifested in the family and the life of the church, especially as the latter embodies the example of Christ's suffering and grace.

The parameters of this practical theology are further explicated by examining how family members participate in an ethic of equal regard and mutuality through different stages in their respective life cycles. Although a 'process of biological, psychological, historical, and religiocultural negotiation' enables personal fulfilment, it is tempered by a family's intersubjective and covenantal relationship, as pursued in the dialogue among unique and changing identities.[95] Furthermore, families are important in their own right, but they are subordinate to the common good and reign of God. Unlike Aristotle, who saw citizenship as an extension of familial affection, Christians insist that such affection is drawn out towards the church. Similar to Maurice, kinship is the base from which larger spheres of affection are extended. Humans cannot learn to love their neighbours if they cannot learn to love their kin. Marriage is thereby the first step in forging larger familial and social covenants.

[92] See Browning *et al.*, *From Culture Wars to Common Ground*, 247–68.
[93] Ibid. 271–2.   [94] Ibid. 275–9.   [95] Ibid. 287–301.

This practical theology concludes with a recommendation on how the church and civil society should cooperate in supporting critical familism. The most pressing problem, at least for Protestants, is to model the family as a non-hierarchical 'domestic church', requiring a dialogical relationship with the church as 'first family'. The authors assert:

Our model grounds parental authority in a *dialogue* between parents' own covenant with God and the church's covenant. This assumes that God has a covenant with both church and family. Parental authority, therefore, should evolve from a dialogue with a church that itself is dedicated to an appreciative yet critical inquiry into its traditions.[96]

Armed with this recognition of parental authority, the church should seek ecumenical cooperation and form strategic alliances with other segments of civil society in promoting a culture of critical familism.

The authors' principal goal is to establish a new basis of authority for promoting a culture of critical familism. To what extent they have succeeded, as well as the consequences of their relative success or failure, is examined in subsequent chapters. What is most pertinent to note at this juncture is that their concept of the family as 'domestic church' in dialogical relation to the church as 'first family' is portrayed as a *means* of implementing their practical theology rather than its *foundational* principle. In this respect, it incorporates many late liberal presuppositions in which the rationale for this relation is ultimately to promote the self-fulfilment of family members. I now turn attention to an account of marriage and family that is more critical of these presuppositions as reflected in its understanding of the relation between family and church in foundational, rather than instrumental, terms.

Church as first family

Rodney Clapp is an American evangelical attempting to recover a biblically inspired understanding of the family. His book, *Families at the Crossroads*, is a reaction against both a conservative espousal of

---

[96] Ibid. 308–9 (emphasis original).

so-called family values, and what he characterizes as unacceptable postmodern options. Similar to Thatcher, Clapp contends that a contemporary Christian exposition of the family must take into account the pervasive influence of the postmodern world. With its emphasis on expressive individualism, a rampant consumerism is well-suited for fulfilling the desires of autonomous persons. Choice is the dominant value, because an 'ideal world is one with as many choices as possible, about everything possible'. The supermarket is an apt symbol of this postmodern culture.[97] This imagery distorts the family by placing a 'premium on novelty rather than fidelity'.[98] Marriage is little more than a precarious contract, enduring so long as it serves the interests of its parties, and children are either avoided as constraints against pursuing one's interests, or seen as commodities enabling one's self-fulfilment. Consequently, the family is a haven that autonomous persons use in pursuing their private interests, effectively stripping the family of any substantive social or political meaning.

Clapp, however, rejects tradition and nature as the primary sources from which the social and political significance of the family can be recovered. Appeals to a nostalgic 'traditional family' hearken back to the nineteenth-century bourgeois family, of the kind championed by the Bergers, based on romantic love, heightened concern for children, and sentimentality. This model portrays the family as a 'private refuge', reflecting a cultural construct of a particular era.[99] Since such a model is not found in the Bible, it cannot provide an authoritative guide for theological deliberation. Nor can the family be understood as an institution grounded in nature. It is instead an 'unnatural' social construct serving the 'natural' needs to 'sanction and regulate sexual mating', assist the 'reproduction, survival and socialization of children', and 'apportion roles, labor and goods between the sexes'.[100] As the Bible, cultural anthropology, and the postmodern world attest, familial structures accommodating these needs vary among historical epochs and contemporary societies.

If Christians are to recover any normative content for the family, they must look to the church for their model. The centrepiece of

---

[97] See Rodney Clapp, *Families at the Crossroads* (1993), 60–2.
[98] Ibid. 62–6.   [99] Ibid. 30–4.   [100] Ibid. 39–45.

Clapp's argument is that, contrary to Bushnell, it is not the family but the church that is 'God's most important institution on earth. The church is the social agent that most significantly shapes and forms the character of Christians. And the church is the primary vehicle of God's grace and salvation for a waiting, desperate world.'[101] Accordingly, the family embodies covenantal rather than biological relationships. In the Old Testament, the covenant between God and the people was admittedly expressed through Abraham's lineage. This did not imply, however, that salvation was the result of biological descent, but that procreation was an obedient response to God's salvific promise. In fulfilling the old age and inaugurating the new, Jesus displaces lineage as the means of keeping the covenant. It is not kinship, but doing God's will that give witness to this new age. Familial relationships and loyalties are tempered and transformed within the community bearing Christ's name. The importance of Mary, for example, is not that she is Jesus' mother but his disciple.[102] It is by being 'born again' into the church that 'families and individuals gain a distinctive Christian identity', empowering them to resist the corrosive influences of a postmodern world. Within the church the natural fate of 'family ties' is replaced with the 'gift' of God's destiny. Clapp insists that reconfiguring familial bonds does not weaken the family; to the contrary, it is 'enriched when it is decentered, relativized, recognized as less than absolute'.[103] The veracity of this claim is demonstrated by examining how singleness is related to the family.

Evangelical Protestants, according to Clapp, are plagued by a 'flawed vision of the Christian family' that 'denigrates and dishonors singleness'. Single persons denote the abnormal status of not being married instead of a way of life that may be better for some to follow. What is needed is a recovery of singleness as a vocation, because '*it uniquely witnesses to true Christian freedom*'.[104] This denigration is rooted in the 'wrong turn' taken by Augustine. Although Augustine affirmed marriage, he nonetheless insisted that sexual intercourse

---

[101] Ibid. 67–8.
[102] Ibid. 80–1; cf. Michael Banner, *Christian Ethics and Contemporary Moral Problems* (1999), 225–51.
[103] See Clapp, *Families at the Crossroads*, 84–8.
[104] Ibid. 89–92 (emphasis original).

was always 'attended by the sin of lust'. Consequently, virginity is a more holy calling.[105]

The significance of singleness, however, is not sexual renunciation, but where one's hope is placed. This is seen more clearly against the Old Testament background in which hope was lodged in lineage. For Christians, hope is transferred to Christ. This transfer is behind Paul's counsel that, in this 'awkward' time of transition between the old and new ages, singleness may prove to be a superior calling, for the 'married person is likely to sink more deeply into the affairs of passing world'. A conjugal relationship is not 'inherently corrupting', but may prevent some persons from devoting themselves to Christ. As a vocation, singleness is an ultimate act of trust that places one's hope exclusively in Christ.[106] 'Christian singles are thus radical witnesses to the resurrection. They forfeit heirs—the only other possibility of their survival beyond the grave—in the hope that one day all creation will be renewed.'[107] This radical witness enables singles to exercise a greater range of freedom; they are, for instance, liberated from marital and parental duties. Moreover, singles are also *free*, rather than compelled, to marry, for if 'we are not truly free to be single, we are not truly free to be married'.[108] There are a variety of spiritual gifts empowering Christians to serve God through the vocations of singleness *and* marriage. Instead of seeing either as superior, singleness and marriage provide 'complementary missionary advantages': the former mobility and the latter hospitality.

For Clapp, marriage is a life of fidelity bearing witness to the story of God's fidelity to Israel and the church. Such fidelity entails bodily acts. Contrary to the postmodern dualism between the will and the body, the one-flesh unity of marriage and lifelong monogamy are ideals upheld by Christians, because they express not only what we think about fidelity, but that they are also something 'we do with our bodies'.[109] Elaborating on this notion of fidelity, Clapp contrasts contractual and covenantal models of marriage. A contractual model portrays marriage as an economic transaction between two autonomous persons; it strives for a 'union of interests rather than a union of selves'. The arrangement presumes that marriage is defined

---

[105] See Clapp, *Families at the Crossroads*, 92–5.   [106] Ibid. 98–101.
[107] Ibid. 101.   [108] Ibid. 107.   [109] Ibid. 123–5.

and structured in accordance with the 'wants and needs' of the parties who are not accountable to any larger 'tradition, community, or institution'. A covenantal model joins two persons together who are 'unconditionally' committed to each other. More importantly, their covenant is made before God and witnesses, making them accountable to the church.[110]

These models of marriage produce two contrasting interpretations of fidelity. First, they situate spouses within differing contexts of accountability and possibility. Since contractual fidelity is restricted to the contracting parties, marriage is 'limited to the possibilities of two people rather than the potential of an entire community'. Covenantal fidelity enfolds a couple into a 'quest or venture' that is larger than their marriage, because they are accountable to the church.[111] Second, the two models produce divergent types of histories. Since contractual fidelity attempts to satisfy the changing desires of two autonomous persons, there is no agreement where a marriage has been or where it is headed. By being grounded in the church, covenantal fidelity gains its bearing from a more expansive story, inspiring the emergence of a 'unique history' of a couple's 'life together'.[112] Third, the two models create differing conceptions of relationships. Contractual fidelity is premised on the power of techniques that individuals employ to improve their marriage, whereas covenantal fidelity is based on 'complex commitment' of enduring and mutual trust.[113] Fourth, the two fidelities shape contrasting expressions of love. In the contractual model sex is a means of self-fulfilment, and thereby not necessarily related to procreation. Offspring may present obstacles in pursuing one's romantic or occupational interests, so 'children fit awkwardly at best into a contractual scheme of fidelity'. In a covenantal model, spouses are bound together within a larger community of service. Conjugal love is a 'celebration of communion with another and the means of "creating" others who will live on' as fellow stewards of creation. A love for children 'flows naturally' out of covenanted fidelity.[114]

Children are the first step in establishing a family as a mission base for extending hospitality to strangers. Covenantal fidelity embodies

[110] Ibid. 125–8.   [111] Ibid. 128–9.   [112] Ibid. 130.
[113] Ibid. 130–1.   [114] Ibid. 129–30.

an expansive love, embracing larger spheres of affection and service. Taking its cue from Israel and the church—both of which are enjoined to welcome strangers in their midst—the family is called to 'put hospitality at the center of its life'.[115] As a mission base, the family is not a private haven but a public witness to God the Lord of creation, and a saviour who 'reaches out to those who are forgotten or oppressed'.[116] Consequently, it is only the church that can provide the normative content, as well as the social and political significance, of the family by calling it to embrace a mission greater than itself. 'Christian families commit themselves to the church; the church commits itself to the kingdom. When affection wanes, spouses are still committed to witnessing God's fidelity, to rearing children who can serve the world in Christ, to providing a place hurt people can come for healing.'[117]

Although Clapp explicates in detail the formation of families in relation to strangers and singleness as mediated through the church, it is unclear what kind of social and political ordering is needed to sustain families in their mission of hospitality. Particular households draw upon the church in embracing their mission, but it is performed largely 'outside' rather than 'within' the 'first family'. In Clapp's account, the distance between formation and performance is largely uncharted territory. It is mapping this terrain that the next proposal undertakes.

Household management

According to David Matzko McCarthy, marriage cannot be sustained by romance. The late modern emphasis on romance and interpersonal intimacy has corrupted love as the proper moral foundation of marriage and family, making both institutions captives of a pervasive 'consumer capitalism and nation-state individualism'.[118] In response to this situation, McCarthy proposes that the more expansive concept of *household* should replace the nuclear family as the proper social

---

[115] See Clapp, *Families at the Crossroads*, 137–40.
[116] Ibid. 155–7; see also pp. 161–2.   [117] Ibid. 163–4.
[118] David Matzko McCarthy, *Sex and Love in the Home* (2001), 3.

setting for ordering marriage, procreation, and childrearing. The principal task, then, is to articulate a theological account of the household that is grounded in vocations that sustain the family. Specifically, this requires an ordering of marriage and family within household and neighbourhood economies, as opposed to capitalistic markets, thereby enabling a more virtuous pursuit of the foundational vocations.

This shift in economic context is crucial, for capitalistic markets promote values that are antithetical to establishing and sustaining households. These markets, for instance, instantiate the assumption that sexual expression is *the* central feature in developing individual personalities. For many individuals, marriage is a primary instrument of this expression, but its fulfilment is often in tension with the more mundane tasks of maintaining a home and raising children. The household is thereby an impediment to the sexual expression of spouses, and they turn increasingly to outside agencies and experts to help them manage these conflicting interests. As McCarthy notes, it is ironic that couples must often flee their homes for romantic trysts in order to keep their love alive. Although McCarthy agrees with Nelson that sexuality is a 'basic expression of the true self, and sexual experiences and fulfilment are goods of life for which we struggle and strive',[119] these goods are distorted when sundered from the formative environments of marriage, families, and households. It is the economy of the household, as opposed to the market, that nourishes the necessary commitments and virtues to sustain the pursuit of these goods over time, for they ground marriage in particular times and places.

McCarthy is highly critical of late liberal theorists, especially Rawls,[120] who have turned the family into an abstraction, stripping the household of any social and political significance by relegating it to a unit of economic consumption. A family is reduced to a voluntary arrangement in which dependent individuals are allied with productive ones. Yet the latter, as Lasch notes, must spend increasing amounts of time outside the home to maintain this relationship. The net effect is to isolate the family from larger social or kinship networks that might challenge the dominant demands of

---

[119] Ibid. 34.   [120] Ibid. 78–9.

'political and economic life' which are based on autonomous self-interests and anonymous exchange.[121] For late liberals, households are little more than convenient staging areas where individuals refresh themselves for the important tasks of production and consumption. This expedient quality is required by the public life of a liberal, contractual society which is predicated on isolated selves pursuing their respective self-interests. Making households increasingly dependent on external institutions and expertise is therefore a form of political control, for '[c]ontractual politics reduces the home to a private place, and in doing so, undermines the possibility of alternative social forms'.[122] Late liberal families are by definition 'closed families'.[123]

In opposition to the closed family, McCarthy proposes a restoration of 'household networks' designed to sustain the open households that are structured in various configurations.[124] 'Open families have loose and porous boundaries, whether they are thought to be nuclear, extended, traditional, or untraditional.'[125] These open families are sustained by a series of 'three distinct, but sometimes overlapping, kinds of networks' comprised of kin, friends, and neighbours,[126] forming together what may be described as a neighbourhood economy and social setting. Gift-giving is the medium of exchange in this economy which provides the foundation of the 'wider social network'.[127] These exchanges offer an alternative social reality to that proffered by capitalist markets, for they presuppose a common life of neighbours rather than contractual relationships among autonomous individuals. One person, for example, mows a neighbour's lawn in exchange for repairing a roof rather than both contracting the respective services of a gardener and roofer.[128] McCarthy grounds his account of the neighbourhood economy in contemporary Catholic social teaching in which marriage and family play crucial roles in promoting a culture of love. Following John Paul II, marriage is the basis of a genuinely civilized life, because it reflects the Trinitarian nature of the creator. Similar to Nelson, McCarthy insists that a spouse cannot be the sole source of fulfilling a person's identity. Marriage is supported and enriched by

---

[121] McCarthy, *Sex and Love* (2001), 67–72.
[122] Ibid. 96.   [123] Ibid. 95–7.   [124] Ibid. 97–101.
[125] Ibid. 97.   [126] Ibid. 101.   [127] Ibid. 103–4.
[128] These exchanges are derived from a spectrum of informal to formal agreements.

friends, but unlike in Nelson these friendships are not open to the possibility of sexual intimacy since their purpose is to strengthen the exclusive bond of marriage. In turn, the family is a form of human association based on mutual love that underlies all other social relationships. In taking its proper 'place in the order of love', however, the family must not 'have a direct relation to the world'.[129] Rather, it is through the church as a social body that families are related to the world, because the church precedes and transforms all other social bonds.

Explicating the *instrumental* role of open households in the order of love receives the bulk of McCarthy's attention. His essential premise is that 'love in its basic and highest form is cultivated in ordinary friendships and duties of neighborhood and home'. Yet 'love of the household and neighborhood is not complete, but moves beyond itself through its grounding and its end in the love of God'.[130] The principal characteristics of these friendships are reciprocity and mutuality. Reciprocal relationships assume a high degree of familiarity and affinity in 'stark contrast to disinterested and unilateral conceptions of neighbor love'.[131] These relational qualities are required in an economy based on gift exchange rather than contractual performance, for both givers and recipients are transformed in their exchange.[132] Consequently, reciprocity brings together mutual benefit *and* self-regard in instantiating the order of love within the social network of the neighbourhood. The reciprocal exchanges of the household promote a mutuality to counter altruistic and incomplete expressions of love. Altruism is inadequate, because it reinforces the fragmented and detached character of contemporary life. The poor, for example, cannot be truly loved through disinterested acts of generosity, but only by sharing their lives through a mutual breaking of bread within the church. Again agreeing with Browning and his co-authors, altruism or self-sacrifice is appropriate only under extraordinary circumstances. The family thereby points to the reciprocal and mutual nature of love, as mediated through the

---

[129] See McCarthy, *Sex and Love*, 124.
[130] Ibid. 128.   [131] Ibid. 133.
[132] Cf. Stephen H. Webb, *The Gifting God* (1996).

church, for love's 'basic habitat is the household economy, not necessarily the biological family, but primarily the household of God'.[133]

It is within love's proper habitat that the neighbourhood economy
orders sexual and parental practices within particular households that
promote a larger process of social reproduction. These practices
are needed to counter the corrosive influences of late liberalism
which reduce sexual intercourse and parenting to contractual relationships that are unable to promote genuine reciprocity and mutuality.
According to McCarthy, this corrosive influence is exemplified in the
increasing use of reproductive technologies in which infertility has
created a market in scarce children. In contrast, there is a plenitude of
children in the neighbourhood economy, for 'all adults have children'
through an informal system of patronage.[134] Since all adults have a
parenting role, parenthood itself is adoptive, rather than biological, in
character, and is a chief feature of the neighbourhood's common life.
Moreover it is this shared and adoptive emphasis on parenthood that
links together the normative ordering of sexual and parental practices,
for married couples and their households are embedded within a nexus
of lineage, kinship, and friendship. In these households, the relationships between spouses, children, and neighbours cannot be easily
demarcated or disentangled. Consequently, in agreement with contemporary Catholic social teaching, McCarthy contends that marriage is
properly oriented towards procreation, but for the purpose of social,
not biological, reproduction. The family alone, then, cannot bear the
heavy burdens of procreation and childrearing, because it is properly a
'dependent social institution that requires a fit within broader systems
of reciprocity, patronage, and gift-exchange'.[135] While McCarthy's proposal challenges conservative appeals to 'family values' and their close
affiliation with market capitalism, he also rejects 'personalist' emphases
which ground marriage in a vacuous romantic love. In this respect,
marriage is not the foundation of the family, much less civil society,
but enjoys a privileged position at the centre of a household that
participates in a larger neighbourhood economy.

---

[133] McCarthy, *Sex and Love*, 141.   [134] Ibid. 206.
[135] Ibid. 213.

4

Retrospect and Prospect

This chapter marks an important transition in this enquiry. The emphasis shifts away from a critical overview of some of the more salient features within the Christian theological tradition on the normative, social, and political ordering of the family, and towards a constructive proposal that appropriates this tradition in the light of late liberal social and political contexts. In this respect, the preceding chapters may be viewed as a resource to be drawn upon in developing subsequent arguments. Consequently, this chapter may also be characterized as a pause to catch our bearings by briefly surveying territory already traversed, and identifying some key landmarks on the horizon which lies ahead.

The earliest Christians were ambivalent about marriage and family. This was due in part to their Lord's teaching which did not condemn familial bonds, but relativized them in accordance with the gospel he proclaimed. Marriage and family were assessed to the extent that they either enabled or impeded one's devotion to God. Paul in turn heightened this ambivalence. He allowed marriage but did not commend it, preferring that everyone follow his example of continent singleness in order to devote their lives fully to Christ. This nonchalance was welcomed by early Jewish converts who, in the turmoil of violent Roman suppression, found it difficult to maintain or be associated with stable households. As socially and economically displaced people, being embraced as members of God's family that was tied to neither land nor lineage was simultaneously a gesture of solidarity and grace.

Yet as the number of gentile converts increased in relatively peaceful cities throughout the Roman Empire, the problem was not finding a home, but maintaining households in a Christian manner. The authors of the Deutero-Pauline literature undertook this task through their formulation of the household codes. These codes maintained the structure of pagan households, comprised of three sets of relationships: husbands and wives, parents and children, masters and servants. Unlike their pagan counterparts, however, these roles represented functional rather than ontological distinctions. This subtle, though significant, shift in emphasis was necessitated by the belief in a radical equality in Christ as reflected in the codes being addressed to both the 'stronger' and 'weaker' parties of each relationship. Augustine initiated a millennium of subsequent theological reflection on the normative requirements and duties of these household roles, particularly in respect of marriage and parenthood, which were gradually codified in canon and civil law.

It was with the Reformation that substantial changes to this household structure were introduced. In removing the sacramental status of marriage, Protestants transferred the formal regulation of this institution from ecclesial to civil authority. Although marriage remained a holy estate, the church was merely blessing a relationship that was inherently natural as opposed to religious. Consequently, divorce and remarriage were permissible. Catholics refined the sacramental status of marriage, and resisted attempts to regulate it through civil as opposed to canon law. Given this sacramental status, divorce was forbidden, but annulment and separation were allowed. In both instances, friendship and intimacy between spouses received greater emphasis, effectively weakening the purportedly intrinsic orientation of marriage towards procreation and childrearing.

More obvious was the disappearance of strangers, as represented by household servants. Although the tripartite structure was maintained in theological, especially Puritan, discourse for nearly four centuries following the Reformation, by the mid-nineteenth century the roles of masters and servants had become conspicuous by their absence. The Christian household became largely indistinguishable from the more profane bourgeois, and later nuclear, family. Coextensively with this disappearance of strangers, the family may be said to have turned inward, transforming itself into a secluded enclave of interpersonal relationships, rather than an institutionalized form of human association which mediated the participation of its members with other social institutions.

Accompanying this inward turn was an emerging understanding of marriage and family in isolation from singleness. To a large extent, previous theological discourse had been coined to differentiate the ways of married householders from those of singles. The Reformation effectively eliminated this need. Protestants simply had no use for singleness. It was at best an aberration, and at worse an enemy of the family as characterized, for instance, in the works of Maurice and Bushnell. There was, in short, no reputable alternative to the vocations of marriage and parenthood. Although Catholics preserved vocational singleness, celibacy was understood largely in isolation from marriage and family. The ways of the married and single followed parallel paths that never intersected. The former was a sacrament that benefited laity, while the latter was a prerequisite for religious vocation. When combined with the collateral changes in marriage and perceptions of strangers, the Protestant loss of vocational singleness and its Catholic isolation signalled that the links between the family and civil society, and more importantly with the church, had become ambiguous and tenuous.

These structural changes in the Christian household mirrored significant developments in the rise of modern liberalism. Early liberal theorists, such as Grotius and Althusius, continued to portray civil society as an association of households, emphasizing the priority of the social over the political. Marriage and family, for example, were natural associations predating the state, and were thereby not subject to the will of the sovereign. Government could be entrusted to regulate marriage and assist families, but it had no authority to prevent or require qualified individuals from marrying and becoming parents. Yet early liberals failed to prevent the erosion of the household's political significance, because they could not protect it against the withering effects of Protestantism's latent individualism. They could not offer a compelling reason why participation in civil society and political community should be mediated through households, particularly since no such mediation was a prerequisite for one's relationship with God.

The contractarians, especially Hobbes and Locke, seized this lack of the household's necessary mediation to reconceive civil association as a society of individuals that were related to families. This

move effectively turned early liberal principles upside down by
emphasizing the primacy of the political over the social. The social
contract that enabled humans to escape the terrifying state of nature
was negotiated among individuals, not households. Marriage and
family were outcomes, not formative contexts, of individuals satisfying their respective needs and desires. The contractarians, however,
failed to incorporate familial bonds into their scheme of political
ordering. They could account for marriage as a contract that was
subject to the state's power to sanction and enforce, but such
a contractual relationship could not be extended to parents and
children. Consequently, the family was tolerated and sequestered as
the last, but necessary, vestige of the state of nature.

Kant presumably overcame this necessity through his programme
of a politically ordered civil society. The social sphere is defined by
and supportive of the political. It is the state, comprised of free and
equal citizens, that generates and perpetuates all forms of human
association. Parents are therefore agents of the state who have
been authorized to oversee the preparation of their children for
citizenship. Marriage and family are not natural institutions that
place limits on the scope of political authority, but useful devices in
preserving the peace and prosperity of the state. Kant's scheme,
however, breaks down at a crucial point, for he fails to guarantee
the equality of individuals within marriage and family. If individuals
are genuinely free, then they are at liberty to enter into unequal
relationships. Yet if children are to be educated to become free and
equal citizens, how can this vital formative task be entrusted to
parents whose roles are embedded in the institutions of marriage
and family that are based on inherent inequalities?

Kant's late liberal disciples, such as Rawls and Okin, purportedly
solve this problem by proposing a form of civil association based on
the empowerment of autonomous individuals. Justice is the underlying rationale of this ordering, consisting of a universal application
of radical equality and fair opportunity that cuts across any so-called
social spheres or associations. The requirements of justice in the
household, for instance, are no different in principle than those of
the workplace. The principal role of the state, therefore, is to ensure
that just practices are enacted and enforced in all social and political
relationships. Indeed, there is no precise line separating the social

from the political, for civil association is the outcome of individuals pursuing their respective interests. All social and political arrangements are thereby constructs which are subjected to frequent reform and reconstruction in accordance with the demands of justice as equality and fair opportunity. Consequently, the state is obligated to regulate families, primarily by removing parental responsibilities and assigning them to other agencies in order to protect the equality and autonomy of its individual members. The state effectively assumes the role of mediating familial relationships. What remains puzzling in this programme is why Rawls and Okin fail to take the next logical step of simply abolishing the family as the last bastion of institutionalized inequality and dependency.

Late liberal critics are alarmed by the prospect of abolition, but they fail to slow, much less stop, the gathering momentum. The Bergers, for instance, appeal to the bourgeois family as the only social location that can form the chief values of freedom and autonomy that are the bedrock of liberal civil society. Yet curiously they appeal to the very values that have been used to dismantle the family they wish to protect. If their argument is to succeed, then it must ultimately be an illiberal one. On the one hand, they must demonstrate that individuals enjoy certain benefits within the bourgeois family that cannot be duplicated in any other form of association. But that is a utilitarian rather than a liberal argument. On the other hand, they can attempt to recover the contractarian mystery that a vestige of the state of nature must be tolerated for the good of civil society. Yet given the decaying line between the social and political spheres, this strategy amounts to a libertarian plea for privacy.

Lasch is more sanguine about the acidic effects of late liberalism on the family. He offers an exacting diagnosis of the family's gravely ill condition, and he realizes that a remedy can only be had through an alternative normative account which challenges the basic presuppositions of late liberal social and political thought, namely, that in subsuming the former into the latter—a process initiated by Kant and nearly culminated by Rawls and Okin—any rationale for preserving, much less protecting, the family was stripped of substantive content. Lasch knows that the culture war over family values is waged largely with empty rhetoric. But he has no cure to proffer, for he is either unwilling or unable to offer an alternative normative account of the family, and therefore no accompanying moral and political discourse to counter that of late liberalism.

Despite the structural changes undertaken, there has been an enduring legacy of Christian marriage and family that has survived and adapted to the changing fortunes of social and political changes, especially those prompted by the rise of modern liberalism. This should not imply that there is an unchanging essence that has stubbornly maintained itself over time, or that structural forms are peripheral or unimportant considerations. Rather, it is simply the admission that certain trajectories present themselves when one is reflecting on the theological and moral significance of marriage and family within the Christian tradition, and what this significance might suggest for questions of social and political ordering.

These trajectories correspond roughly with Augustine's three goods of marriage that may be characterized as *proles*, friendship, and fidelity. Although these qualities are inherently good, they also serve to embed marriage and family within a nexus of social, political, and ecclesial relationships, providing a useful point of departure for formulating a counter-form of moral discourse to that of late liberalism. *Proles* (i.e. offspring, descendants) serve as a reminder that the link between *natural and social* cannot be easily separated or discounted. Social bonds are intrinsically intergenerational. The perpetuation of civil society is thereby invariably dependent upon and grounded in nature. Marriage and family, however, are not merely accretions that have attached themselves over time to the need for breeding. Rather, marriage and family serve to link the task of biological reproduction with the task of social reproduction.[1] Despite late liberal proposals that these tasks can be easily separated and assigned,[2] there is a growing body of counterfactual evidence that disregarding the link between procreation and childrearing has detrimental effects upon all other social affinities, as Browning and his co-authors demonstrate.

The *friendship* afforded by marriage provides a bridge between the *social and political* spheres. Marriage is an institution based on

---

[1] In this respect, reproductive technology assists, rather than displaces, this dependence and grounding.

[2] See Bertrand Russell, *Marriage and Morals* (1929); John A. Robertson, *Children of Choice* (1994); and Ted Peters, *For the Love of Children* (1996).

mutuality and equal regard which is ensconced in the principle of consent. Consent, however, is not a private agreement, but a public covenant and contract, sanctioned by both ecclesial and civil authority. In the absence of public witness afforded by the political spaces of the church and civil government, marriage, and its related office of parenthood, is stripped of any moral or social significance. This does not mean that either the church or civil government authorizes marriage, but that both acknowledge its appropriate role in the tasks of social and political ordering. More importantly, marital friendship provides a base, though not the only one, for interaction with other social spheres. Through their life together a family, comprised of persons both of and not of one's choosing, learns to negotiate a world of strangers. Without this base of friendship, it is arguable that the resulting social and political order is little more than a series of temporary alliances among strangers that endure for relatively short or lengthy periods of time, as was noted in McCarthy's critique of capitalistic markets. This does not imply that citizenship is merely a political form of friendship, for the state is neither a family nor neighbourhood writ large. Politics is properly the task of ordering a life together among strangers, but nor does this mean that the friendship marriage promotes is irrelevant in establishing a political order that is genuinely civil.

The good of marital *fidelity* is an avenue over which the traffic of the *political and ecclesial* may travel. At its root, fidelity is specified loyalty. A woman and man pledge their loyalty to each other in terms of what it means to be wife and husband. Moreover, this pledge is declared publicly to the church and civil community, to which they are also accountable in performing the requisite marital duties. Yet their mutual loyalty is never absolute or all-encompassing, for it is tempered by their primary loyalty to God. Similarly, familial fidelities owed by parents, children, and siblings are also limited by this constraint. Consequently, in blessing marriage the church reminds the state that by extension political loyalty is penultimate and not ultimate, and that political ordering should honour rather than disregard this limitation. If the principle is not honoured, then there is little to prevent the state from becoming totalitarian, either in terms of overt and oppressive tyranny, or in late liberal forms of making every aspect of life political. In this more Augustinian sense, marriage

may be understood as a sacrament. As borrowed from Roman political vocabulary, a sacrament is a pledge of fidelity that is delineated
and limited by the terms and dictates of particular, exclusive, and
often overlapping, loyalties at stake. Yet unlike the Roman demand of
ultimate fidelity to Caesar, such loyalty is reserved to God alone.
Consequently, the sacramental status of marriage is a reminder that,
unlike the ecclesial and political spheres where dual citizenship is
possible, the pledge of marital fidelity, like the pledge of loyalty to
God, offers no such option. It is not coincidental that, for many
biblical writers, adultery and idolatry are often closely related.

Taken together the goods of *proles*, friendship, and fidelity form
the base of the family as *providential witness*. As developed more
extensively in subsequent chapters, the family bears witness to a
created order that has been vindicated by Christ. This witness is
intelligible only when in embedded in a larger social and political
vision, a vision that may be characterized, in brief, as a series of
affinities integrally related to socially constructed associations tem-
porally ordered in accordance with creation's *telos* in Christ. The
structural mutations that occurred following the Reformation were
not so much a result of accommodating a Christian understanding of
the family to rapid social and political change, as it was a loss of
witness due to its being dislodged from a teleological vision that was
incommensurate with modern liberalism. This loss can be seen most
vividly in the attenuation of three crucial relationships.

The first relationship involves the virtual disappearance of
strangers as a formative category. A family cannot be a self-defined
association in isolation from other social spheres. Strangers are
needed in both a definitive and operative manner. A family is defined
by differentiating itself from strangers through a process identifying
and maintaining what kinds of relationships are properly familial,
and which are not. It is also through strangers that families mediate
their relationships with broader spheres of social and political association. In the absence of normative standards to guide these defini-
tional and operative tasks, we may say that the late modern family
lost its public pole, and in the ensuing disorientation collapsed in
upon itself, becoming a private enclave; Lasch's haven in a heartless
world. This is precisely why the household codes retained the role of
servants, for they served as both a symbolic and practical reminder

that any family claiming to be Christian could not be delineated solely by lineage or kinship. The family's witness ceases to be providential when its attention and actions are self-referential, and cannot point to affinities larger than itself.

This occluded perspective leads to the second lost relationship, namely, singleness. Similar to strangers, singles provide a normative category against which the family is defined and its actions are shaped. The ways of the household are not the ways of singleness, and the former must pattern its life in accordance with what it is, and what it is not. In this respect, the family is not in a position to either denigrate or emulate the operative virtues and advantages of singleness, but it is also perilous to ignore them. When singles are rendered invisible, the family is tempted to succumb to one of two temptations: to either bestow kinship with an unwarranted value and hope, or to operate as an alliance of individuals who are effectively little more than singles cohabitating. In either case, the family's providential witness is again distorted, because there is no complementary eschatological witness that singles embody. The family can only bear witness to creation's vindicated order when it is tempered by a witness to its end and transformation in Christ. In the absence of singleness, the family's penultimate witness attempts to take on an ultimacy for which it is not suited and cannot sustain.

The tension between the family's providential witness and the eschatological witness of singleness anticipates the third estranged relationship between the family and the church. The witness and vocation of singles are made intelligible and sustained by the church as the eschatological community; the community that awaits creation's consummation in Christ, thereby judging the inadequacy of all penultimate loyalties. The challenge is to order this tension in ways that do not debilitate either pole, a particularly daunting task for Protestants who have largely withheld from singleness any theological significance, but no less challenging for Catholics who have tended to isolate it as a prerequisite for religious vocation. In the latter instance, the tension is relaxed by maintaining the familial and the ecclesial as separate spheres which do not overlap, but are traversed by individual Christians. But this results in a theologically vague account of how the family *per se* should be related to the church, an ambiguity reflected in John Paul II's *Familiaris Consortio*.

In the former instance, the tension is collapsed by making the family and the church mirror images of each other, the difference being that of scale. But this results in either portraying the church as a family, or the family as a church. In either case, the eschatological witness the church is called to embody is blunted either by incorporating the church into the present reality of the familial (Bushnell) or absorbing the familial into the eschatological (Clapp).

The principal issue at stake is that familial roles and relationships are not easily transferable to the life of the church. Its members are not spouses, parents, children in Christ, but sisters and brothers awaiting full fellowship with their Lord. As the second clause of the preceding sentence indicates, familial images have been used to describe the life of Christians. But it must be remembered that this imagery is anticipatory rather than descriptive, otherwise the very power of the familial images to qualify and transform present relationships would be lost. In this respect, it should be remembered that the early church took great care to maintain a distinction between the familial household and the household of God. The tension between the family and the church is a necessary one that cannot be resolved without doing grave damage to the eschatological orientation of Christian faith, for it is unfulfilled expectation that is the source of its vitality. Christian hope is not placed in a future family or church, but in a kingdom and new city in which there is no need for either families or churches.

The following chapters attempt a theological and normative recovery of the relationship among the family, strangers, singleness, and the church. Or posed more expansively as a question: how should the family be ordered in respect of civil society, political community, and the church? And how in turn should the church, political community, and civil society be ordered in respect of the family? Answering these questions requires both a critical appropriation and constructive exposition of the principal claims and arguments summarized in the preceding chapters, a task of simultaneously drawing upon and addressing the deficiencies of the theological tradition these writers claim to represent. Some the chief issues upon which this critical and constructive recovery concentrates are noted briefly below, signalling the basic lineaments of the arguments developed in subsequent chapters.

Baxter emphasized an understanding of the Christian family defined in part to its relation to strangers, and more broadly to civil society. He accomplished this by retaining a tripartite structure which included household servants, and stressing the duty of parents to preparing children for vocations useful to church, society, or government. In failing to make virtually any mention of singleness, however, he loses an eschatological witness to delineate and complement his account of the family. Consequently, his description of the relationship between the family and church is vague, and his emphasis on vocational preparation admits a growing individualism accompanying the contractarian shift away from a society of households towards one composed of individuals.

These weaknesses in Baxter's account of the family were exacerbated in subsequent theological reflection which further blurred its relationship with the civil and ecclesial spheres. Schleiermacher, for instance, retained the tripartite structure of the household codes, but, following Kant, he transformed the family as a political agent of social control, thereby collapsing its providential witness and the eschatological witness of singleness into the security and fate of the state. In contrast, Bushnell reasserted the family as an autonomous association by portraying it as the principal agency of evangelism. Yet in doing so he condemned singles and strangers as enemies, effectively making the Christian family superior to the church and all other forms of social association, a particularly dangerous notion given his belief, borrowed from Baxter, in 'holy seed' that pious parents passed on to offspring.[3] Maurice reclaimed the primacy of the church as *the* social and political sphere satisfying the family's natural longing for greater affiliation. But like Bushnell, he too dismisses singleness and strangers as irrelevant considerations for social and political ordering, thereby asserting the primacy of the church over the family and all other civil associations.

Schleiermacher's, Bushnell's, and Maurice's attempts to resolve the underlying tension between providence and eschatology by collapsing both poles in the state, family, or church respectively proved untenable, however, with the late liberal shift towards the political empowerment

---

[3] See Brent Waters, 'Engineering our Grace', in Gerard Magill (ed.), *Genetics and Ethics* (2004).

of autonomous individuals. Contemporary theological reflection on the social and political significance of the family has been formulated largely in response to this shift in emphasis, and these formulations have tended to take one of three dominant approaches.

The first approach of reformulation recognizes that the late liberal social and political tasks of empowering autonomous individuals should not be ignored or castigated, but embraced in revising Christian attitudes towards marriage and family. Yet to what extent can these revisions be said to be peculiarly Christian? Nelson, for example, establishes a fundamental equality between women and men based on reciprocity and mutuality, which is grounded in the natural and healthy impulse towards sexual expression and personal fulfilment. But given his thin theological grounding, his fixation on sexual expression is reduced to a means of asserting the will, effectively disembodying his purportedly embodied ethic. This reduction strips marriage and family of any normative content or social setting as seen in his analysis of adultery and same-sex union. Thatcher's revision embeds many of Nelson's themes in thicker theological soil, which enables him to recover the moral significance of embodiment, and therefore the social and political importance of marriage and family. His theological soil, however, is not suitable for garnering the kind of harvest he anticipates as seen in his discussions of betrothal and same-sex union in which ecclesial and civil communities are reduced to ambivalent affirmation or indifferent acceptance of private agreements. Curiously, Thatcher undermines the public square that he wishes the church to engage in a more relevant manner.

A diametrically opposite approach is one that resists any extensive accommodation with contemporary values and mores that are undermining marriage and family. This stance asserts the primacy of the Christian theological tradition as the source of a counter social and political discourse to that of late liberalism. Yet to what extent does such resistance succeed in lodging marriage and family in their proper social and political locations? John Paul II, for instance, rebuilds the social location in relation to singleness and the church within a lush theological landscape. But he grants too much primacy to the church, effectively reducing the family to a tiny and dependent replica, thereby weakening its normative relation to strangers. Grisez endeavours to strengthen this relationship by arguing that married couples have moral obligations to children beyond their own offspring that are exercised through adoption and charitable work. His attempt is not entirely successful, however, for his argument is aimed primarily at infertile couples rather than parents in general, implying they are alternative methods for satisfying natural parental desires, thereby distorting the moral significance of these acts.

Critical adaptation offers an alternative stance to those of reformulation or resistance. This approach takes into account, albeit selectively, contemporary social and political circumstances, while simultaneously recovering neglected themes from the Christian theological tradition. Yet to what extent do these synthetic constructs solve the problems they purportedly address, and what additional issues do they leave unaddressed? Critical familism, for example, establishes equality, reciprocity, and mutuality in marriage and family in functional social terms, in contrast to Okin's politically mandated terms. But Browning and his co-authors provide a theological framework that is too thin to address the issue of how families should be related to singleness and the church other than in an attenuated posture of dialogue and support. Clapp reclaims the providential witness of the family by establishing its relation to the eschatological witness of singleness, and its evangelistic mission to strangers. But in recasting the Christian household as a domestic church he diminishes the social and political significance of the family. Moreover, in portraying the church as first family, he distorts the providential and eschatological witnesses that he is attempting to clarify. In his account of household management, McCarthy proposes the neighbourhood as the social context in which to locate marriage and the family. The neighbourhood economy he proposes, however, cannot bear the moral weight he wishes to place on it, effectively diminishing marriage and parenthood.

With these theological landmarks in mind, this enquiry may now move on into the territory of formulating a proposal that is both critical and constructive. Rather than beginning with the assumption that late liberal society is the background against which Christians must develop a reformulated, resistant, or adapted account of the family, this proposal prefers to start by formulating theological answers to the questions posed earlier regarding the family's normative relationships to civil and ecclesial associations. This does not imply that the context of late liberal society should be ignored, only that it not be granted the privilege of forming the shape of theological argumentation. The preceding chapters, then, may be seen as representative conversation partners, both in terms of their respective strengths and weaknesses, in developing the following proposal. The principal goal of this constructive task is to determine whether a more stable theological foundation can be developed in which an essentially Augustinian framework can be embedded, and if so, what the ensuing implications might mean for larger questions of social and political ordering.

5

Alternative Conceptual Themes

This chapter develops an alternative form of discourse on the relation between the family and social and political ordering, initiating a search for concepts to counter those that have come to prevail in late liberalism, as well as drawing on countervailing strands that were summarized in previous chapters. Developing a comprehensive alternative theory, however, is beyond the scope of this study. Rather, the more modest goal is to identify promising paths for how a normative account of the family might illuminate larger issues of social and political ordering. The following enquiries into selected philosophical, theological, and moral themes provide a base from which the direction of these paths is subsequently mapped.

PHILOSOPHICAL THEMES

Nature, history, and culture

Life is sustained and perpetuates itself through natural processes. Without certain physical, chemical, and organic elements there would be no living creatures, rightfully inspiring a response of awe and wonder. This does not entitle nature to be romanticized, however, for it is also a source of pain, suffering, and misery predicated on the necessity of death. The natural means for expediting the survival of a species often proves inimical to the flourishing of individual creatures. There is within nature's order a quality of threatening disorder, inspiring humans to speak, without irony or contradiction, of such evils as earthquakes, droughts, and deleterious genes. Humans are wondrously dependent upon *and* frightfully at the mercy of nature.

We may also use the term 'nature' to describe a crucial characteristic of an object or process, or ascribe a certain purpose or quality. We may say, for instance, that when a fault shifts it is natural that the ground shakes, or that the purpose of a heart is to pump blood, or that human parents have an innate proclivity to care for their offspring. We may even speak of an underlying *human nature* which in turn shapes our assessments of the behaviour of individuals and various forms of associations. Yet these descriptions and ascriptions do not eliminate our ambivalent dependency upon nature.

It is due in part to this ambivalence that we must also refer to history. Humans are endowed with a capacity for purposeful and cooperative action, enabling them to exploit natural processes to their benefit or allaying some of their more threatening aspects. This capacity has been described variously as dominion, a social human nature, or survival advantage in the evolution of the species, but what these claims hold in common is the acknowledgement of a human capability to impose a limited reordering of nature, creating what we may call history. Through such pursuits as agriculture, industry, commerce, and medicine, humans sustain themselves in a more efficient and less burdensome manner.

In using 'nature' and 'history' as heuristic devices we must be careful in perceiving how they are correlated. If we try to force them to stand as two unrelated, antagonistic, or irreconcilable realms then we are forced to straddle two modes of existence and to pursue two lives, one of the body and one of the will. This is precisely the perception ensconced in modern liberal social and political theory, in which history is used to distinguish human existence from that of other creatures.[1] History refers to a realm of free and purposeful human will, whereas nature denotes a mechanistic determinism. Humans, then, live inescapability in two conflicting realms. As George Grant has argued, the seeds of this dichotomy were sown by Rousseau, Kant, and Hegel in which history

was used to describe the particular human situation in which we are not only made but we make. In this way of speaking, history was not a term to be applied

[1] See George Grant, *Time as History* (1995), 3–15.

to the development of the earth and animals, but a term to distinguish the collective life of man (that unique being who is subject to cause and effect as defined by modern science, but also a member of the world of freedom).[2]

Beginning with the contractarians, nature and history have been posed as antithetical realms of human life. It is the state of nature humans must escape if they are to become historical beings, and in pursuing this deliverance liberal social and political theory reduced nature to instinct, and history to the assertion of human will. Neither of these diminished categories, however, can sustain a vision of social and political ordering that can, to any significant extent, be regarded as natural or historical. Nature is not simply a random collection of purposeless processes, nor is history merely an account of humans asserting their will against or over nature.

Although the relationship between nature and history offers a heuristic foundation upon which we can build, these categories alone remain too abstract for the purposes of this inquiry. We must also turn our attention to *culture*, for it is within this realm that the relation between nature and history is manifested in its most concrete form. It is within culture that natural resources are used to construct various artefacts. It is within particular cultural settings that various intellectual and artistic endeavours are pursued. Most importantly it is within a cultural milieu that beliefs, symbols, and values are created, refined, and reformed, collectively generating an emerging ethos that inspires and shapes the principal institutions directing the dominant patterns of social and political ordering. Thus we may speak about the ethos of an age as a shorthand reference to these various activities and pursuits.

As discussed in Chapter 2, early liberals placed cultural formation within the realm of history, but culture itself was not divorced from nature as a consequence. Institutions governing the cultural processes of social and political ordering possessed inherent natures which must be honoured, thereby imposing not only practical limits on what humans could will but also normative limits on what should be willed. The decisive move in the development of modern liberal thought was the insistence that it was precisely these imposed natural constraints that must be overcome, or at least tempered, to create social and political orders less inimical to human flourishing.

[2] Ibid. 12.

The move was further reinforced in late liberalism's adoption of a technical rationality that seeks not merely to carve out a domesticated sphere within a hostile state of nature, but its complete mastery and accompanying transformation of human nature.[3] Although the effects of this alliance between technical rationality and late liberalism are examined in greater detail in subsequent sections of this inquiry, it suffices at this juncture to note that the principal consequence is that the task of social and political ordering, as well as other forms of private and public associations, become projects and artefacts of the human will. Ironically, it is the cultural projects undertaken by humans that become the nature of their corporate life.[4]

In contrast to an ethos of mastery, we must instead speak of an unfolding nature that is historical in character, so that nature must be *safeguarded* if humans are to *evoke* a history from it. Nature without history is purposeless mutation over time, and a history unrelated to nature is a chronicle of episodic events. For nature to be nature necessitates a law-like pattern of structural formation over time, while history to be history requires an ordered movement through time. Nature and history are not separate or antithetical domains but integrally related dimensions of a larger created order. Thus in respect to the central topic of this enquiry, we may also speak of the nature of *procreation and childrearing* that must be safeguarded in order to evoke a *familial* history from it, and this evocative process in turn induces the unfolding and enfolding of larger spheres of human association. Yet before we can investigate further the cultural manifestations of this process, we must develop a vocabulary for ascribing how history is integrally related to nature.

Sphere sovereignty

To entertain the possibility that nature and history are integrally related is not to suggest that our attention should become fixated

---

[3] For critical accounts of technical rationality, see Albert Borgmann, *Technology and the Character of Contemporary Life* (1984); Jacques Ellul, *The Technological Society* (1964); and George Grant, *Technology and Empire* (1969) and *Technology and Justice* (1986); and Brent Waters, *From Human to Posthuman* (2006).

[4] Cf. James M. Gustafson, *Ethics from a Theocentric Perspective* (1981), i. 214–19.

on the minute or causal details of physical processes. We cannot, for example, examine an underlying physics and derive from it a normative pattern of social and political ordering, for at the atomic and sub-atomic levels nature is apparently characterized more by chaos than order. Rather, it is to pose the question: is there an inherent nature to various forms of human association which when safeguarded properly evoke their historical unfolding? And can this evocative unfolding be ascribed in a normative manner? Similar types of questions prompted the early liberal theories of Grotius and Althusius, and a more contemporary inquiry along similar lines is provided by Herman Dooyeweerd's account of sphere sovereignty.[5]

Sphere sovereignty is founded on the 'scriptural ground motive' of 'creation, fall, and redemption through Jesus Christ', which 'operates through God's Spirit as a driving force in the religious roots of temporal life'.[6] Creation should be ordered in accordance with this ground motive, and although sin distorts our perception of this order, through grace its 'multifaceted aspects and structures'[7] can be nonetheless discerned. Temporal reality is constituted by a range of discrete yet integrally related aspects, likened to light passing through a prism and refracted into various hues.[8] These aspects share a common origin and deeper unity that cannot be disclosed in any single dimension. Consequently, the temporal ordering of creation has a pluriform character.

Pluriform ordering does not imply that nature is subject to human domination. The underlying principle of sphere sovereignty[9] dis-closes the *'mutual irreducibility, inner connection,* and *inseparable coherence* of all aspects of reality in the order of time'.[10] The world

---

[5] The primary texts consulted are *Roots of Western Culture* (1979); *A New Critique of Theoretical Thought*, 4 vols. (1953–8), and *A Christian Theory of Social Institutions* (1986). A comprehensive exposition of Dooyeweerd's sphere sovereignty is beyond the scope of this chapter. Consequently, the selected concepts drawn from his work are employed in a suggestive and interpretive manner.

[6] Dooyeweerd, *Roots of Western Culture*, 40.

[7] Ibid. 40.   [8] Ibid. 40–1.

[9] According to Dooyeweerd (ibid. 43), the phrase 'sphere sovereignty' was coined by Kuyper. Elsewhere he asserts that Althusius offers the 'first modern formulation of the principle of internal sphere-sovereignty in the social relationships' (*New Critique*, iii. 663).

[10] Dooyeweerd, *Roots of Western Culture*, 42 (emphasis original).

consists of a series of sovereign spheres incorporating levels of micro and macro complexity,[11] and the totality of temporal existence cannot be reduced to the structure of any single sphere. Rather, they cohere in their mutual ordering to and with each other. There is, for example, an inherent integrity to one's 'psychical aspect of reality'[12] which is connected to the physical, logical, historical, cultural, lingual, social, economic, aesthetic, and moral dimensions of one's life. The integrity of an individual is distorted if reduced to any one aspect, or if her inherent structures are disrupted. No single sphere may be imposed as the foundation for ordering temporal reality because it is the *totality of creation* that orders the sovereign spheres comprising it.

As parts of a created order, human associations reflect a series of integrally related social spheres. Sphere sovereignty

> applies to the structure of societal forms, such as the family, the state, the church, the school, economic enterprise, and so on. As with the *aspects* of reality, our view of the inner nature, mutual relation, and coherence of the different *societal spheres* is governed by our religious point of departure. The christian [sic] ground motive penetrates to the root unity of all the societal spheres that are distinct in the temporal order. From the root unity, it gives us insight into the intrinsic nature, mutual relation, and coherence of these spheres.[13]

For Dooyeweerd, all forms of social ordering are based on some type of *religious foundation*. It is never a question of whether civil society will be religious or secular, but if the foundational myth is true or false. Social ordering always reflects a religious faith regarding the fundamental structure of reality. Such myths as the original position, general will, or state of nature, for instance, inspire differing accounts of what constitutes a well-ordered society, as opposed to one established on creation, fall, and redemption in Christ.[14] A civil society founded on a true religious ground motive reflects the created order, consisting of a series of independent, integrally related, and coherent

---

[11] See Dooyeweerd, *New Critique of Theoretical Thought*, i. 99–107.

[12] Dooyeweerd, *Roots of Western Culture*, 45.

[13] Ibid. 47 (emphasis original). See also Dooyeweerd, *Christian Theory*, 64–78.

[14] The veracity of faith is known through revelation rather than reason. See Dooyeweerd, *New Critique*, ii. 298–330.

social spheres, again like light passing through a prism and refracted into various hues. Moreover, it is only through faith that the light and its source may be perceived, whereas philosophy is limited to investigating the narrow bands of the refracted hues. This is why social theory, according to Dooyeweerd, must penetrate back through the temporal spheres of reality to their created origin.

Although each sphere has its own inherent nature and structure, this does not imply a static quality. Sphere sovereignty is also premised on a temporal unfolding of *social differentiation*.[15] According to Dooyeweerd, undifferentiated societies are kinship-based associations of clans or tribes. With extensive population growth more complex forms of association are needed, requiring a division of labour in such areas as agriculture, industry, commerce, governance, education, and the arts. Within these social spheres cooperative activities are pursued among individuals not linked directly to kinship. It is important to emphasize that this social differentiation discloses the unfolding history of a created order, and the temporal development of its social spheres proceeds along the lines of their respective natures and structures. The latent qualities of a differentiated society, then, were always present in the historical unfolding of human associations.

Dooyeweerd admits that the social spheres have a great deal of plasticity in regard to how they are ordered, but a point can be reached that breaches their internal sovereignty.[16] Maintaining spherical integrity is crucial because an individual as such can only exist within the *structure of a given social sphere*. An 'individual' is not a subjective consciousness cutting across various social spheres, but one who embodies a given relationship within a particular social sphere.[17] A woman, for example, who is known as the individual called 'mother' within the sphere of the family is not the same individual within the sphere of commerce. This does not mean that a person is comprised of multiple personalities, for personhood is derived from one's status as God's creature. It is one's individual identity that changes in accordance with the nature and structure of a particular social sphere.

---

[15] Ibid. iii. 157–261; see also *Roots of Western Culture*, 73–81.
[16] See Dooyeweerd, *New Critique*, ii. 542–98.
[17] Ibid. iii. 53–153.

Sphere sovereignty and autonomy, however, are *not* synonymous concepts because they are based on antithetical principles:

Autonomy of the parts of a whole and sphere sovereignty of radically different societal relationships are principially [sic] different matters. In a differentiated society the degree of autonomy depends upon the require- ments of the whole of which the autonomous community remains a part. Sphere sovereignty, however, is rooted in the constant, inherent character of the life sphere itself. Because of their intrinsic natures, differentiated spheres like the family, the school, economic enterprise, science, and art can never be parts of the state.[18]

It is important to highlight that, in contrast to the dominant strands of late liberal social theory in which autonomy is politically *protected* in respect to the needs of the state, the sovereignty of each social sphere is *inherent*. In the former instance the family, for example, is a voluntary affiliation whose members are granted a limited autonomy to conduct their affairs along a specified range of activities that enable a more efficient pursuit of shared interests. In the latter instance, the family is a social sphere, whose individuals perform their roles in accordance with the nature and structure of the familial association. In late liberal accounts emphasizing autonomy, an individual's identity is a subjective will that remains relatively stable in pursuing a range of interests within various social spheres; it is the same individual pursuing her interests through the family or commercial institutions. In respect to sphere sovereignty, the identity of an individual is determined by the respective roles of mother or banker, while her personhood remains fixed; she is the same person but not the same individual performing certain roles within the spheres of the family or commerce. For late liberal social theory, the social spheres offer malleable constructs for expressing the identities of autonomous persons, whereas for sphere sovereignty the social spheres are the structures which form the individuality of its members.

According to Dooyeweerd, autonomy is a holdover from undiffer- entiated societies that has exerted a corrupting influence on the historical unfolding of the social spheres in the modern era.[19]

---

[18] Dooyeweerd, *Roots of Western Culture*, 56.

[19] Sphere sovereignty cannot be expressed in an undifferentiated society because there is nothing against which the nature and structure of a sovereign sphere can be contrasted (ibid. 74–5).

In undifferentiated societies autonomy was a legal status granted to a community without recourse to any higher political authority. Such a community possessed no value or integrity in its own right. With the rise of the modern nation-state, the undifferentiated aspects of civil society were eliminated by incorporating them as differentiated dimensions of a political body. Autonomy became a provisional status granted to citizens or voluntary associations in line with changing perceptions of what constituted the general will. Despite attempts to construct stable autonomous spheres within liberal regimes, these efforts largely failed to resist the state's penetration into virtually every aspect of private and public life, resulting in a transient concept of autonomy because it is premised on the necessity of a hierarchical political order. In short, sphere sovereignty is not synonymous with autonomy because it is grounded in a created order rather than a historicist assertion of political will.[20] Consequently, sphere sovereignty provides a superior foundation for social and political ordering because it reflects the nature of reality as the 'work of God's creation, which is integral and complete'.[21]

We may now draw out some implications of sphere sovereignty regarding its alternative understanding of the relation between nature and history in contrast to that presumed by late liberal social and political theory. The scriptural ground motive of creation, fall, and redemption in Jesus Christ provides an underlying pattern of temporal order. Although this order is pluriform in character, especially as it is manifested in history and culture, there is nonetheless an underlying unity; the nature of creation is diverse but not divided. Temporal reality is neither self-contained nor atomistic but relational, and its ordering encompasses a harmony of the whole without negating the integrity of the parts. Recognizing such an order resists an epistemological and moral imperialism asserting the sovereignty of one sphere over the whole, as well as opposing an autonomy denying any unity other than what can be willed. Social differentiation enabling the emergence of sovereign spheres discloses a *historical unfolding of the nature of a created*

---

[20] For Dooyeweerd's critique of historicism, ibid. 61–87, and *New Critique*, ii. 192–229, 337–62.
[21] Dooyeweerd, *Roots of Western Culture*, 58.

order. Consequently, we may speak of moral ordering as safeguarding the inherent natures of the social spheres, while evoking from them a social and political history.

A well-ordered civil community resists the presumption that unity and pluriformity are mutually exclusive or incompatible. This presumption is exhibited in two prevalent accounts of social and political ordering:

1. Collectivist regimes in which the value of social institutions is derived from the needs of the state: emphasizing the primacy of the state incorporates the imposition of its sovereignty over the social spheres, and should be opposed as a denial of creation's pluriform character.

2. Political programmes founded upon the primacy of autonomous persons, as propounded by such theorists as Rawls and Okin, are to be rejected for failing to protect the sovereignty of the social spheres. Such regimes attempt to displace the given character of social institutions with malleable qualities that can be easily recast at will, thereby denying creation's underlying unity. Although the social spheres possess inherent goods, the common good is not simply their aggregate. Rather, the common good is related to, but greater than, the sum total of the respective spheres' individual goods, and these individual goods are related to, but not derived exclusively from, the common good. Sphere sovereignty promotes forms of social and political ordering embodying the underlying unity of creation *and* its temporal pluriformity.

These twin foci may be seen more clearly by concentrating on the familial sphere.[22] Since the family is not an instrument of the state, it does not exist for the purpose of accomplishing a regime's quantitative or qualitative population goals. And since the family is also not an artefact of the collective will of its members, it is not a means of personal fulfilment. In both of these instances, the inherent nature and structure of the family may be easily abandoned or altered in accordance with changing political objectives or social mores. The familial association is itself a sovereign sphere, integrally related

---

[22] For Dooyeweerd's account of the 'natural family', see *New Critique*, iii. 157–345, and *Christian Theory*, 79–85.

to the other social spheres comprising a differentiated society. Contrary to the claims of some late liberal theorists, the family is not a relic of undifferentiated societies. As Dooyeweerd contends, the 'natural community between a couple of parents with children under age is not a relationship with an undifferentiated inner destination. If it were, it would disappear in the advance of the differentiating process in historical development. It would be a rudiment of a former historical phase.'[23] This is clearly not the case, for the family has survived, even flourished, within this historical process of social differentiation. Moreover, since the inherent goods of the familial association are expressed through a normative structure,[24] the family can only contribute to the common good when it is ordered towards exercising its rightful sovereignty. Thus the family provides the natural and social contexts for properly ordering procreation and childrearing.

The most important implication to be drawn is that sphere sovereignty proposes an alternative conception of the terms 'private' and 'public', in contrast to those propounded by late liberal theorists, especially in respect to the social and political ordering of the family. We may say that what is private pertains, invoking themes suggested by Althusius and Grotius, to the law and right of the familial association as exhibited in its inherent *nature and structure* as a social sphere, whereas public denotes cultural institutions and political acts evoking its *historical unfolding* in relation to other social spheres. Rather than construing the family in terms of how it assists the interests of the autonomous persons comprising it, emphasis is placed on the integrity of the familial association in relation to other social spheres. To illustrate this contrast, in late liberal social and political theory autonomous persons pursue their reproductive interests within the boundaries of self-imposed constraints as required by the terms and limitations of relevant contracts, effectively dividing the family into a private realm of procreation and a public realm of childrearing. Whereas for sphere sovereignty, persons are individual spouses, parents, or children within the familial sphere, so

---

[23] Dooyeweerd, *New Critique*, iii. 269.
[24] According to Dooyeweerd, the 'natural derivation and consanguinity of children under age, issuing from the same parents, is the necessary structural foundation upon which ... a family is built' (ibid. 266).

a family's private dimension includes procreation *and* childrearing, while its public dimension entails relationships with other social spheres to protect and enable the family's sovereignty within its sphere. This private dimension, however, is *not* synonymous with an absence of external constraints, but is a freedom to pursue those vocations, virtues, and practices pertaining to the inherent nature of the familial association. Nor is the public dimension synonymous with constraining or facilitating the rights of individual family members, but it entails the moral, social, and political ordering of the spousal, parental, and filial roles in relation to the other social spheres comprising a differentiated society.

It is important to note the contrast between the underlying psychologies. For much of late liberal social and political theory, *individuality is assumed while personhood is acquired.* Every human is an individual but not all individuals are persons because they lack the requisite capacities for asserting or developing autonomy.[25] Although individuals may possess interests, only persons have the necessary will to pursue them, so it is only persons who possess rights. Moreover, these rights pertain to persons regardless of particular social contexts. A person, for example, may be a mother and a banker, but she does not possess her rights in virtue of these roles. Rather, she exercises her rights as a person in pursuing her parental and commercial interests. This psychology reflects an abstract understanding of personhood, cut off from concrete circumstances in which persons exercise their so-called rights. A late liberal person combines a socially conferred status with a volitional capacity to calculate and pursue one's interests. A woman must be able to identify her reproductive and commercial interests before she is able to exercise her rights to become a mother and banker in pursuing them. This volitional capacity is required if autonomous persons are to submit themselves to self-imposed restraints, for in pursuing her reproductive and commercial interests a woman does not have the right to neglect her children or defraud her clients. Yet this also means that the dividing line between private and public domains is

[25] It is not clear what modern liberal theorists mean when they refer to individuals independently of their social roles and political relationships. For a critical discussion of the modern invention of the individual and its influence on subsequent developments in moral, social, and political theory, see Alisdair MacIntyre, *After Virtue* (1985), 51–78; cf. John E. Hare, *The Moral Gap* (1996), 17–22.

an abstraction, disregarding the structures of the social spheres in which these interests are identified and pursued. There is nothing pertaining to the natures of the family or political economy ordering the suitability of one's reproductive and commercial interests, because such ordering depends on the will of autonomous persons independently of these social spheres—persons, in short, who can deliberate behind an imaginary veil of ignorance. Persons must simultaneously calculate their private interests while submitting to self-imposed constraints in publicly pursuing them. Consequently, human associations are the public outcomes of private interests. The family, for instance, is the sum total of its members' interests, or the economy is the aggregate of commercial interests.

In contrast, the underlying psychology of sphere sovereignty asserts that *personhood is a given quality whereas individuality is an acquired status*. Humans are persons because they are created in the image and likeness of God, and persons become individuals by virtue of their associations within particular social spheres. It is the same persons who are associated with various social spheres, but they do not exercise their subjective rights derived from their personhood within these associations. There are instead objective duties and privileges performed in virtue of the right of the roles being performed. A woman, for example, does not exercise her reproductive and commercial rights within the spheres of the family or commerce. Rather, she assumes parental privileges or contractual duties because of her status, respectively, as mother or banker. Furthermore, these privileges and duties are delineated by the nature and structure of the social sphere in question. In respect to the familial association, its inherent nature and structure entails an unfolding, expansive, and enduring love. It is in and through this love that a bond of mutual belonging is established among individuals in virtue of their roles as spouse, parent, child, or sibling, each enjoying designated privileges and duties pertaining to their familial association.

The implications of these contending psychologies may be further drawn out by revisiting the separation between procreation and childrearing that has been propounded by many late liberal theorists. As was discussed in Chapter 2, Rawls and Okin argue that there is a strong public interest in childrearing, because it is as young children that we learn basic values (such as self-esteem and respect for others) that will promote good citizenship later in life. The public interest, however, should not impinge unduly upon individuals exercising their private reproductive rights. Consequently, neither Rawls nor Okin contend that there is any necessary or even implicit continuity between procreation and childrearing. And both imply that if more suitable childrearing arrangements for inculcating basic values could be constructed that would exclude biological parents, there would be nothing inherently wrong in doing so since both young children and society would benefit. A line is effectively drawn between the private pursuit of reproductive interests, and a public interest in childrearing.

This line, however, is misplaced because the familial association is *not* a contractual affiliation of autonomous persons. The family is a uniquely voluntary *and* involuntary association of *both* natural *and* social affinities. The familial association has both private and public dimensions that are invariably intertwined rather than easily divisible. The private dimension more directly embodies the familial nature of mutual belonging, entailing a normative and integral ordering of procreation and childrearing, in which individuals perform their roles within a given structure of familial relationships. The public dimension involves the family's moral and political ordering in other social spheres which assist it in evoking a history of its unfolding, expansive, and enduring love. The social and political ordering of the family is not predicated on a procedural balance between the rights of private persons to pursue their reproductive interests, and a public interest in childrearing. Rather, it entails a political ordering of civil society respecting the right of the family as a unique association of natural and social affinities. As Althusius recognized, familial ordering is more a political than economic issue, but it is a politics of individuals tied by bonds of association rather than a politics of autonomous persons divided by conflicting interests.

The limits of sphere sovereignty

Although sphere sovereignty offers a promising philosophical framework for drawing out some of the chief implications that the familial association holds for broader questions of social and political ordering, it nonetheless provides too narrow a foundation for building a normative account of the family. For Dooyeweerd, a family exists only when the genetic offspring of two parents are living together in a common household.[26] Adoptive or foster parents, for instance, offer 'motherly' and 'fatherly' affection, but they cannot provide genuine 'maternal' or 'paternal' care.[27] Furthermore, with the death of parents or maturation of offspring the 'family-bond' is broken, sundering the familial relation between adult children and ageing parents. When children leave home the parents revert to being a married couple.[28] Reducing the family to a genetic relationship between parents and dependent offspring, however, results in a highly attenuated portrayal of familial relationships, because they endure over time and physical proximity. It is not clear why intergenerational love and mutual commitment cannot emerge in the absence of a biological connection or filial dependency.

The problem is not that out of a variety of family models Dooye-weerd commends one particular model as a universal norm. He may account for this diversity by appealing to cross-cultural studies of the family which disclose more similarities than differences, arguing that these variations reflect peculiar or localized circumstances within the broader historical pattern of social differentiation, or distortions introduced by false religious ground motives.[29] The problem with Dooyeweerd's account of the family is that he pays insuffi-cient attention to the *telos* of the familial association. To what end the social sphere of the family as part of a created order is being drawn towards is a question he does not address.

Although Dooyeweerd acknowledges that familial structures have changed over time, the significance he assigns to these changes is misplaced. Dooyeweerd is correct in claiming that, since there is an underlying created order to the historical development of the social spheres, it should be possible to trace a normative pattern of development over time, implying a familial nature that remains constant throughout the stages of social differentiation. The struc-tural changes reflect attempts at moral and social ordering motivated by a true or false faith. If Dooyeweerd is right, then he would have us believe that the essence of a family based on a true religious ground

---

[26] See Dooyeweerd, *New Critique*, iii. 343–4.   [27] Ibid. 292, n. 1.
[28] Ibid. 304–5.   [29] Ibid. 262–368.

motive is seen most clearly, if not exclusively, in the genetic and social relationship between parents and dependent offspring. But it is difficult to understand how this 'essence' accords with his construal of the family as a social sphere integrally related and ordered to other social spheres, because the imagery is entirely centripetal. Dooyeweerd's attenuated account of the nature of the familial association entails a circular unfolding within history, for the purpose of the family is little more than maintaining a relatively brief parent–child relationship based on a genetic bond. Such a family turns in upon itself, focusing on its own internal ordering rather than suggesting patterns that may inform larger patterns of social and political ordering. Dooyeweerd's family appears to be more a secluded enclave than a social sphere. He fails to entertain the possibility that, because of the fall, the historical unfolding of a normative family structure may also disclose an inherent deficiency within the nature of the familial association. Although a normative ordering of the familial association based on a true religious ground motive will reflect an underlying created order, if such a created order is itself in need of redemption, and is being drawn towards a transformed destiny, then the family cannot exist as an end in itself.

The principal problem with Dooyeweerd's account of the family is *theological*. Dooyeweerd tends to use 'creation' and 'nature' as interchangeable terms. Although the fall distorts the temporal ordering of creation, its nature remains unaffected by sin. It is only history, not nature, that needs to be redeemed. Humans may look to nature, aided by grace, to discern normative patterns of social and political ordering. Dooyeweerd's portrayal of redemption is fixated almost solely on the historical unfolding of the social spheres. Consequently, there is no attempt to forge a link between creation and redemption, and little attention directed towards creation's eschatological destiny. Since the essence of creation has not been perverted by sin it would be superfluous to speak of its radical transformation in the fullness of time. If the sovereign spheres are ordered properly then we will come to see the inherent perfection of creation, but it is a temporal process that will not be completed until Christ returns to bring history to an end. This implies, however, that redemption is more a recovery of creation's pristine origin than its transformation in Christ; more an attempt to restore the old than to be drawn into the new.

What does this lack of a direct relationship between creation, redemption, and eschatology have to do with the family, particularly in respect to questions of social and political ordering? Although Dooyeweerd is correct in contending that a normative family structure discloses an underlying created order, its historical unfolding also reveals the incomplete nature of the familial association. The family is always accompanied by a divine judgement on the limitations of its internal affinities. The roles of spouse, parent, and child are to be displaced by sisters and brothers in Christ. The family intimates an end beyond the nature of its temporal association if it genuinely affirms a created order being drawn towards its destiny. Consequently the family must bear witness to creation's hope in the New Jerusalem instead of a restored Eden. If sphere sovereignty is to provide an alternative foundation for portraying a normative account of the familial association as a font of social and political ordering, then it must first be placed in a more explicitly theological framework.

THEOLOGICAL THEMES

The vindicated order of creation

According to Oliver O'Donovan, the death, resurrection, and ascension of Jesus Christ vindicates creation and its divinely ordained order.[30] The word 'creation' implies a given order, otherwise the world, if it could be called that, would consist of an undifferentiated and unintelligible collection of matter and energy. Rather, creation is vertically ordered to its creator and this in turn is reflected in the horizontal ordering of the parts to the whole. We cannot simply perceive created order, however, for our perception is distorted by what classic theology described as the fall.[31] Humans exhibit a 'fateful leaning towards death' or inclination to 'uncreate' themselves and to 'uncreate the rest of creation'. Yet in Christ's resurrection, creation and its ordering toward life is vindicated in that humans have 'not been allowed to uncreate what God created'.[32]

[30] See Oliver O'Donovan, *Resurrection and Moral Order* (1986), 31–52.
[31] Ibid. 19–20.   [32] Ibid. 14.

The vindicated order of creation provides an objective and expansive focal point for moral deliberation because God's created order includes all creatures and the natural processes upon which they depend. This does not mean that we may simply look to nature and discover given norms or ethical principles.[33] This would entail reducing creation to nature, thereby diminishing the moral and redemptive significance of Christ's resurrection. Rather, the vindicated order of creation discloses a *natural ethic*[34] that can only be perceived by its ordering in and to Christ as the head of creation and first born from the dead. It is through Christ's resurrection that we are enabled to perceive a created order, rather than a more narrowly construed natural one, for 'only in Christ do we apprehend that order in which we stand and that knowledge of it with which we have been endowed'.[35]

The vindication of creation cannot be seen, however, in isolation from the redemptive, providential, and eschatological dimensions of what is revealed in Christ's resurrection, for they are of one piece. Redemption, if it is to avoid Gnostic and historicist distortions, implies a created order which in turn orders the acts and roles of its creatures; a recovery of the whole from which the parts derive their intelligibility in a mutual and integral coherence. Moreover, God in Christ is not rescuing humans, as well as their history, *from* nature but is transforming creation in its entirety. Although the vindicated order of creation suggests this salvific contour and providential trajectory, Christ's resurrection serves as a redemptive *promise* rather than fulfilment.[36] The created and redeemed order is irreducibly eschatological, proleptic, and teleological. As O'Donovan argues:

we must go beyond thinking of redemption as a *mere* restoration, the return of a *status quo ante*. The redemption of the world, and of mankind, does not serve only to put us back in the Garden of Eden where we began. It leads us on to that further destiny to which, even in the Garden of Eden, we were already directed. For the creation was given to us with its own goal and

[33] For O'Donovan's distinction between natural law and his 'exposition of created order', ibid. 85–7.

[34] Ibid. 16–21.   [35] Ibid. 20.

[36] Ibid. 22–3. O'Donovan contends that in Christ's resurrection creation is 'renewed and vindicated in principle', but 'awaits its universal manifestation' (22). Cf. Stanley Hauerwas's discussion of creation as eschatological confession (*In Good Company* (1995), 195–6).

purpose, so that the outcome of the world's story cannot be a cyclical return to its beginnings, but must fulfil that purpose in the freeing of creation from its 'futility' (Rom. 8: 20).[37]

In Christ, creation's pristine state is not recovered but transfigured into the new creation. It is because of creation's destiny in Christ that nature and history are intelligible. The 'eschatological transformation of the world is neither the mere repetition of the created world nor its negation. It is its fulfilment, its *telos* or end. It is the historical *telos* of the origin, that which creation is intended *for*, and that which it points and strives *towards*.'[38] No arbitrary lines may be set demarcating a pattern of creation–redemption–eschaton. God's vindication of creation prevents its degeneration or nullification, because all other destinies are ruled out other than the one ordained by God.

This means that as humans we do not possess an inherent capacity to vindicate and perfect ourselves. Contrary to late liberal faith in the efficacy of the human will, history is not an account of humans overcoming or mastering nature in determining their own fate. A created order does not embody its own destiny, but is drawn towards its recreation. This teleological imagery inspires a model of social and political ordering that attempts to safeguard the nature of human associations. The tasks corresponding to this ordering are in turn received as gifts eliciting a response of grateful stewardship, a stewardship premised on a mode of life being drawn towards its perfection in Christ, as opposed to fabricating its own imagined perfection. In short, the temporal ordering of human life acknowledges creation as the historical unfolding of *mutual and timely belonging* that in turn is being enfolded into a new mode of belonging in the fullness of time.

Although the theme of mutual and timely belonging is examined in greater detail below, it may be noted at this juncture that in between creation's origin and end we must order our lives as creatures within the vindicated order of God's creation. For the timeliness of our belonging is manifested in the providential trajectory of creation's vindication. In the absence of providence, nature becomes little more than an indifferent or inimical force we attempt to overcome in fashioning a history of sorts, but ultimately proving to be little more than an assortment of

---

[37] O'Donovan, *Resurrection and Moral Order*, 55 (emphasis original).
[38] Ibid. 55. (emphasis original).

episodic and futile acts. There can be no order other than what we might concoct and impose, and there is no reason to believe that our efforts will lead to anything more than nihilistic displays of despair since there is no given end guiding our efforts. Yet if Christ's resurrection has vindicated creation then its providential ordering towards its end is also confirmed, so we may look, through the lens of revelation, to nature as a reliable source of moral wisdom that can help fashion a meaningful history in conformity to its underlying order. It is in the cruciform character of providence that we learn 'from the regularities of the created order',[39] coming to trust and know 'that the God who rules the world is the same God who made it, and that the outcome of history will affirm and not deny the order of its making'.[40] It is in conforming ourselves to the providential unfolding of a creation groaning in travail that we catch a glimpse of its vindicated order, seeing there, albeit imperfectly, a divinely given *is* and thereby the *ought* of our actions. To further explicate this temporal unfolding of a vindicated creation being drawn towards its destiny in Christ, we now turn our attention to the relation between providence and eschatology.

Providence and eschatology

The trajectory of the providential ordering of creation is *teleological and proleptic*. It is teleological in that creation is comprised of given affinities, natural processes, and social spheres possessing inherent purposes and relations integrally ordered to each other. These components become disordered when these purposes are not adequately safeguarded, or when they are improperly ordered to each other. The family, for instance, is disfigured if its purpose is reduced solely to procreation, or when its integrity is not protected against unwarranted incursions by other social spheres which assume parental privileges and duties. A providential ordering of creation is proleptic in that destiny has priority over origin. Although these two qualities are related, hope is drawn more by the future than pushed by the past, incorporating, in the words of Ted Peters, an 'awareness and anticipation ahead of time of the future whole'. This proleptic trajectory discloses a 'destiny–wholeness–integration formula'

---

[39] O'Donovan, *Resurrection and Moral Order*, 44 (emphasis original).
[40] Ibid. 45.

in which Christ is the divine assurance embodying the 'future God has promised for the whole of creation, namely, new creation'.[41] It is only in the light of God's future that what appears to be the fragmented character of creation can be seen in terms of its pluriformity being drawn towards its uniformity in Christ. The past and present are interpreted, drawn together, and redeemed in the light of this future, so that the temporal ordering of creation has a dynamic quality. Family roles, for instance, have changed over time since the familial social sphere is embedded in a historical process of social differentiation.

As Paul attests, however, hope is unseen; we cannot gaze at nature or history and discern an obvious imprint of creation's destiny. This hope is seen only through the eyes of faith, and even then only as puzzling reflections in a mirror. Yet we *do* see, and the sign of creation's destiny, the object of its enigmatic hope, is the resurrection of Jesus Christ from the dead. What is revealed in the resurrection does not provide additional knowledge about creation, but offers an understanding and interpretation of its unfolding over time in accordance with its appointed end.[42] It is through Christ's resurrection that we may catch a glimpse within creation's vindicated order of the promise of destiny, a destiny that is neither a restoration of its origin, nor a future discontinuous with its past. The resurrected Christ is not a resuscitated Jesus, yet nor do the disciples fail to recognize continuity between Jesus and their living Lord.

Nor is the new creation, unlike the old, created *ex nihilo*. The old gives birth to the new, and thus the old becomes enfolded into the destiny of the new. Through faith we see in Christ's resurrection intimations of creation's destiny, and thereby signs of providential trajectories refracted in its temporal ordering. What may appear as a random interplay of purposeless natural events and pointless historical acts may be interpreted, from the vantage point of creation's vindication, as a providential ordering of creation towards its appointed end in Christ. It is in Christ that nature and history find both their prox-

---

[41] Ted Peters, *God: The World's Future* (1992), 19.

[42] As O'Donovan contends, 'revelation in Christ does not *deny* our fragmentary knowledge of the way things are, as though that knowledge were not there, or were of no significance; yet it does *build on* it, as though it provided a perfectly acceptable foundation to which a further level of understanding can be added' (*Resurrection and Moral Order*, 89; emphasis original).

imate and ultimate meaning and harmony. One practical import of perceiving this providential trajectory is its formative influence on how the tasks of social and political ordering are undertaken. The familial association, for example, is not expressed through malleable institutions or social constructs that can be easily altered in response to changing historical circumstances to accommodate the need of perpetuating the human species. Rather, the task of social and political ordering is to enable families to bear witness to the providential ordering of natural and social affinities by providing a mutual and timely place of belonging. Recognizing this providential pattern and trajectory, however, does not imply that the cultural manifestations of the familial social sphere must embody a universal and unchanging structure. Such insistence not only denies the pluriform character of created order, but attempts to reduce divine action to predictable technique. Acknowledging the providential ordering of creation not only provides a moral standard for guiding the social and political ordering of the familial sphere, but also preserves God's freedom to act within creation's vindicated order. Providence necessarily entails inscrutability if God is to remain the creator, redeemer, and sustainer of creation, and not a hapless spirit or cosmic observer of earth's progressive and evolutionary history.

In its most basic sense providence means *provision*.[43] God foreknows and thus provides what is required to sustain creation as it is drawn towards its destiny in Christ. Or more prosaically, God provides human creatures with what they need to pursue those ends for which they have been created and ordained by God. Thus we may speak of a providential ordering of creation as a trajectory of integral relationships that enable creatures to become what their creator intends them to be. Nor can creatures become what God intends them to be if the integral ordering of relationships is ignored or perverted. Karl Barth, for instance, has observed that the 'life of man is ordered, related and directed to that of woman, and that of the woman to that of the man'.[44] This 'natural dualism'[45] cannot stand as a perpetual dialectic or incongruity, but must be mutually ordered.

---

[43] See Paul Helm, *The Providence of God* (1993), 18; see also Karl Barth, *Church Dogmatics* (1960), iii/3. 48.

[44] Barth, *Church Dogmatics* (1961), iii/4. 163.   [45] Ibid. 120–1.

Nor can this ordering be pursued properly in isolation, for 'there is no such thing as a self-contained and self-sufficient male life or female life'.[46] Nelson's objection that Barth's account of the male–female relationship discriminates against singles and homosexuals because only heterosexual relationships embody the *imago dei* is misplaced,[47] for Barth is not making any ontological claims regarding this relationship.[48] Rather, he is noting that the temporal task of ordering creation cannot be pursued by women and men in isolation from each other, a task and relationship from which singles and homosexuals are either relieved or forbidden from undertaking. Simply because one is not married does not imply that cooperation between women and men should not pursued. There must instead be a genuine encounter and engagement premised on a mutual ordering of similarity and difference, for it is only as woman *or* man, and woman *and* man, that both together may become what God has created them to become *as* female *and* male.[49]

Consequently, we may also speak of a providential purpose imposed by God upon creation and its creatures, for the sake of ordering the form of creaturely life oriented toward ends ordained by God. God commands humans to pursue those purposes which enable them to become the creatures God intends them to be, and in pursuing any other purposes they become other than what God has intended. The purpose of the relationship between woman and man, for example, is to enable a fellowship reflecting the nature of the triune God in whose image they are created.[50] It is for the purpose of fellowship that God created humans as female and male, for without this distinction there can be no genuine communion, nor could humans pursue those purposes which God commands them to accomplish. If we defy the providential ordering of our relationship as female *and* male, then nor can we become women *and* men in an unfolding fellowship intended for us by our creator.

Thus we must also speak of the providential trajectory of creation. The providential ordering of creation as established by God is not

---

[46] Ibid. 163.
[47] See James B. Nelson, *Embodiment* (1978), 135–6.   [48] Ibid. 191–2.
[49] See Mary Stewart van Leeuwen, *Gender and Grace* (1990), 33–51.
[50] See Barth, *Church Dogmatics*, iii/4. 116–17; cf. Emil Brunner, *The Divine Imperative* (1937), 347–9.

oriented towards merely sustaining itself, but enables creation to move through time until it is recreated in Christ. Its creatures have not been created to maintain a fixed point or holding pattern in time, but are proleptically oriented towards their renewal and perfection in Christ. In this respect, the fellowship between woman and man is drawn towards marriage as a disclosure of the mutual and divinely ordained encounter between female and male. It must be emphasized, however, that not all women and men are called to marry. Some are called to singleness, which also honours the fellowship of woman and man. Although marriage discloses the providential ordering of the female–male relationship, there is nevertheless, and contrary to Luther and subsequent generations of Protestant theologians, no obligation to marry.[51] Within the generic categories of female and male, humans are drawn towards each other as particular women and men, and it is in the one-flesh unity of marriage that their fellowship finds a full and deep expression. We may point to marriage as a sign, covenant, and practice bearing witness to creation's providential trajectory towards the enfolding love of its creator and redeemer.

Since providence orders creation towards its eschatological end in Christ, then so too are nature and history ordered to, and find their completion in, this destiny. If nature and history are two antithetical domains, then we would be forced to pursue two lives, one of the body alongside that of the will. The fellowship of woman and man would really be two, culminating in a dual marriage of body and will, but never a unity of will and body. It would also be mistaken, however, to believe that this dualism is overcome through the ultimate victory of nature over history, or history over nature. If nature is the end of providential ordering, than we can accomplish little more than futile gestures in the face of forces that will eventually obliterate us. The fellowship of woman and man would be little more than playing out instinctual drives, reducing marriage to a form of ritualized breeding or sexual pleasure. Nor does providence entail the ultimate victory of history in which the eschaton is reached through the complete mastery of nature. This would mean that humans

---

[51] See Barth, *Church Dogmatics,* iii/4. 181–4; cf. Stanley Hauerwas, *After Christendom?* (1991), 113–31, and *A Community of Character* (1981), 186–93.

are largely what they will themselves to be, measuring the veracity and efficacy of their acts against subjective standards which they construct and alter as they please. The fellowship of woman and man would be an expedient contractual arrangement that is kept so long as it satisfies the desires of particular females and males.

These portrayals of the relationship between nature and history are mistaken, because the moral ordering of creation requires a response honouring the providential trajectory imposed by God. To leave nature and history as a dualistic enigma, or to use one to negate the other, is to reject the very means God has provided to achieve the ordering of creation vindicated by Christ. To choose to live in an irreconcilable tension, or deciding in favour of one over the other, is a false dilemma. Both nature and history have been provided by God to order creation towards its appointed end in Christ. It is in conforming the ordering of creation in accordance with this providential trajectory that we discover the genuine meaning of our acts, and hence the gift of our freedom as creatures. God has created humans as female and male, for instance, so that in their differences they may seek fellowship as women and men. Nor is this relationship the outcome of deterministic instinct or wilful choice, but an obedient response to God's provision of a fellowship in which we are offered our freedom to be women and men, reflecting the triune image and likeness of our creator. Moreover, the attempt to maintain an irreconcilable dualism between nature and history, or using one to negate the other, must fail, for they incorporate reductionistic understandings of human instinct or will that cannot bear the weight placed upon them. The will alone cannot yield a full sense of history nor can instinct portray nature adequately, for they tear themselves asunder as conflicting and incomplete accounts by ignoring creation's providential trajectory. Responding to nature and history as gifts given by God will not diverge but converge, for history to be history involves a temporal ordering of natural goods, while nature to be nature entails a proper order of these goods that grant humans their meaning and history.

We cannot simply look at nature *or* history, or nature *and* history, however, to discern a providential trajectory. A quick glance or prolonged investigation may divulge little more than a fortuitous happenstance of events; more a collection of haphazard sentences than a coherent storyline. To see nature and history in providential terms we must first know what we are looking for. There must be a revealing point in the storyline that interprets and ties together seemingly unrelated events into an unfolding narrative. The revealing point of creation's providential storyline is, as has already been implied, the resurrection of Jesus Christ. In raising Christ from the dead, God vindicated creation, manifesting the first fruits of a destiny that will bring its movement through time to its appointed rest. In short, the providential trajectory of creation ties together its origin, redemption, and destiny in Christ.

It is only in looking at nature and history through the lens of a vindicated order of creation that we may perceive its providential trajectory. Nature and history are not antithetical realms, but interrelated dimensions of God's creation being opened up and drawn out towards its destiny; an order which is pluriform in character so that it may become uniform in Christ. The trajectory of this providential storyline is crucial in terms of how we undertake the tasks of social and political ordering that have been entrusted to us by God, for it is a storyline pulled more by its end than pushed by its origin. The emphasis is upon the final day of creation in which the heterogeneity of the preceding days find their rest and completion. Creation's movement through time does not entail its perpetual differentiation but its eschatological unfolding into Christ, so that its providential trajectory does not suggest the ultimate victory of either nature or history, but their redemption in the fullness of time. Providence, then, entails safeguarding nature and history, *and* evoking history out of nature. Yet what role are humans called to play in this storyline?

Dominion and stewardship

To raise the question of the role humans are called to play in creation's providential unfolding begs the issue of purpose or teleology: to what end does God create, redeem, and sustain humans? And what is God calling and enabling them to be and to do in accomplishing this end? A succinct answer is suggested by God's command to exercise dominion over creation.[52] Humans are created by God for

---

[52] See Gen. 1: 24–8.

the purpose of exerting dominion over what God has created; they are fashioned in the *imago dei* to the end that God's creation be properly governed in accordance with the providential trajectory of its vindicated order. There are three general precepts that may be derived from this divine command.

First, *dominion is a blessing*. The charge to govern creation is neither a crushing burden nor an insufferable challenge, testing humans to determine if they are worthy of bearing the divine image. Dominion is a gift enabling humans to be the creatures God intends them to become, namely, the creatures authorized by God to tend creation. If humans refuse or neglect this blessing they reject their own nature, as well as the One whose image they bear. This does not imply that exercising this divine commission is free of demanding responsibilities, but they are labours inspired by gratitude for being entrusted by God with a gift reserved only for creatures bearing the *imago dei*.

Since dominion is a divine blessing, its recipients are entrusted by God to exercise it *in accordance with creation's vindicated order and appointed end*. As creatures bearing the divine image, humans are the designated caretakers of creation, possessing the ability, albeit often incomplete and fragmentary, to discern God's commands and the capacity to execute them at God's bidding. As stewards, humans are authorized to govern creation in ways which accord with its providential trajectory being drawn towards its recreation in Christ. Consequently, humans must perform certain acts to exercise their dominion and stewardship, performing the tasks accompanying the gift entrusted to their care. Humans cannot assert their dominion faithfully or be faithful stewards in isolation from each other. Thus the blessing of dominion is given equally to woman and man; they are commissioned together by God as female and male. Although the *imago dei* is imprinted fully on both as discrete beings, it is not wholly expressed in their separation. Their intrinsic integrity depends upon their fellowship, for they have been created by God to be together. They cannot govern creation in accordance with its vindicated order if it is divided between them. They cannot receive the blessing of dominion or discharge their stewardship as female *or* male, but only as woman *and* man in fellowship.

Second, *humans are the creatures commanded by God to subdue the earth*. Although Christ has redeemed and vindicated creation, it is not yet suitable to be enveloped fully within its appointed destiny. The natural and historical processes enabling creation to be a hospitable place for its creatures must be channelled along its providential trajectory. Subduing the earth may be understood as subjecting it to creation's vindicated order and sovereignty of its creator. This requires a delicate balance between asserting and restraining the cooperative powers which God authorizes humans to discharge in exercising their stewardship.

Since humans are commanded by God to subdue the earth, they are also mandated to *act in ways corresponding to the providential unfolding of creation towards its appointed destiny*. Humans are not authorized to recast the earth in their own image or to plunder it to satisfy their desires.[53] They are not called to vanquish nature in asserting the primacy of their history, but to safeguard the former in order to evoke the latter. The proper governance of the earth requires honouring the integrity of its constituent spheres, and that the social and political ordering of human life is congruent with the inherent natures and ends of these sovereign spheres. In bearing the *imago dei*, humans are called to be obedient and trustworthy stewards, subjecting the earth to creation's vindicated order so the imprint of its creator and redeemer becomes more deeply emblazoned upon a work of divine love being drawn towards its consummation.

Consequently, humans must acknowledge and receive God's *authority* if they are to accomplish the cooperative tasks God commands them to perform. The earth cannot be submitted to the vindicated order of creation if there are no creatures authorized by God to govern on God's behalf. And if this governance is to be organized properly, then there must be sufficient authority to compel the requisite acts. The ability to act in a genuinely free and responsible manner requires that we accept divinely imposed constraints. Acts undertaken in performing certain tasks must conform to a given

---

[53] As O'Donovan argues: 'Man's monarchy over nature can be healthy only if he recognizes it as something itself given in the nature of things, and therefore limited by the nature of things. For if it were true that he imposed his rule upon nature from without, then there would be no limit to it. It would have been from the beginning a crude struggle to stamp inert and formless nature with the insignia of his will' (*Resurrection and Moral Order*, 52).

pattern and end, for, as O'Donovan contends, 'since freedom is not indeterminacy or randomness but purposive action, this means describing the world as a place in which actions may have ends, that is to say, as a teleological system'.[54] We are not, for instance, authorized by God to impose our will upon nature as if it were formless or chaotic matter. Rather, our dominion and stewardship entail cooperative tasks, limited to safeguarding nature while evoking a history *within* creation's vindicated order and along its providential trajectory. In this respect, the temporal governance of creation involves its purposeful ordering toward a Sabbath rest.[55] Consequently, humans are authorized by God to regulate procreation and childrearing in exercising their dominion and stewardship across generations.

Third, *humans are commanded by God to be fruitful and multiply.* Humans cannot exercise their dominion and stewardship if they are unable to flourish over time, failing to become the creatures embodying God's intention that creation be ordered towards life rather than death. If humans come to prefer sterility over fertility, they are no longer discharging the duties entrusted to them by God, because they will have rejected the life-giving end for which creation was called into being. This does not imply that humans can, or should, do anything possible to perpetuate themselves, for then they would be turning themselves into an end instead of serving *the end* for which they have been created. Rather, they are summoned by God to govern their transmission of life in accordance with creation's vindicated order and providential trajectory through time.

Consequently, humans have been given a divine *mandate to procreate.* This mandate, however, is proximate rather than ultimate. The orderly transmission of life requires procreative stewardship, enabling humans to accomplish the tasks that God calls and empowers them to accomplish. The command to be fruitful and multiply is not pro-natalist but procreative, because it is conducted 'for, or in behalf of (*pro*), the creator of all things'.[56] The dominion and stewardship entrusted to us places procreation in a normative category beyond, though integrally related to, biological necessity.

[54] Ibid. 122.

[55] See Augustine, *City of God* 22. 30; see also O'Donovan, *Resurrection and Moral Order*, 61–2, and *The Desire of the Nations* (1996), 181–6.

[56] Paul Ramsey, *One Flesh* (1975), 4.

We must organize our pursuit of procreation as a cooperative and divinely ordained task, for sustaining ourselves over time towards an end established by God entails more than passing on our genes. It is through our full and complete fellowship as woman and man that progeny are brought into being and prepared to carry on the cooperative tasks required by our dominion and stewardship.

The family is the locus of authority established by God for organizing the cooperative tasks of procreation and childrearing. The structure and roles comprising the familial association promote the wellbeing of its members through a series of mutual obligations and duties. Moreover, performing these roles, obligations, and duties does not reflect an implicit agreement to cooperate for the sake of personal benefit. A family is not a convenient means of assisting each other in pursuing our respective self-interests. Rather, the family is greater than the sum of its parts, its structure reflecting a natural *and* social ordering of the parts to and with the whole. Thus the family is authorized by God to organize those cooperative tasks which safeguard the nature of its association, while evoking from it a particular familial history.

Since God's blessing of dominion enables us to exercise our stewardship of creation in accordance to its vindicated order and providential trajectory, and if the family as a sovereign social sphere is the locus of authority for organizing the cooperative tasks of procreation and childrearing as an expression of our stewardship, then we must also enquire into the moral themes which should inform the social and political ordering of the familial association.

MORAL THEMES

If a moral account of the family incorporating the philosophical and theological themes examined above is to disclose implications for broader issues of social and political ordering, then we must also investigate the following themes. First, if the nature of the familial association is encompassed within the temporal unfolding of a differentiated society, then what are the normative roles and relationships comprising the structure of the family? Thus we must say something about the family providing a place of *mutual and timely belonging.* Second, what standards should be used in safeguarding the nature of the familial association in its ordering to the other social spheres? Thus we must say something about the family engendering an *unfolding and enfolding love.* Third, if familial belonging is being drawn towards an end transcending its own nature and history, then how does its moral, social, and political ordering point to a mode of association beyond and more expansive than itself? Thus we must say something about the family's *witness and destiny.*

Mutual and timely belonging

'Mutual and timely belonging' is a shorthand reference to the ordering of human life prior to creation's consummation in Christ. It emphasizes the incomplete quality of creaturely life, juxtaposing the given relationships entailed in its temporal ordering. Timeliness implies a historical development of human associations, while belonging denotes their inherent natures as disclosed through particular social structures and institutions. The rough contours of mutual and timely belonging can be seen in representative themes examined previously. Althusius's account of a social human nature acknowledges that human associations incorporate some type of agreement, but the structure of these compacts should conform to the nature or right of the association in question rather than the subjective will of the contracting parties. Dooyeweerd's sphere sovereignty affirms a changing family structure within a process of social differentiation, but the historical unfolding of the familial social sphere is governed by its inherent nature as a dimension of a created order. O'Donovan's teleological account of created order stresses the necessity of purposive initiatives in the pluriform ordering of creation towards its *telos* of uniformity in Christ.

The family as a place of mutual and timely belonging offers a focal point for developing these themes further, because it is the most basic and intense form of human association. It is simultaneously a voluntary and involuntary association, and the ordering of these contrasting affinities does not entail reconciling two antithetical principles, but maintaining a creative tension between two complementary poles. Establishing and sustaining a household requires subjective decisions involving marriage, procreation, and childrearing, but these choices are shaped in accordance with the nature and *telos* of the familial association. Once a child has been entrusted to the care of parents, a new relationship exists that is not dependent solely upon the ongoing will of the parties. The familial association is greater than the sum of its parts, having interests in its own right beyond those of its individual members. The common good, and the goods of the parts, are intertwined, inter-dependent, and integrally related.

It is in this respect that we may speak about a familial *covenant* rather than a contract. A covenant requires an ordering of internal and external goods binding individuals together by its imposed terms. Unlike a contract, the terms of a covenant are not subject to periodic negotiation in response to the changing interests of the parties. A covenant confirms and embodies the given nature, structure, and *telos* of an association or social sphere, whereas a contract assists autonomous persons in achieving their respective goals and objectives. The former guides the will of those in covenant, while the latter is a means of asserting the will of the contracting parties. Within a covenantal framework an institution enables individuals to perform their roles within a social sphere, whereas in a contractual setting institutions reflect the needs and desires of autonomous persons. A covenant encapsulates and gives substance to the inherent nature, structure, and *telos* of the family as a sphere of temporal belonging, thereby incorporating elements that are both chosen and given. We may account for a moral bond between parents and children that transcends natural instinct, a relationship that vexed the contractarians and was only 'resolved' by late liberal theorists by transforming children into satisfactory outcomes of parental will, thereby negating any inherent bond between parents and offspring.

In providing a place of mutual and timely belonging a family is not an abstract or idealistic concept, but a concrete association of particular individuals bound together under circumstances largely not of their choosing, and enduring independently of what they might will. *This* woman belongs with *this* man in marriage; *this* child belongs with *these* parents in *this* family. A particular person is (or was) my spouse, parent, child, or sibling, and the fact of this affinity cannot be erased through a sheer force of will. Although a woman and man may choose each other in marriage, with parenthood they become mutually related with someone they did not choose nor chose them. Yet it may be said that together they share a relationship unlike any other. As the individuality of their family roles unfold, they come to know themselves and each other as spouse, parent, child, and sibling. The nature of the familial association requires an enduring fidelity among persons who are related by both voluntary and involuntary bonds, and performing one's role within this relationship entails the given or imposed duties of a covenant rather than the conditional obligations of a contract. But what are these duties, and how should they be performed? To answer this question we must turn our attention to the vocations, virtues, and practices which are inherent to the family.

A vocation marks an obedient response to a particular command of God in which one way of life is followed to the exclusion of other possible ways. Pursuing a vocation entails ordering one's life within the given circumstances where one is called to follow Christ. The particularity of a vocation, however, is not synonymous with receiving private instructions from God. Although one's vocation reveals a unique facet of providence, there is nonetheless continuity with how the nature of a vocation has been disclosed in its historical unfolding. Otherwise, we could not discern the difference between an obedient response to God's command from one that is disobedient.[57]

Every vocation encompasses an inherent set of virtues and practices. A virtue is a quality denoting the excellence of an object or person. Objects or persons are excellent when they embody or personify the requisite quality for which they are fitted. To designate an object or person as being excellent, we must be able to identify that they possess a required quality. In respect to conduct, a virtue provides a foundation for habitual behaviour that is recognized as being excellent. A person attains a virtuous status when her character personifies the requisite quality, and in order to attain this status she must master a fitting set of practices. Determining which virtues

---

[57] For discussions on vocation, see Barth, *Church Dogmatics,* iii/4. 596–647; Dietrich Bonhoeffer, *Ethics* (1955), 222–9; O'Donovan, *Resurrection and Moral Order,* 70–1, 220–2.

should be practised, however, is not left to personal judgement, but is set by one's vocational end or *telos*.[58]

Every vocation is comprised of a teleological ordering of its inherent virtues and requisite practices, for its *telos* determines which virtues must be practised, given a vocation's natural quality. Over time a pattern of how certain vocational virtues should be practised is established, enabling a vocation to accommodate change while also ensuring continuity. For various reasons, how certain virtues are practised may change, promoting a more faithful pursuit of a vocation, yet these changes accord with the nature and *telos* of the vocation in question. This does not imply that new virtues or established practices may be arbitrarily introduced or altered, for such innovations may distort the integrity of a vocation. Rather, continuity is safeguarded and change evoked within a larger social context to which a vocation is related.

Consequently, every vocation is embedded in a tradition-bearing community that discerns whether a change in how a virtue is practised is continuous with the *telos* it is ordered to serve. It is this embedding that safeguards the nature of a vocation while also evoking a history of its practice. In the absence of such a tradition-bearing community it is doubtful if one can speak meaningfully about vocation, because the 'virtues' which are 'practised' are employed as a means of asserting certain preferences rather than ordering a normative pattern of conduct. If removed from its appropriate community, a vocation may become perverted into something other than it attests to be, 'practising virtues' which are neither inherent to its nature, nor continuous with its history. It would seem odd, for example, to speak of a community of violent crime whose members practise the virtues of assault and robbery. Yet in the absence of a tradition-bearing community in which lawful and criminal conduct are not clearly differentiated it would presumably be possible to entertain a vocation of liberating assets from individuals in which mastering the practice of inducing terror is recognized as a virtue. Although such a description of crime as a vocation is plausible, it is nonetheless perverse given

[58] For discussion on the relation between virtue and practice, see Stanley Hauerwas *et al.*, *Truthfulness and Tragedy* (1977), 40–56; James McClendon, *Systematic Theology* (2002), i. 160–77; MacIntyre, *After Virtue*, 121–80; and Gilbert Meilaender, *The Theory and Practice of Virtue* (1984).

the normative connotations of such terms as community, virtue, and practice.[59] In sum, a vocation derives its intelligibility from a tradition-bearing community, for it is only in such a setting that a fitting set of virtues may be formed, practised, and sustained over time.[60]

We may say that the family is a community *in* which certain integral vocations are embedded, and *from* which they derive their intelligibility. In obedience to God's command a woman and a man are called to the vocation of marriage, thereby foreclosing the alternative vocation of singleness. Their marriage marks a unique unfolding of God's providential ordering of their lives, yet their exclusive commitment to each other is continuous with an established pattern of what it means to be married. And if God should call this couple to become parents, then in obedience they follow the vocation of parenthood. This not only entails changes in their marital fellowship, but also the recognition that their new vocation is built upon and grows out of the exclusive cooperation of their marriage. God has not called them to obtain any child, but to receive and be with the one whom God has entrusted into their care as wife and husband. The particularity of this new relationship discloses another facet of the providential ordering of their lives, yet their life with a child is continuous with an established pattern of what it means to be a parent, and what it means to belong together as a family.[61]

The family encompasses the practice of an inherent set of marital and parental virtues. A good spouse, for instance, personifies the

[59] See Philippa Foot, *Virtues and Vices* (1978), 1–18.

[60] For discussions concerning the embedding of virtues and practices in tradition-bearing communities, see Stanley Hauerwas, *A Community of Character* (1981), 111–28; MacIntyre, *After Virtue*, 181–225, *Three Rival Versions of Moral Enquiry* (1990), 102–215, and *Whose Justice? Which Rationality?* (1988), 349–403; Gilbert Meilaender, *The Limits of Love* (1987), 113–43.

[61] Childhood is not a vocation because a child, unlike a spouse or parent, is not called to adopt this way of life to the exclusion of others. Rather, childhood denotes a set of conditions referring to a particular familial relationship. Although there is no vocation of childhood, children do incur certain obligations to parents and siblings given the nature of their affinity. In addition, behaviour learnt in a family can serve as a base for practising religious and civic virtues as the child grows older. See Barth, *Church Dogmatics*, iii/4. 240–85; cf. Horace Bushnell, *Christian Nurture* (1960), 3–51.

virtue of fidelity.[62] The term, however, connotes more than resisting adultery, for its nearest synonyms are loyalty, truthfulness, and steadfastness as facets of the marital covenant. There are the requisite practices of trust, truth-telling, and mutual submission a couple must master if they are to become habitually faithful spouses.[63] In this respect, the traditional marriage vows express the virtue of mutual fidelity as a promise to remain fully present to each other, despite what good or ill fortune may accompany a couple in their life together.[64] We may also speak of parental fidelity to a child God calls a couple to belong with. Again, there are requisite practices of truth-telling, patience, and discipline if a couple are to become habitually good parents. Yet the foundation underlying these practices is different from that of marriage, for parenthood is not a contract but a trusteeship whose duties are exercised within the *given* terms of the familial covenant. Contrary to late liberal presumptions, parents do not choose to love and care for their children, thereby constructing a relationship with them. This false presumption is seen in Peters's contention that individuals 'choose to make a covenant that they will love their children to such an extent that the well-being of the children is regarded as equal to, if not given priority over, their own striving for self-fulfillment'.[65] It is difficult to imagine, however, how an adult can *make* such a covenant—which Peters likens to the marital vow of 'for better or worse, for richer for poorer, until death us do part'[66]—with an unborn or newly born child. Not only can a child not consent to such a mutual commitment, but how is this reciprocal relationship to be construed when the child is linked to the parent's self-fulfilment, as Peters argues elsewhere? Given the nature of

[62] There are, of course, other marital virtues, but fidelity is at the heart of a marriage especially in terms of the mutual duties that instantiate the relationship. For discussions of marital fidelity, see Gustafson, *Ethics*, ii. 159–84; Meilaender, *Limits of Love*, 115–29; and Oliver O'Donovan, *Marriage and Permanence* (1984). For general discussions of fidelity, see H. Richard Niebuhr, *Radical Monotheism and Western Culture* (1993), 16–23, and Josiah Royce, *The Philosophy of Loyalty* (1995).

[63] Being faithful to one's spouse is more a matter of practising fidelity so that one becomes habitually loyal, rather than choosing not to be unfaithful. See Stanley Hauerwas, *The Peaceable Kingdom* (1983), 129–30.

[64] This does not imply that divorce is never warranted. A grievous violation of fidelity (e.g. adultery, abuse, or abandonment) may bring a marriage under God's judgement and command that it be dissolved. See Barth, *Church Dogmatics*, iii/4. 210–13; cf. Grisez, *The Way of the Lord Jesus* (1993), ii. 574–80, 584–90.

[65] Ted Peters, *For the Love of Children* (1996), 12.   [66] Ibid. 32.

the parent–child relationship which is intelligible within the context of the familial association, a parent incurs obligations, as well as lifelong affinity, to children. In this respect, parental love and care is unconditional and one-sided rather than contingent and reciprocal.

Marital and parental virtues, however, are not idealistic constructs; they are not practised for the sake of spouses and parents in general, but in terms of a *particular* spouse and child commanding one's loyalty. Yet nor does this imply that each parent–child relationship has its own unique set of virtues and practices, for if this were the case we could not discern the difference between fidelity and infidelity. Rather, we see in a particular practice of marital and parental fidelity its continuity with a teleological ordering of marriage and parenthood. But what is the source and pattern of this ordering?

An unfolding and enfolding familial love

An orderly practice of marital and parental fidelity is based on, and discloses, an *unfolding and enfolding familial love*. When God calls a woman and man to marriage, a new and more expansive love unfolds in their exclusive affection and mutual devotion. Their one-flesh unity embodies their fully shared being. Should God call this couple to become parents, a further unfolding of their love occurs in extending their fellowship to children entrusted to their care. The two become one and bring into being a new life. There is a continuous thread in the unfolding of such a familial love, originating in marriage and extending through the begetting and rearing of children. The birth of a child does not simply inaugurate a parallel relationship; a family is not merely a container for its separate spousal, parental, filial, and fraternal relationships. Rather, they are aspects of a larger loyalty, mutual belonging, and common love. We may speak of marital love unfolding into parental love, and a consequent unfolding of a familial love in turn enlarging, enfolding, and transforming the forms of love preceding it. Although the family includes marriage, procreation, and parenthood, they are not its sum total, nor can it be reduced to or determined by any one of these constitutive elements.[67] Marriage is the normative foundation of the family

---

[67] Gustafson, for example, argues that 'marriage and family are more than the sum of their individual parts, more than the aggregate of the persons who belong to them'.

because it embodies the natural and social contours of those relationships that offer a mutual and timely place of belonging.

It is at this juncture that I must part company with Barth for, in examining the relationship between parents and children,[68] he avoids the term 'family' because it holds 'no interest at all for Christian theology'.[69] This is due to the family's association with politically organized units such as households, clans, and tribes, and their corrupting influence on social and political ordering. Consequently, he restricts his analysis to the parent–child relationship in the absence of any explicit familial context. Although Barth is correct in arguing that marriage is an end in its own right[70] and that not all married couples are called to procreate,[71] it is not clear why he severs a direct relation between marital, parental, and familial forms of love. If the relationship between female and male and the fellowship of woman and man are disclosed in marriage and form the normative basis for parenthood, then why is the resulting familial relationship not an object of theological interest? Moreover, it is difficult to imagine the types of marital and parent–child fellowships he expounds without presupposing a familial context, much less how these fellowships are to be related to near and distant neighbours in its absence.[72]

Sadly, Barth's curt dismissal of the family removes a significant form of fellowship which enables us to respond faithfully to God's command to exercise our stewardship of creation. Familial love is not merely affection or sentiment, but an outgrowth of following those vocations and practising those virtues that are inherent to the nature and *telos* of the familial sphere. The family is a community incorporating its members into a common life, but not as a collective diminishing the individual for the sake of the whole, or as a contract enabling its parties to pursue their respective interests. The family entails an integral ordering of individual goods with the common good. And it is an ordering which occurs between the poles of its particularity and continuity with an established pattern for expressing

---

The good of the parts and the whole, however, are 'intricate' and 'reciprocal', so that one cannot be sacrificed or diminished for the sake of the other (see *Ethics*, ii. 162–3).

[68] See Barth, *Church Dogmatics*, iii/4. 240–85.   [69] Ibid. 241.
[70] Ibid. 189.   [71] Ibid. 187–8.   [72] Ibid. 285–323.

familial love. Thus marriage and parenthood are not a means for fulfilling personal desires, but vocations embedded in the family as a community from which their inherent virtues and practices derive their intelligibility. Consequently, contrary to Locke, familial relationships are neither a series of negotiated *quid pro quo* arrangements, nor do its roles, contra Okin, institutionalize a wilful assertion and passive reception of power. Rather, familial authority is exercised in the giving and receiving of loving commands in ordering the good of a family to the wellbeing of the individuals and relationships comprising it. A daughter, for instance, may command her father to fulfil responsibilities incumbent upon him as her father, not only for her sake but the good of their family as well.

It must be emphasized, however, that although children are properly brought into being through the fully shared being of their parents, children are not parental possessions or property. Rather, children and the parents they are with find their mutual belonging in their association together as a family. In a restricted sense, there is an adoptive element in every family, for although procreation and childrearing extending from the one-flesh unity of marriage is the norm, God nonetheless intends all children to be provided with a place of mutual and timely belonging.[73] Parents with children who are not their biological offspring constitute an authentic family so long as such a place of belonging is provided.[74] Adoption serves as a reminder that, although the family is enmeshed in a complex nexus of biological and social affinities, it cannot be reduced to either set but requires their suitable ordering, under both ideal and adverse circumstances.

We may also speak, then, about the normative structure of the family as both a means of safeguarding the nature of procreation, *and* the nature of the familial association as a social sphere. The contrast between the categories of 'being' and 'will' is illuminating

[73] In this respect, Hauerwas is correct in insisting that children are gifts and signs of hope so that parenthood is a calling or office rather than a means of natural necessity or personal fulfillment (see *Suffering Presence* (1986), 148–52, and *Community of Character*, 168–74). Although he does not discount biology in his account of parenthood, he contends that it 'cannot be biologically derived' (*Suffering Presence*, 152). Thus 'everyone in the Christian community is called in quite different ways to the office of parenthood' (*After Christendom?* (1991), 131). See also Brent Waters, *Reproductive Technology* (2001), 70–5.

[74] See Brent Waters, 'Welcoming Children into our Homes', *Scottish Journal of Theology*, 55/4 (2002) and 'Adoption, Parentage, and Procreative Stewardship', in Timothy P. Jackson (ed.), *The Morality of Adoption* (2005).

in this regard. As noted previously, late liberal theorists routinely endorse artificial and collaborative reproductive techniques not only to enhance the freedom of autonomous persons, but also to remove the final impediment on the primacy of the human will which has haunted modern liberalism, namely, how to accommodate society's need to perpetuate itself without recourse to the family's seemingly inherent inequality. Modern liberalism went far by widening the gulf between procreation and childrearing initiated in the Kantian revision, but apparently not far enough. Rawls, for example, admits that his account of justice suggests that the family should perhaps be abolished, yet he cannot bring himself to commend the illiberal measures which would be required. It is not clear if reasonable people deliberating behind a veil of ignorance would countenance such constraints upon their liberty.

It is the category of being, as opposed to will, which should inform the moral and social ordering of procreation. When the will is given priority, procreation becomes a reproductive project in which the finished product (as an artefact of the will) is alienated from its maker. A fundamental alienation and unfamiliarity is presupposed in the parent–child relationship. When being is stressed, procreation is an act of begetting another with whom one shares a fundamental equality. A basic affinity and familiarity between children and parents is presumed. It is within a social sphere of shared being that they develop their individuality based on the equality of familial fellowship. Late liberalism's faith in autonomous personhood as the foundation upon which equality may be established is misplaced. A contract expressing the will of the parties, as opposed to a covenant codifying the nature of a relationship, merely confirms the self-imposed limitations of the stronger over the weaker party. There is a procedural, instead of an ontological, equality. The alienated relationship between the parent as maker and child as product purportedly aids the development of the latter party as an autonomous person, for although adults have virtually unrestricted freedom in pursuing their reproductive interests, childrearing is subject to public regulation. Although this alienated status constrains how children are subjected directly to the will of their parents, it fails to acknowledge that through other social spheres supplanting parental prerogatives, children are still subjected to the will of stronger parties. Beginning with birth, children are progressively introduced into various contractual relationships which they must negotiate from relative and varying positions of strength and weakness.

Safeguarding the nature of procreation and equality of the familial association, however, are not the only tasks entailed in its moral, social, and political ordering. Such ordering must also evoke a familial history. Thus we must also examine the question of teleology: to what end or destiny does the family bear witness?

Destiny and witness

As demonstrated in the preceding section, an unfolding familial love entails practising certain virtues inherent to the vocations of marriage and parenthood. How these virtues are practised shapes what may be described as an ensuing procreative pattern. The ends *and* means of procreation are inseparable, for the unfolding of the latter enfolds the former; the means bear witness to, and are shaped by, the end which they are employed to achieve. Late liberal social and political thought offers a destiny that is a projection of the human will. A liberal account of the vocations, virtues, and practices (if these terms may be regarded as such by liberals) associated with the family forms an ensuing procreative pattern reflecting satisfactory outcomes for persons pursuing their respective reproductive interests. This account offers a striking contrast to one of marital and parental virtues and practices embedded in the familial association which in turn accords with the providential trajectory of a vindicated created order being drawn towards its destiny in Christ. Although a more detailed analysis of these contrasting accounts, particularly in terms of their implications for larger questions of social and political ordering, will be undertaken in the next chapter, at this juncture I shall sketch out the principal issues at stake as a way of bringing to a close this inquiry into the alternative conceptual themes that will be used and further developed throughout the remainder of this book.

Given the anticipatory character of the following discussion, I may begin with an objection rather than an assertion, namely that late liberalism tends to *disfigure the pattern of an unfolding and enfolding familial love into acts of wilful assertion.* Reducing parenthood to an act of will denies that there are given affinities ordered by the family, for such an affiliation is merely the outcome of a person or persons asserting the will to obtain a child. Evoking a familial history, however, requires a normative ordering of these affinities, necessitating a limited range of options. In this respect, late liberal theorists incorporate an impoverished understanding of *particularity*, making it synonymous with autonomy instead of recognizing the unique characteristics persons bring with them in practising parental virtues. Moreover, late liberalism has failed to comprehend that genuine freedom is not a capacity to be asserted, but a quality to be embraced in the acknowledgement that the very act of choosing necessarily forecloses the possibility of entertaining other options. Accepting one's calling to singleness or marriage, for example, forecloses participation in the ways of the other. The parental vocation does not entail that any woman may collaborate with any man to produce a child, but that a particular woman and man become one to receive the gift of a child entrusted to their care. In reducing parenthood to an act of will, the family bears witness to a destiny of wilful assertion rather than familial love against which the will is conformed.

When procreation bears witness to a destiny of wilful assertion, offspring are effectively reduced to artefacts. Children are fashioned, within a shrinking circle of technical limitations, in the image and likeness of what their parents will them to be, rather than received as gifts bearing unique and unanticipated qualities. There is a significant difference in the relationship between a maker and artefact, as opposed to that between a recipient and entrusted gift. In the former instance, a product may be manipulated because it is subject to the will of its maker, while in the latter, parent and child partake of a larger and common source of being but are nevertheless unique beings. Consequently, as Hauerwas has observed, children are not raised 'to conform just to what...the child's particular parents think right', but in accordance with more expansive 'commitments that both child and parents are or should be loyal to'.[75]

It is this larger loyalty that enables the evocation of a familial history. A family does not share an affiliation based entirely on natural instinct or wilful agreement. Rather, a family is bound together by

---

[75] Hauerwas, *Truthfulness and Tragedy*, 151–2.

affinities that are simultaneously oriented towards a deep *and* expansive affection. The familial association manifests a mutual and sacrificial love underlying both creation's vindication and destiny, so that the natural unfolding of a particular familial love also enfolds it in a greater destiny of universal love. Maurice is correct in noting that the family has a natural desire for social association greater than itself, but he fails to acknowledge that this is an outgrowth of the familial association itself rather than as a means of achieving more extensive affiliations. The exclusive nature of the marital covenant brings a woman and man together in a unity that does not destroy their respective identities, yet it is a unity enabling them to extend their fellowship to include children. Parents in turn do not own but belong *with* their children, for the nature of parental love is not possessive, inspiring a mutual belonging that neither reduces a familial identity to a collection of its members, nor negating its members within a collective identity. Members of a family do not possess themselves or each other, for the nature of their timely belonging requires a shared being for and with each other. Consequently, children are not projections of a reproductive will, but gifts entrusted to the care of parents precisely 'because they draw our love to them while refusing to be as we wish them to be'.[76]

We may say, then, that safeguarding the nature of marriage and parenthood prevents procreation and childrearing from dissolving into a series of discrete acts, while evoking a familial history prevents a family from collapsing in upon itself. The family exists within a creative and fragile tension between a centripetal pole of its *providential* affinities, and a centrifugal pole of its *eschatological* destiny. The unfolding and enfolding of familial love becomes stunted and distorted if either pole collapses. If the former pole is ignored, procreation and childrearing become a series of episodic events, strung together by the will of autonomous persons pursuing their reproductive interests. If the latter pole is ignored, a family becomes a secluded enclave, protecting and promoting the interests of its individual members. It is in preserving the tension provided by these complementary attractions that the core of a natural love may be established, and from which a familial history may be evoked. Evoking such a history, however, requires a transcendent *telos*.

[76] Ibid. 153.

Although the character of timely belonging afforded by the family entails an exclusivity defining the boundaries of its association, the family *per se* is not oriented towards insularity. Rather, it is from a core of natural or given affinities that a familial love may be opened up to embrace, or provide the basis for, broader forms of human association. Thus the social sphere of the family must be ordered to a *telos* beyond itself in order that its history will unfold along its teleological trajectory.

In contrast, late liberal social theory has displaced a teleological unfolding of history with a voluntaristic pursuit of interests, goals, and objectives. There is admittedly an element of transcendence in this strategy, for a goal may serve as an end directing a course of action. This end, however, originates in, and is projected by, a subjective will, validating a chosen course of action rather than delimiting which acts may be undertaken in pursuing a given end. Nor can these goals be formulated in terms of the nature of a relationship or association, because they are derived from the varying interests of autonomous persons. The primacy of the will promotes a differing account of the social ordering of procreation and child-rearing than those inspired even by early liberal theories. In late liberalism, a family marks the accomplishment of reproductive goals instead of establishing a familial association. Such a family also signifies the outcome of contractual negotiation among persons pursuing their reproductive interests, especially if reproductive technologies are employed, so there are few objective standards defining what a family is, and what means may be used to form it.

Consequently, there is no nature of marriage, procreation, or childrearing to safeguard, because these acts are simply the means deployed by a person to pursue his or her self-defined interests. Yet this means that a familial history cannot be evoked, for such a family does not disclose a particular facet of the teleological unfolding of human life, but reveals a wilful collaboration to obtain a child. In late liberal social theory, timely belonging is diminished to contractual negotiation, and providence is displaced by process. But if there is a vindicated order of creation, then there is also a nature of the familial association to be safeguarded, and thus a history to be evoked out from it. The impetus of the family is not, so to speak, *pushed* by a progressive mastery of natural necessity, but *pulled* by its eschatological destiny, thereby serving as a reminder that the fate of creation and its creatures do not depend upon, nor are constrained by, *either* human will or biology.

Late liberal social theory attempts to collapse the centripetal and centrifugal poles of the familial association, displacing their tension with a singular assertion of will. This strategy, however, effectively eliminates the categories of strangers and singleness, both of which are crucial in defining and delineating the familial social sphere. A family cannot be recognized as such unless placed against a backdrop of strangers. The members of a family are bound by a series of affinities whose intensity cannot be duplicated in any other social sphere. Within the familial association there is a given familiarity which, unlike any other social sphere, is not subject to negotiation among strangers. Contrary to Okin, the social and political practices of the political sphere are not easily transferred to the household. Spouses, parents, children, and siblings may seem strange to each other or become estranged, but they are not strangers to each other for otherwise the very term 'family' has no meaning. Nor is marriage intelligible in the absence of singleness. This is not because marriage is merely a public declaration of a voluntary relationship between a woman and a man, for if this were the case it would simply disclose their willingness to enter a contractual arrangement that could be easily dissolved when it is in their interest to do so. Or put more cynically, marriage would be temporary abstinence from singleness. But what is most important for this discussion is the different ends to which the vocations of marriage and singleness bear witness. Since marriage is the normative foundation of the familial association, we may say that it bears witness to the providential ordering and trajectory of creation, whereas singleness bears witness to the eschatological end of this ordering. Without the exclusivity and fidelity of marriage, the family loses much of its centripetal force in creating a bond of mutual and timely belonging, whereas in the absence of singleness, the family is largely deprived of a centrifugal force that draws it out as a basis for a more universal belonging. In short, the nature of the familial association provides a core of temporal belonging that is drawn out as an open-ended community in accordance with its *telos* in Christ,[77] and by way of contrast,

---

[77] See Grisez, *Way of the Lord Jesus*, ii. 569–74.

strangers and singleness accentuate the family's providential and eschatological witness.

The tactic employed by late liberal social and political thought to collapse the family's centripetal and centrifugal poles is to treat *everyone* as if they are strangers and single in pursuing their reproductive and affiliative interests. This assumption is echoed in Nelson's pallid account of sexual expression in which he contends that every person requires multiple contacts to be fulfilled. If true, then marriage is effectively reduced to a series of one-night stands between two consenting adults, both of whom enjoy a preferred but certainly not exclusive status. Autonomy serves as a myth enabling autonomous persons to construct whatever types of relationships are required in pursuing the kinds of associations they choose to create. This myth inspires a deconstruction of the family, for marriage, procreation, and childrearing are distinct contractual relationships through which the parties attempt to forge bonds of familiarity. When everyone is a stranger, then the only remaining channel of social communication is a continuing will to cooperate. Procreation, for instance, *always* entails some type of implicit or explicit reproductive contract, especially when reproductive technologies are employed. Other than procedural con- siderations and technical complexities, there is little difference between a married couple attempting to conceive naturally, and an infertile man securing the necessary gametes, fertilization techniques, and gestational services in attaining the same end, namely, obtaining a child. Moreover, when unfamiliarity is presumed then constructing a family entails negotiating with strangers. Decisions must be made to determine whose gametes shall be used, what method of fertilization will be employed, who will provide gestation, and who will play what roles in childrearing. When a baby is delivered to her 'parents', she is both an artefact of their will, and a stranger with whom they must build a relationship. A family, then, denotes little more than a pragmatic line that has been drawn to identify who is and who is not a party to specific reproductive and childrearing contracts. Strangers, by way of contrast, disclose nothing about the nature of the family as an association of both chosen and given affinities.

With this loss of the stranger's role, the ordering of the family to other social spheres is also distorted. The social spheres are not related to the family, but enable those affiliated with it to pursue their respective interests. As Lasch recognized, the spheres of commerce, medicine, school, and government, for instance, may assist family members to pursue various economic, health, and educational interests, but they do not assist families directly. Moreover, the state will only intervene when the rights or welfare of individual citizens are threatened, but not for the sake of the familial association as such. The family does not provide a core of familiarity through which its members may communicate with strangers, but is a contractual arrangement in which a collection of autonomous persons are more closely related to each other as a particular company of strangers. This means, however, that the family is deprived of any transcendent *telos* drawing it out beyond itself, for when it is presumed that everyone must create their own bonds of familiarity there is no core to be drawn out. Late liberal social and political ordering renders any moral difference between marriage and singleness meaningless, other than to the extent they enable autonomous persons to pursue their reproductive and affiliative interests. Being married or single does not reveal anything about the contrasting natures, practices, and witness of two distinctive vocations, but only discloses differing lifestyles.

Yet if a more robust contrast among the family, singleness, and strangers is to be recovered, particularly in terms of how this contrast might inform questions of social and political ordering, we must first explicate in greater detail what is at stake in a normative and teleological account of the family as opposed to what is offered in late liberal accounts.

6

The Teleological Ordering of the Family

This chapter outlines a teleological account of the family, drawing upon the philosophical, theological, and moral themes developed in the previous chapter. The first section describes the principal structural elements of the familial association that is required for ordering its inherent affinities, and which in turn provide the basis for ordering the family to larger spheres of civil association. The next section examines the providential significance of the family as social sphere, while the final section draws out this significance in regard to the family's economic ordering. It was argued in the previous chapter that the family's significance for social and political order is intelligible only in its distinction from strangers and singleness. This chapter further explicates this distinction by concentrating on the family's relationship with strangers, whereas the next chapter focuses on the relation between the providential witness of the family and the eschatological witness of singleness.

THE TIMELY ORDERING OF AFFINITY

The familial association bears a providential witness to the vindicated order of a creation being drawn towards its destiny in Christ, because at the very least families involve an ordering of human life over *time*. Humans perpetuate themselves through progeny. No generation comes into being *ex nihilo*, cut off from ancestors and descendents. Every person is a recipient, and many are potential progenitors of a genetic legacy. Humans, however, do not merely propagate themselves upon the crest of biological processes, for each generation is brought into being through what may be characterized as a socially ordered particularity. As Maurice noted, every child has a particular mother and father, and each parent begets a particular daughter or son. Humans are not related, either biologically or socially, to a general humanity, but to specific people. Although all humans were once children, all the women and men preceding them were not their parents, nor or all children succeeding them their offspring. Without particular biological and social bonds a sense of continuity between generations is lost. This loss weakens the family's providential witness by denying the vindicated order of creation, for humans do not merely perpetuate themselves as a species, but pursue a purposeful transmission of life from one generation to the next. It may be said, then, that a family embodies a *lineage* that helps situate its members within creation's unfolding history.[1]

Lineage suggests that the family is something more than a biological bond extending over time, for it entails a matrix of voluntary and involuntary relationships within various social spheres. Although the family orders natural reproduction, its meaning and purpose are discerned and ascribed within broader social and cultural traditions. The concept of lineage forces the recognition that an orderly transmission of life requires the cooperation of persons who are both related and unrelated by any common genes. The family is not exclusively a natural institution or social construct, but a unique and intense blending of biological and social affinities. A family usually consists of a symmetrical relationship among parents genetically unrelated to each other, but sharing such a relation with offspring, while siblings share both a biological and social lineage inherited from their parents.[2] Lineage serves to situate humans within a series of given, overlapping, and interlocking biological, social, and historical settings. A family exists as a particular sphere in which one is associated with individuals largely not of one's choosing. Although one may select and be selected by one's spouse,

---

[1] According to Lisa Sowle Cahill, maternal, and to a lesser extent paternal, lineage is a universal foundation of all familial and kinship structures (see *Sex, Gender, and Christian Ethics* (1996), 102).

[2] Ibid. 247.

individuals do not choose their parents or children in the same manner. Families are in turn related to larger communities, institutions, and traditions. Within these more expansive spheres the particular and given qualities of one's origin become more pronounced. Individuals do not choose the culture, civil society, and nation in which they are born and reared. Yet these given factors, in tandem with a particular family and its lineage, shape their identities. Nor are these larger spheres mere social contrivances, for they emerged from, remain dependent upon, and are circumscribed by a variety of natural processes and environments. Consequently, the family encapsulates an ordering of both natural *and* social affinities. The principal normative elements of this ordering are described below.

Procreation

If lineage and affinity may serve as signs indicating a providential trajectory of creation, then the family is necessarily dependent on *procreation*. Procreation alone, however, is not synonymous with a family. A birth does not in itself connote any providential significance, for a birth does not automatically establish a place of mutual and timely belonging for the one born. A woman surrendering her child for adoption, for example, has given birth, but she will not (in most instances) be a member of the child's family. Although the family cannot be reduced to procreation, nor must it be forgotten that every family presupposes a birth. Each child has a biological origin, entailing, to date, the joining of egg and sperm, and a woman bearing and giving birth to that child. Although the natural means of ordering procreation may, with technological assistance, be discounted, the biological and physiological elements of conception, gestation, and birth cannot be denied. Every family, even one in which no member is genetically related, remains grounded in human biology. Moral deliberation on the family must take into account this biological substructure, discerning to what extent the techniques and social structures employed in pursuing procreation distort the ordering of familial affinities, and whether the degree of this distortion is telling in shaping the family as a place of mutual and timely belonging.

Parenthood

Providing children with a place of mutual and timely belonging requires that something be said about *parenthood*. It is difficult, if not impossible, to describe a family without reference to parents. Defining what parenthood means, however, is elusive because it is comprised of natural and social aspects which are divisible yet ineluctable. For instance, gamete donors, surrogates, and women surrendering their babies for adoption *are* parents, and yet they are also *not* parents. Or adoptive couples, step-parents, and infertile spouses *are* parents, and yet they are also *not* parents. These perplexing depictions suggest a twofold understanding of parenthood. On the one hand, there is a weak construal associated with biological aspects of procreation, while on the other hand, there is a stronger social sense involving childrearing. Dividing these natural and social dimensions arbitrarily results in a truncated understanding of parenthood, either emphasizing one dimension to the detriment of the other or striking an artificial balance—hence, the emergence of hyphenated forms of parenthood, or attempts to transform it into parenting.[3] The dilemma becomes even more pronounced with the advent of reproductive technology: if the social relationship between parent and child is the overriding consideration, then why should infertile couples be assisted in obtaining genetically related offspring, or if a biological bond is paramount then why should gamete donation be employed? Using various technologies to assist procreation presupposes an ordering of *both* biological and social relationships in line with certain values and objectives. The question at stake is what standard should shape this ordering? Contrary to late liberal social theory that answers this question in terms of an assertive will to obtain a child, what is required is an explication of parenthood within a familial context. Parenthood does not designate the successful completion of a reproductive project undertaken by strangers, but is defined in respect to the familial end of providing a place of mutual and timely belonging, and it is in virtue of that end that the methods of pursuing procreation should be assessed.

[3] For an example of the contemporary dilemma of defining parenthood, see Oliver O'Donovan's critique of arithmetical proposals (*Begotten or Made?* (1984), 46–7).

Marriage

The normative relationship underlying parenthood is the vocation of *marriage*. In their one-flesh unity, a wife and husband provide the foundation for ordering the natural and social affinities delineating the familial association. As Ramsey contends, marriage is a covenant of mutual love and fidelity binding together the full and embodied being of a particular woman and man.[4] The marital covenant is teleologically and christologically oriented, providing a temporal setting in which human life originates, is lived out, and drawn towards. 'Men and women are created in covenant, to covenant, and for covenant. Creation is *toward* the love of Christ.'[5] Procreation outside of marriage severs the unitive and procreative dimensions of covenantal love, stripping sexual intercourse of its deeper meaning when reduced to either reproduction *or* gratification, for it is within marriage where the dual aspects of this love are expressed fully. In this respect, Thatcher's claim that, if a pregnancy occurs it should prompt a couple to become married, or at least betrothed, is correct but cumbersome. It is correct in terms of the best interests of the child, but cumbersome given his attempt to simultaneously *endorse as a matter of Christian morality* both marriage as an exclusive covenant open to procreation, *and* sexual experimentation prior to marriage (or betrothal). Yet Thatcher contends, rightly, that pregnancy should be an outcome of, and not the reason for marriage. For the sake of consistency should he not be making the decidedly un-postmodern claim that any couple engaging in sexual acts that could result in pregnancy are in fact already, or at least presumptively, married?

Furthermore, although the marital covenant draws a wife and husband together, it does not, given the nature of their mutual love and fidelity, collapse in upon itself. As both Clapp and McCarthy argue, children are rendered inexplicable in late liberal social theory

---

[4] See Paul Ramsey, *One Flesh* (1975), 4–14.

[5] Paul Ramsey, *Fabricated Man* (1970), 38–9; emphasis original. Ramsey argues that the *telos* of sexual love is Christ because it prefigures the love of God in Christ. Thus pursuing procreation outside of marriage 'means a refusal of the image of God's creation in our own' (39). For Ramsey's discussion of the *imago dei*, see *Basic Christian Ethics* (1993), 249–84.

unless they are perceived as a means of self-fulfilment, for they are largely liabilities upon one's mobility and financial resources. In contrast, the nature of the one-flesh unity of marriage denotes a fellowship that is open to including children. In short, marriage is oriented towards becoming a family. Sexual intercourse is simultaneously an act of love and procreation, regardless of whether conception is intended, prevented, or achieved. 'This means that sexual intercourse tends, of its own nature, toward the expression and strengthening of love and towards the engendering of children.'[6] If contraception, for example, should fail, the resulting child is not an accident or unwanted burden, but welcomed as a proper outcome of marriage. To do otherwise is to deny the nature and *telos* of the marital covenant, for it is a 'covenant whose matter is the giving and receiving of acts which tend both to the unique one-flesh unity between the partners and to the unique one flesh of the child beyond them'.[7] In marriage, a woman and man, unrelated by blood but bound together in mutual love and fidelity, bring into a being a child to whom both are related and drawn together in love. In this respect, the spousal relationship, contrary to Maurice, is prior and foundational to other familial relationships. Consequently, lineage is not merely a line of genetic descent, but also traces a legacy of love and fidelity embodied in and enabled through marriage.

Although the family is based on marriage, it does not itself constitute or inaugurate a family. A wedding, for example, concludes with a pronouncement that a couple has become husband and wife, not a family. An unmarried couple or single person, a widowed, divorced, or abandoned spouse, can certainly provide parental care. Although such families may in many instances prove commendable, they are nonetheless exceptions rather than exemplars of the norm. In the absence of marriage the provision of a mutual and timely place of belonging is, to varying degrees, impaired because the family's peculiar source for ordering its affinities cannot be drawn upon fully. Contrary to McCarthy's portrayal of thriving 'open families', a neighbourhood economy is not fully compensatory.

---

[6] Ramsey, *One Flesh*, 4.   [7] Ibid. 13.

Childrearing

The family involves *childrearing*. This may appear obvious, but a child means something more than the outcome of a reproductive project. What is this 'something more' regarding the meaning of a child? We may begin searching for an answer by revisiting the curious circumstances in which one can simultaneously be, and yet not be, a parent. Gamete donors, surrogates, or women surrendering their babies for adoption are parents of offspring, while adoptive couples, step-parents, or infertile spouses are parents of children. The former are childless parents, while the latter are parents *with* children. This does not imply that the social aspect of parenthood negates or subsumes the biological dimension. Rather, it shifts the focus away from parents and offspring to children and families. It is the place of mutual and timely belonging that defines what a child is or, phrased differently, it is within a family that offspring become children. Consequently, children do not belong to their parents, but they do belong with parents in a family. Familial belonging acknowledges both the biological and social aspects of parenthood, while resisting attempts to reduce it to either pole. This familial emphasis is seen in the difference between childless parents and parents with children. A boy, for example, may say that the woman who surrendered him for adoption is his mother and he is her son, but she is not the mother of the family in which he belongs.

This does not suggest that the biological and social aspects of parenthood may be divided haphazardly and rearranged arbitrarily. There is a normative ordering of these dimensions, and it is the one-flesh unity of marriage that provides the moral contours of this ordering. There is a presumption that children should be brought into being *and* reared through the fully shared being of their parents, instantiating a continuity of parentage in providing a place of mutual and timely belonging. Marriage is both the institutional embodiment of this fully shared being and the foundation of parental continuity. The birth of a child, however, does not merely create a new parent–child relational track. A family is not a container for the parallel relationships among wife and husband, children and parents, sisters and brothers, but defines and enriches these relationships within a more expansive context of mutual love and fidelity.

Covenant

The birth of a child initiates the unfolding and enfolding of a familial *covenant*. We may speak of a spousal love and fidelity unfolding into parental love and fidelity, and a consequent unfolding of familial love and fidelity in turn enfolding, enmeshing, and enlarging the forms of love and fidelity preceding them. Although the normative ordering of the family entails the characteristics of marriage, procreation, parenthood, and childrearing, they are not its sum total, nor can the family be reduced to any one of these elements. As Gustafson argues, the good of the family and the goods of its members are 'intricate' and 'reciprocal', so that one cannot be sacrificed for the sake of the other. The family is more than a means of physical survival and emotional attachment, but is a setting in which the 'joy of mutual love [is] freely given and freely received'.[8] Nor is the family an outcome of its various characteristics, but rather, they derive their meaning and structure from the nature of the familial association. Consequently, the one-flesh unity of marriage is the normative foundation of the family, because it most clearly embodies the range of affinities inherent to a place of mutual and timely belonging.

An important qualification must be noted that, although children are properly brought into being and reared through the fully shared being of their parents, children are not parental possessions. Children are gifts from God entrusted to the care of parents. Thus offspring do not belong to their parents; rather, children and the parents they are with find their mutual belonging in their familial association. In this restricted sense, there is an adoptive element in every parent–child relationship, because the principal purpose of a family is to provide a place of mutual and timely belonging rather than perpetuate a lineage or satisfy parental longings. Parents with children who are not their offspring constitute a genuine family, so long as they fulfil their vocation to care for the gifts entrusted to their care. Contrary to Clapp, this does not mean that children are strangers, implying that the methods employed by adults to be with children are unimportant. Procreation within the one-flesh unity of marriage remains the

---

[8] See James M. Gustafson, *Ethics from a Theocentric Perspective* (1981), ii. 162–3.

norm, because it most clearly encapsulates the ordering of the biological and social affinities characterizing the family. Parents do
not beget or rear strangers, but particular individuals with whom
they share a relation that cannot be replicated with any other persons.
Adoption is not, therefore, a reproductive option, but an act of
charity in response to unfortunate circumstances in which a place
of mutual and timely belonging cannot be provided by parents who
have begotten offspring.[9]

Cohabitation

Mutual and timely belonging implies that families are comprised of
persons who, to varying periods of time, live together or *cohabit*.
There is a voluntary dimension of familial cohabitation as exemplified by marriage. Yet a family does not exist only for as long as its
members agree to reside together, nor do individuals cohabiting
necessarily constitute a family. Divorce, for instance, does not erase
familial affinities, nor is a convent a family. There is also an involuntary aspect of familial cohabitation. Children do not choose the
families in which they belong. A family does not exist for only as
long as its members are forced to reside together, nor does involuntary cohabitation compose a family. Familial affinities do not cease
when unhappy children reach the age of emancipation, nor is a
prison a family. Familial cohabitation need not be perpetual or
necessarily continuous. The maturation of children does not bring
a family to an end, nor does extended separation of children from
parents (for example, boarding school or parental incarceration)
suggest that a family does not exist during that period of time.
Familial cohabitation signifies a voluntary and involuntary association comprised of biological and social affinities from which a
familial identity unfolds, demarcating a time of living together
which is indelibly etched (albeit for good or ill) in the identities of
the individuals comprising a family. The persons sharing such a
history of cohabitation may wish to affirm or disavow it, but they
cannot truly deny it simply because it involves circumstances beyond

---

[9] See O'Donovan, *Begotten or Made?*, 35–40.

their control. Familial cohabitation serves as a reminder that the providential trajectory of creation entails associations of mutual belonging, and the forging of shared histories with persons both of and not of one's choosing.

Household

The most apparent manifestation of familial cohabitation is the *household*. A family requires a place where its physical and affective needs may be met. Family members need shelter, rest, and sustenance, as well as amity, care, and affection. Admittedly, these needs can be met by other institutions or organizations. Yet there is a qualitative difference, for a household encompasses familial vocations and practices which are not present in these other settings. A household embodies a singular and intense blending of affinities that is not a natural feature of any other form of human association. The familial qualities of marriage, procreation, parenthood, childrearing, and cohabitation are uniquely present in a household. Although other institutions may incorporate one or more of these characteristics, none captures the entire range of their breadth and depth. The tasks entailed in ordering a household cannot be broken down into component parts and assigned to alternative social spheres, for they derive their meaning and vitality from the totality of familial vocations and practices.

Living together in a household, for example, is not the same as students residing together in a boarding school, even though they have similar characteristics. A household and school both provide shelter, rest, and sustenance, as well as opportunities for amity, care, and affection, but these similar qualities serve differing purposes or ends. Although a boarding school provides a place of cohabitation, it is not a place of timely belonging; a homecoming to *alma mater* is not the same as coming home. Although a school produces generations of students it does not generate offspring. Although teachers may function as *in loco parentis*, they are not parents with children. Although a school may etch itself deeply upon the identities of its graduates, it does not embody a lineage and familial history. Although a school may engender deep and lifelong friendships, it is not a place where individuals become loving spouses, parents, or siblings. A school, like many other institutions, may in many respects resemble a family, but it is not itself a household, nor can it serve as a surrogate without distorting its own, as well as the family's, inherent integrity.

It must be emphasized, however, that the family cannot be reduced to a household. A family is not synonymous with a physical structure or geographic location. Unlike a household, a family can be displaced and still remain a family. The homeless, transients, and refugees may maintain their mutual belonging despite the uprooted character of their lives. Although the lack of a stable household may jeopardize familial wellbeing, a family is not absolutely dependent upon it. Nor can a household be diminished to a secluded enclave. Rather, a household is simultaneously an *openly sequestered and intimately open space* for ordering the private and public poles of the family. What this, admittedly awkward, phrasing attempts to convey is an acknowledgement that the family's privacy depends on a public context, and that the ordering of familial affinities derives their meaning within broader spheres of civil association. The family cannot provide mutual and timely belonging if either of its private or public poles is collapsed, for it then loses the necessary parameters for demarcating the line separating these realms. A household is a concrete means of assisting unfolding families towards broader associations. A household prevents familial love from turning in upon itself when, as Clapp contends, it is ordered towards extending hospitality to strangers. As marriage orders a narrow bond of affinity to a particular lineage and familial history, likewise a household helps link the family to a greater range of social spheres.

Kinship

The first step in extending familial affinities towards more expansive forms of human association is through *kinship*. Members of a family are related, through blood and marriage, to a larger network of people. The family is embedded in both a biological and social lineage that cannot be reduced to either aspect. Augustine affirmed the need for this balanced ordering of kinship.[10] His argument for exogamy prevents kinship from being construed too loosely or too tightly. On the one hand, if kinship is ignored then individuals will share no common bonds leading to social strife. On the other hand, if individuals marry and reproduce within families this would not only result in a confusing array of familial roles,[11] but would also fail to enlarge other spheres of affinity, thereby promoting social discord among ingrown families. Properly ordering the biological and social dimensions of kinship helps secure the peace and concord of civil society.[12]

The extended family embodies this exogamous ordering by recognizing that the roles of aunt, uncle, niece, nephew, and cousin denote a bond stronger than that conferred by species, race, nationality, citizenship, or friendship, yet weaker than those of spouse, parent, grandparent, child, and sibling. The relative strengths and weaknesses of kinship magnify the interdependence of the family's affinities, for kin are not related exclusively by either genes or consent. Kinship requires both given and chosen relationships in which one is born and incorporated into a lineage. There must be a covenant between unrelated persons in order for a familial history to unfold over time. In selecting each other, spouses also enter into relationships with other relatives not of their choosing, and children may belong with extended families in which they are related to no one through either genes or marriage. Kinship is not simply a mechanism for tracing a line of genetic descent, but includes integration into the history of a lineage. Adopted children, for instance, are incorporated into the lineage of their adoptive parents because they belong, in virtue of the parents they are with, to an extended

---

[10] See *City of God* 15. 16, pp. 623–6.

[11] 'For marriage of brothers and sisters would at this stage mean that one man would be father, father-in-law and uncle to his own children. Similarly his wife would be mother, aunt and mother-in-law to the children she shared with her husband. And the children of the couple would be to each other not only brothers and sisters and spouses, but also cousins, as being the children of brothers and sisters' (ibid. 624).

[12] 'For affection was given its right importance so that men, for whom social harmony would be advantageous and honourable, should be bound together by ties of various relationships. The aim was that one man should not combine many relationships in his one self, but that those connections should be separated and spread among individuals, and that in this way they should help to bind social life more effectively by involving in their plurality a plurality of persons' (ibid. 623).

family. Nor is the existence of kin a familial prerequisite, for a married couple with no living relatives may establish a place of mutual and timely belonging that is connected to a lineage that is historically embodied in the couple as they become parents.

Seed of civil society

Since familial affinities are related and ordered to extended spheres of kin, the family may also be conceived as the *seed of civil society*. In further explicating this quality, two similar portrayals must be rejected to avoid confusion. First, it is not the same as asserting that the family is the *foundation* of civil society. Civil society may exist without families, as envisioned in Plato's *Republic*. Second, the family is not a *microcosm* of civil society, nor is civil society a *macrocosm* of the family. There is no organic continuity in which the family is a miniature *polis*, or the *polis* is an *oikos* writ large. Rather, the family is a distinct social sphere, integrally related to the other social spheres comprising a differentiated society. Although social differentiation has changed the structure of the family over time, its inherent integrity must be safeguarded if the ordering of the other social spheres is to promote the proper performance of their respective roles. When the normative ordering of familial affinities is ignored or discounted, then other institutions become distorted in attempting to fill the void by assuming roles they are ill-equipped to perform. A school, for example, is not suited for assuming the primary responsibility of childrearing.

Object of political ordering

Civil society requires governance, so the family, as a social sphere, is an *object of political ordering*. Good governance entails the lawful and just ordering of civil society in ways embodying the cultural heritage and traditions of the people being governed. The purpose of political governance is to promote the common good, and such promotion is just when it is enacted in ways that do not benefit the few at the expense of the many, or vice versa. The common good cannot be promoted justly if families are granted unwarranted privileges, or treated with indifference or hostility. A polity incorporates the ordering of various affinities and associations, and the family is the social sphere embodying the perpetuation of this ordering across generations. When the family is weakened, the other social spheres become distorted in undertaking tasks they are ill-equipped to perform, thereby diminishing the common good. A just political regime protects and assists families in providing places of timely and mutual belonging. In practical terms, this requires laws and policies enabling households to meet the physical and affective needs of their members. Although the family may rightly enjoy a privileged status in the political ordering of civil society, this does not imply that the relation between the state and its citizens should be mediated exclusively through familial associations or households. Yet nor does it follow that this relation should be restricted to protecting the rights and freedoms of citizens as autonomous persons. Even a polity founded on the primacy of individual rights and liberties cannot adequately protect them if the state fails to take into account the layers of various affinities and associations in which they are exercised. Moreover, although the family is not the cornerstone of political ordering, political ordering cannot be just in its absence. In this respect, the authors of *From Culture Wars to Common Ground* are correct in their insistence that the common good is promoted through public policies supporting a culture of critical familism. But they are mistaken in believing that such promotion is best achieved by enabling individual members of households to pursue their respective interests, using familial relationships as a means of mutual self-fulfilment rather than enacting policies that address the nature, needs, and structure of the familial association in its own right.

In summary, as a witness to God's providential ordering of creation, the family is a human association comprised of biological and social affinities which provide a place of mutual and timely belonging for its members. The family is characterized by a married couple with children, who are in turn related by blood, marriage, and lineage to an extended range of kin. The family entails voluntary and involuntary cohabitation within a household, and the proper ordering of its private and public poles promotes an extension of familial hospitality to strangers. As a social sphere, the family is integrally ordered to other social spheres comprising civil society, and a political regime promoting the common good safeguards the family by enabling it to meet the physical and affective needs of its members. These principal characteristics mark the contours of a normative familial framework upon which we may pursue further development of the family's role in social and political ordering, as well as providing a standard against which variations may be assessed. It may be asked, however: what is peculiarly providential about this portrayal of the family that it should enjoy a normative status?

THE PROVIDENTIAL MOVEMENT AND WITNESS OF THE FAMILY

As was argued in the previous chapter, since the resurrection of Jesus Christ from the dead vindicates creation and draws it towards its appointed *telos*, we may trace a providential trajectory of its temporal unfolding resulting from this vindication. The family, as a human association grounded in creation's vindicated order, may be said to bear a providential witness to this temporal and teleological unfolding. Yet it was also conceded that this claim runs counter to a prevalent late liberal rationality that rejects any purposeful historical movement other than chronicling a series of wilful human acts. Consequently, the family bears no significance other than indicating the shared interests of its affiliates. In order to further examine the implications of this contrast I will need to demonstrate how the family discloses creation's providential trajectory.

Since the family is a human association comprised of biological and social affinities, it is not rooted exclusively in nature or history, but embedded in both. This is to be expected if it is to provide a place of mutual and timely belonging, for the natural designation that a human being is *homo sapiens,* or the social designation that one is European, are not sufficiently expansive or particular in their own respective right to offer an adequate sense of belonging. The familial association is not a microcosm of a species or culture, but a peculiar blending of the pluriform dimensions of human life, through which humans are naturally and historically situated within the providential unfolding of God's vindicated creation. The family may be said to bear a providential witness to the extent that the ordering of its affinities conform to the providential trajectory of creation toward its destiny in Christ, thereby safeguarding its nature from which a history may be evoked. Conversely, the family fails to be such a witness to the extent that the ordering of its affinities resists the providential trajectory towards its appointed end in Christ, therefore failing to safeguard its nature from which a history may be evoked. These qualities may be sketched out by focusing on how the family is related to this providential trajectory.

Members of a family belong together within a web of voluntary and given affinities. Yet the totality of these affinities does not simply follow biological or social lines. A family is not a collection of parallel relationships among spouses, siblings, parents, and children. Rather, the family is an integral association, emerging from its biological and social antecedents whose members are bound together by mutual love and fidelity. Together, parents with children initiate a patterned movement being drawn towards a greater end, which over time draws them out as an association built upon, but greater than, what preceded it. The family is related to a providential trajectory in that this expansive quality is being drawn towards a transformation of the very affinities of which it is comprised.

This providential trajectory can be seen more clearly in contrast to accounts of the family which subsume it into either nature or history. When the familial association is grounded primarily in nature it is reduced to a means of propagation. Its purpose is to engender offspring for the sake of perpetuating a genealogy. Parents have a common interest in childrearing because of their genetic investment, and siblings share the interests of their common parentage. The family designates an ordering of separate but overlapping spousal, parental, filial, and fraternal relationships rather than the ordering of an expansive familial love. Moreover, such a family is defined largely in terms of cohabitation, effectively coming to an end when children leave their parental home. Although parents and their adult children may continue to share mutual affection, it is an extension of parental and filial relationships rather than an expression of familial love and fidelity. Consequently, the so-called 'natural family' is driven by a circular necessity.

When the familial association is grounded exclusively in history it is reduced to a projection of human will. A family is the outcome of a reproductive project in which a child is obtained to satisfy an adult's parental desire. A biological affinity is an accidental, rather than inherent, characteristic, for familial relationships are structured and maintained by what is willed by the relevant parties within a matrix of changing circumstances and obligations. A family connotes a collection of parallel relationships, formed and held together through force of will instead of given affinities. We cannot speak of an unfolding and expansive familial love and fidelity, because such a family exists only for as long as compulsory duties can (or must) be discharged, or there is sufficient will among the parties to identify themselves in terms of familial relationships. Consequently, the so-called 'social family' amalgamates diffuse and multidirectional trajectories.

The 'natural family' cannot bear witness to creation's providential trajectory, because its temporal movement is circular. Rather than being opened up and drawn out, the family turns in upon itself, ordering its affinities principally along a line of shared genes. In turning in upon itself the family promotes a fear and mistrust of strangers, encouraging a perception of social and political ordering that regulates the public interactions of citizens who do not trust one another. Private associations must be defended from unwarranted intrusions in order that trustworthy relationships may be formed within its secure boundaries. The family is effectively reduced to an enclave whose purpose is to protect the rights and interests of its affiliates. The family is not, nor can it be, the seedbed of civil society, for the natural basis of its affinity is antithetical to the contractual terms governing larger associations of autonomous persons. As depicted by Hobbes, the family remains the last vestige of the state of nature which must be simultaneously tolerated *and* contained. The family is a fortress whose walls defend its privacy while also protecting the peace of civil society from its divisive influence. Such a family, however, is not a witness to the providential unfolding of a vindicated creation, but is a gesture of resistance, in the name of nature, against a history of wilful human pretension.

The 'social family' cannot bear a providential witness because its movement through history is diffuse and multidirectional. Again, the family is not opened up or drawn out towards creation's appointed end, for a family exists only for as long as necessity dictates, or there is sufficient will among its parties to maintain familial relationships.

Such a family does not so much turn in upon itself as expresses and disperses itself through episodic bursts of contractual affiliation. The family is not a social sphere with an inherent nature and structure, but is simultaneously a means and outcome of persons possessing varying stages of autonomy in pursuing their respective physical, affective, and reproductive interests. Consequently, the family is relevant to social and political ordering only to the extent that it enables the effective pursuit of these interests. The family, then, is comprised of a series of descriptive, rather than normative, relationships, and the line separating the private and public aspects of these relationships is a procedural one, in which the former aspect denotes a realm of personal goods, while the latter provides a neutral space for their peaceful pursuit. If, for instance, one is hampered by natural or social constraints in pursuing one's private reproductive interests, one is entitled to enter the public realm to secure the necessary collaboration in pursuing those interests. Such a social and political ordering of familial relationships neither promotes nor discourages a fear of strangers, but presumes inevitable conflict among autonomous persons pursuing their private interests. Moreover, the line separating private from public is mobile, drawn by the dictates of changing individual and corporate values. The family may therefore be treated expediently in respect to whether it promotes or inhibits a pursuit of private interests. The line demarcating the family is not so much a fortress wall as a narrow canal that can be redirected in reaction to shifting circumstances. Such a family, however, is not a witness to the providential trajectory of a vindicated creation, but displays a human attempt to overcome nature in constructing its own history and destiny.

The family bears a providential witness when its movement corresponds to the trajectory of a vindicated creation being drawn toward its eschatological destiny in Christ. As discussed previously, this movement is encompassed in an unfolding and expansive familial love that engenders hospitality to strangers. Moreover, this providential movement resists attempts to ground the family exclusively in either nature *or* history. These attempts distort the ordering of familial affinities because they transpose ends and means. It is in nature *and* history that humans perceive the trajectory of a vindicated creation being drawn towards its destiny, and thus a teleological ordering of the human roles which are performed within the spheres of their various affinities and associations. These respective roles have an inherent nature which is disclosed in their historical unfolding, but they will also be transformed in the fullness of time. Consequently, creation's providential trajectory is not headed towards either a universal family (contra Bushnell) or a universe of autonomous beings (contra Nelson and Thatcher). Nature imposes restraints upon historical pretensions, and history enriches human life in the face of natural limitations, but neither has the final word regarding the end of God's creation.

Neither the 'natural' or 'social' family can succeed, because their foundational premises are conflated to points that cannot sustain the weight of what they assert. In asserting the primacy of nature, the family is reduced to an ordering of reproductive instinct, while asserting the primacy of history distorts the family to an artefact of the will. Both collapse because distilling nature to instinct and history to the human will fails to acknowledge that these two categories are interdependently related in ways which cannot be preserved in their separation. There is a *history of nature and a nature of history* within creation's vindicated order, otherwise we could not distinguish one from the other. The 'natural family' fails because instinct alone cannot disclose a history, and the 'social family' fails because it cannot extract the history it wills. The former is frozen timelessly in place, while the latter ignores its timely location. Safeguarding nature in history, and evoking history out from nature, reflects their converging co-inherence, rather than their mutual incoherence. Moreover, this co-inherence can only be disclosed within the vindicated order of creation, in which the history of nature and the nature of history are given their meaning by being delimited and enfolded within creation's appointed destiny.

Attempts to ground the family exclusively in either nature *or* history are invariably distorted, because correct but partial insights into creation's providential trajectory are elevated into complete, and thereby deceptive, descriptions. Accounts of the 'natural family' are correct in insisting that the ordering of the familial association entails biological affinity, yet they fail to recognize that procreation is not an end in itself, but a means of building upon and enlarging the scope of this affinity. Safeguarding the nature of the familial association requires evoking a history that transcends reproductive instinct.

Accounts of the 'social family' are correct in seeing that the ordering of the familial association is not limited to biological affinity, but they are mistaken in contending that wilful affiliation is a good in itself rather than a means to a more expansive range and ordering of given affinities. Larger spheres of human association depend on a core of given affinities which do not depend on the will of its members. Moreover, both fail to acknowledge the pluriform character of creation as an ordered movement towards uniformity in Christ's new creation. The family is a witness to creation's providential trajectory to the extent that it embodies this movement from pluriformity to greater uniformity. Such a family affirms its given affinities, while also pointing beyond itself as a mutual and timely place of belonging to where a vindicated and redeemed creation belongs in the fullness of time. Yet before I may turn attention towards the eschatological witness which the family also intimates indirectly, I must first further develop the principal features of the family's providential witness.

PROCREATION AND SOCIAL REPRODUCTION

The purpose of this section is to flesh out some of the principal characteristics of the family that have been outlined in this chapter. Or to pose the task as a question: what type of social interactions or economy does the familial association suggest in respect to broader issues of civil and political ordering? In addressing this question I will concentrate on the relationships between parents and children, and between households and strangers. The heuristic devices of the 'natural family' and 'social family' discussed above will continue to be employed, using the contrast to refine the principal normative features of the familial association.

Parents and children

Any normative account of the family necessarily requires that we think about children and parents. Attempting to conceive a 'family' comprised exclusively of adults or entirely of children would stretch the term beyond any useful form. The fact that particular bonds may be identified as familial implies an intergenerational relationship. However varying the structures of families may be, they are all predicated on procreation and childrearing. Yet this common thread is too thin to disclose a normative pattern of the parent–child relationship, and we must look elsewhere for clues, to the reasons why people become parents.

It would appear that the natural family is predicated on the need or desire to perpetuate a genealogy. The parent–child relationship is the crucial link in a genealogical chain which both preserves a particular heritage and projects it onwards into the future. Consequently, parents and children are bound together by a common origin *and* trajectory; they are situated together within a lineage that precedes them, and will presumably endure beyond them. As late moderns we should not be tempted to simply dismiss the natural family as a vestige of a primitive era embodying a quaint biological essentialism. As the quest of many adoptive children to find their natural parents and the growing use of assisted reproduction by infertile couples to have children of 'their own' testify, there is seemingly a deep need to find one's place within a sequenced pattern of relatedness, extending both backwards and forwards through time. Moreover, recent studies in evolutionary psychology presumably document certain advantages for childrearing when parents are genetically invested in their offspring, and as was discussed in previous chapters, much of traditional Christian teaching presupposes marriage and family as natural institutions. There is, in short, no compelling reason, other than ideological presumption, why the biological lineaments of the familial association should be dismissed out of hand.

In many respects the natural family is preferable to its social alternative. Within the social family any biological relation between parents and children is an accidental feature, because some variant of self-fulfilment is the principal reason for becoming a parent. The self-fulfilling motive need not be selfish or egotistical, however, for the desire to have a child may very well exhibit a genuinely altruistic love for children, and such love is not based upon or restricted to a biological or genetic relation between parent and child. Although the vast majority of parents may share a genetic relation with their children, it reflects a method of choice (or convenience) among a growing range of options (such as adoption or technological assistance) rather than any inherent characteristic of the parent–child relationship. Consequently, there are no objective criteria for defining the parent–child relationship other than a subjective love for children which motivates the desire to initiate such a relationship.

Moreover, the parent–child relationship does not presuppose any prior relational foundation, such as marriage, upon which it is based. The social family signifies the successful outcome of one or more individuals pursuing their reproductive interests. In many respects the rhetoric of 'procreative liberty', as the dominant mode of public discourse for how we are coming to think about the parent–child relationship, instantiates the social family, in its myriad forms, as the paradigmatic model.[13] The chief tenet of procreative liberty is that every person has a fundamental right to reproduce or otherwise obtain a child that one may rear as a parent. A person exercising this right should be free to use whatever means are required to achieve this end, so long as the rights or interests of other persons are not harmed in the process. Individuals pursuing their reproductive interests enter into collaborative relationships or contracts with other willing parties to obtain the necessary materials or services such as coitus, gametes, wombs, or technological assistance. Parents are thereby 'commissioners' who initiate and oversee a collaborative reproductive project which, if successful, culminates in the acquisition of a child. Within this framework, commissioners are at liberty to employ various combinations of techniques such as gamete donation, artificial insemination, *in vitro* fertilization, or surrogacy which best suit their needs and personal preferences. And there are no normative constraints on how these techniques may be deployed so long as none of the collaborating parties, and eventual children, are harmed.

It is important to note that, in this depiction, *every* method for forming a parent–child relationship is reduced to contractual

---

[13] See John A. Robertson, *Children of Choice* (1994). For critical analyses of Robertson's account of procreative liberty, see Brent Waters, *Reproductive Technology* (2001), 49–56, and Gilbert Meilaender, *Body, Soul, and Bioethics* (1995), 61–88.

transactions between commissioners and collaborators. A couple attempting natural reproduction, for instance, have simply opted to limit the scope of their collaboration to each other in pursuing the reproductive project they have commissioned. The only difference between this couple and an infertile man acquiring donated gametes, contracting a surrogate, and employing *in vitro* fertilization is the range of collaboration required in accomplishing the identical goal of obtaining a child. Parenthood is ultimately an act of will, and the child is an artefact of that will, and most importantly, it is the force of this will which both establishes and maintains the parent–child relationship.

The principal objection against both the natural and social models of the family is that they distort the teleological nature of the parent–child relationship, effectively disabling the family's providential witness. As was argued above, the parent–child relationship is established by God, who entrusts a child to the care of parents. Children are with parents in a place of mutual and timely belonging. Although the parent–child relationship infers a genetic bond, it is not a prerequisite for extending parental care and affection. Contrary to the natural family, shared genes are not an indispensable component of the relationship between children and parents. To claim otherwise is to disfigure the family into a genealogical conduit, rather than a place of mutual and timely belonging. Contrary to the social family, a child is not simply the outcome of a reproductive project or an artefact of parental will. Children belong with but not to parents. Although a biological bond between parent and child is not an indispensable component of the familial association, neither can it be carelessly ignored or discounted. Even when such a biological bond is absent, it should nonetheless inform the familial structure of the parent–child relationship. The significance of this objection, as well as the implications for larger questions of social and political ordering, can be further explicated by examining how the natural and social families render adoption as being either inexplicable or irrelevant.[14]

---

[14] For more expansive discussions of adoption, see Waters, *Reproductive Technology*, 67–75; 'Welcoming Children into our Homes', *Scottish Journal of Theology*, 55/4 (2002); and 'Adoption, Parentage and Procreative Stewardship', in Timothy P. Jackson (ed.), *The Morality of Adoption* (2005).

As was argued above, an adoptive family may be regarded as a genuine family in every respect so long as it provides a place of mutual and timely belonging for its members, for in doing so it bears a providential witness to a vindicated created order. Adoption, in short, is a means God may use to entrust a child to the care of parents. The idea of adoption is not compatible with either the natural or social family as distinct models. In respect to the natural family, adoption is inexplicable. If the primary purpose of the familial association is to perpetuate a particular genealogy, then there would be no compelling reason for a couple to rear a child with whom they share no genetic bond. An infertile couple might be motivated to adopt a child as an heir in order to keep assets within a family line, but the supposed genealogical rationale of familial relationships would, as a consequence, be rendered fictitious. If the family is an entirely natural institution, then the most plausible and humane response to parentless children would be orphanages. In respect to the social family, adoption is an irrelevant or unproblematic consideration, because it is merely one reproductive option among many. Adoption, for various reasons, may prove to be a convenient or preferable option to natural or assisted reproduction. So long as procedural safeguards are in place for protecting children, as well as their adoptive parents, adoption presents no particular ethical concerns as a means for forming a family.

Yet adoption deserves singular attention, because it is an act that simultaneously affirms the nature of the parent–child relationship while also allowing suitable plasticity for evoking a familial history. Adoption exhibits a love for a stranger or neighbour in need. If the care and affection of a family is withheld, a child will not have a place of mutual and timely belonging. Adoption is a supreme act of charity in which adoptive parents follow a 'pattern of representation by replacement'.[15] Adoptive parents do not simply extend the hospitality of their home to a stranger for an extended period of time, but represent themselves to the child as the parents of the family which now binds them together. Although adoptive parents may be motivated at least initially by a charitable impulse, it is not a form of love that is cut off from or incongruent with a parental and familial

---

[15] See O'Donovan, *Begotten or Made?*, 35–8.

love that develops over time between children and parents. Like the natural family a child is entrusted by God to the care of parents, but there is an elastic quality to the parent–child relationship that allows it to transcend a biological bond while also signifying it. In short, adoption does not nullify natural procreation, but is structured around and informed by it. This is one reason why adoption (as well as foster care) is preferable to orphanages, because it provides a child with a place of mutual and timely belonging that cannot be replicated in an institutionalized setting.

Adoption, however, does not imply that the biological bond of the parent–child relationship is irrelevant. Although God may entrust some children to the care of parents through adoption, it cannot thereby be presumed that the methods employed to establish their relationship are equally suitable. Such a presumption warps the nature of the familial association grounded in the one-flesh unity of marriage. As a representative act, adoption refers to a familial setting instantiated in this one-flesh grounding, otherwise adoption becomes a means of completing a collaborative reproductive project, stripping it of its charitable character. Under these circumstances, adoption is more akin to an informal surrogacy contract rather than an act of parental substitution. As an act of charity, it must be remembered that the sole purpose of adoption is to locate the child in a suitable place of mutual and timely belonging, and not to satisfy an adult's desire to obtain a child.[16] The adoptive act *per se* does not so much emphasize the 'element of adoption' present in every parent–child relationship as it reinforces the nature of the familial association it seeks to represent.

A teleological ascription of the familial association must take into account the biological bonds that demarcate and differentiate it from other spheres of human association. The ordering of these bonds, however, must also incorporate an elastic element, otherwise the family cannot simultaneously bear a providential witness while also intimating an eschatological transformation of its internal relationships. The tension between this providential witness and

---

[16] Although this may very well prove to be the case in many instances, satisfying the reproductive interests of the adoptive parents is a consequence and not the purpose of adoption.

eschatological intimation is examined in greater detail in the next chapter, so it will suffice to indicate in a preliminary manner that although the family bears a unique witness to the vindicated order of creation, it also falls under a judgement that requires its redemption, and therefore transformation, in the fullness of time. Familial roles and relationships will be displaced by sisterhood and brotherhood in Christ. Without some latitude for ordering its internal relationships, as signified in adoption as an act of representation, the best the natural family can bear witness to is a return to an isolated association of shared genes. But this requires bearing witness to an unbiblical eschatology, for it is not flesh and blood that will inherit the kingdom of God, and so the family reminds us that we wait for the coming of the New Jerusalem rather than a restored Eden.

The elasticity of the familial association, however, is not infinite, for if this were the case then its boundaries could not be delineated. A family would designate either parental ownership (albeit temporary and limited) of children, or the consent of autonomous persons to maintain a voluntary affiliation enabling them to pursue their respective interests. The family is reduced to the outcome of a will to obtain children or an expression of an ongoing will to maintain voluntary relationships among autonomous persons. Distilling the family to such a porous state also destroys it as a distinguishable and viable social sphere. Although the implications of the diminishment of the family as social sphere for broader questions of social and political ordering is examined in greater depth in Chapter 8, it will suffice here to contend that in failing to account for its involuntary and given affinities, the involuntary and given affinities of civil society will also grow increasingly inexplicable. If parenthood is simply the outcome of a reproductive project, thereby corrupting the charitable act of adoption into a reproductive option, then acts of charity within and between other social spheres may also become corrupt. The social family has no providential witness to bear or an eschatological destiny to intimate, for it can only magnify itself as both the means and end of those who have willed it to be and what it shall become, for it has nothing larger than a projected mirror of itself on the horizon towards which it may point.

As noted above, the primary purpose of this chapter is to construct the lineaments of a normative account of the familial association based on the philosophical, theological, and moral themes developed in the previous chapter. This section in particular has focused on the crucial nature of the parent–child relationship as a way of describing some of the principal characteristics of a teleologically ordered family which requires *both* a grounding in a given, biological affinity *and* flexibility in extending its social bonds, *if* the family is to simultaneously bear a providential witness to and eschatological intimation of a vindicated creation being drawn towards its destiny in Christ. Adoption, as an act of charity and representation, was in turn used to disclose both the necessity and limits of this ordering. Moreover, adoption was portrayed as an act which simultaneously safeguards the nature of the parent–child relationship while also helping to evoke from it a familial history, a task which neither the natural nor the social family can accomplish. The ground has now been prepared to broach the broader questions of social and political ordering, namely: if the ordering of the natural and social affinities of civil society requires both a given grounding *and* institutional flexibility, what natural qualities must be safeguarded to evoke an unfolding social and political history? Before undertaking this more expansive task, however, some additional preliminary steps must be taken.

Households and strangers

Up to this point I have concentrated primarily on what may be described as the internal ordering of the familial association. What has remained largely unaddressed is how this normative account might order the family to and with the other social spheres comprising civil society. Or posed as a question: how does a household enable or disable a family's relationship with strangers? In order to limit this inquiry to a reasonable length, it will focus primarily on what may be construed broadly as economic relationships; that is, interactions or transactions involving the exchange of goods and services.

Since the natural family is suspicious, if not distrustful, of strangers, it presumably would limit its interactions with them as much as possible, concentrating on exchanges that enable it to pursue its principal goal of perpetuating a genealogy. Two prominent strategies suggest themselves for achieving this goal. On the one hand, a family could acquire assets or property to insulate itself, channelling necessary transactions through a few trusted agents. Or on the other hand, parents could invest heavily in the education and development of their children in order to attract suitable mates for perpetuating the familial line of descent. Components from both of these strategies could also be combined in a number of ways. Although this portrayal of the economic interests and strategies of the natural family is admittedly sketchy, it nonetheless captures the basic elements of the Bergers' portrayal of the bourgeois family, which suggest the following observations.

First, the family is a unit that *accumulates or produces wealth*. By accumulating financial resources or property a family is presumably in a better position to isolate itself from relationships with unwanted strangers, thereby exerting greater control over the quality of its internal life. Although accumulating wealth may require relationships with a more expansive range of strangers in order to preserve, manage, and invest assets, this can be controlled through interactions with a limited range of trustworthy institutions or agents, a situation not entirely unlike the relationship between masters and household servants that were present in the household codes, and preserved and refined by subsequent theological reflection as exemplified in Baxter's and Schleiermacher's respective accounts of the family. Moreover, the natural or bourgeois family also has a strong interest in passing on accumulated assets to offspring, for a substantial inheritance would presumably assist the perpetuation of a lineage.

Second, the family is a unit of *consumption*. By investing in their children, parents purchase or otherwise obtain various goods and services related to their education, health, and physical and emotional wellbeing. Other items may also be obtained to improve the quality of life for various members of a family. In addition, even a family dedicated to accumulating wealth must nonetheless consume certain goods and services to maintain a household and protect its assets, a goal that cannot be achieved in isolation from the other social spheres. Although increased consumption requires contact with a greater range of strangers, thereby seemingly working against the natural family's inclination towards insularity, some protection is afforded through legal, regulatory, and market mechanisms.

Third, the *private domain denotes a secluded enclave* in which a family accumulates wealth, and determines household values that sets its patterns of consumption. A family, in this scheme, is necessarily secluded because it requires both a physical and social space that demarcates itself from other human associations comprised of strangers. A family is also necessarily an enclave, for a household is not the home of a hermit, but is comprised of individuals sharing certain purposes and objectives. A household thereby requires certain configurations of authority and cooperation in meeting the needs of its members and pursuing its common good, especially in respect to accumulating wealth, and consuming goods and services. Admittedly the borders of such a secluded enclave are not as solid and protective as the imagery suggests. Such external factors as taxation, shifting markets, cultural mores, and marketing surely limit a household's ability to accumulate wealth, as well as influencing which goods and services it consumes. It is, however, within the confines of a household that these external factors are filtered, interpreted, and investment and consumption strategies are formulated.

Fourth, the *public domain is an 'open space'* in which a family (or its agents) engages in exchanges with strangers to accumulate wealth, and consume goods and services. These exchanges with strangers are a prerequisite if a family is to achieve its accumulative and consumption objectives, for no household can be entirely self-sufficient. Although these exchanges are more often than not accomplished by individual members of a household, the benefits (as well as the liabilities) rebound back to the family, especially in respect to pursuing its principal objectives of perpetuating a genealogy, and passing on accumulated wealth to subsequent generations. We may say, then, that the model of the natural family inspires forms of political ordering that protect simultaneously the seclusion of the private domain and openness of the public domain. The former is achieved through policies designed to maximize parental authority to oversee the education and physical and emotional welfare of their children, while the latter is accomplished by ensuring that households will have ample opportunities to accumulate wealth, and consume goods and services. Presumably, these objectives are best achieved through minimal governmental involvement in or regulation of free markets, even though various households will be competing unevenly on a field of scarcity to achieve their respective goals. Yet if government is to simultaneously protect the seclusion of the private domain and the openness of the public domain, then its role is not to treat certain types of households preferentially or level the playing field, but to ensure that opportunities to compete are open, and that competition is conducted fairly.

In contrast, the social family is presumably less suspicious of strangers, because it is itself comprised of strangers attempting to form various familial relationships over time. These relationships are undertaken ultimately as a means of self-fulfilment for the individual members of an association designated, at least for a period of time, as familial. The boundaries demarcating a family, then, are necessarily porous, enabling exchanges with a range of strangers that varies over time in line with how its members choose to pursue their respective interests. It should be stressed that this portrayal of the social family is *not* pejorative. It may very well prove to be the case that many social families develop more loving and caring relationships than their natural counterparts, but they result from the will of the respective parties rather than any so-called natural structure of their association as a family. Consequently, the social family may adopt strategies for its economic exchanges with strangers which appear identical to those employed by the natural family characterized above. But, as demonstrated below, the principal rationale for accumulating wealth and consuming goods and services differs markedly. Again, although this sketch of the social family is sparse, it encapsulates the rudiments of the late liberal theorists and their sympathetic theologians, such as Nelson, Thatcher, and to a more limited extent Browning and his co-authors, suggesting again the following observations.

First, the family promotes the *self-fulfilment of its members*. Familial relationships are established as a means to enable the individual parties to pursue their respective interests. This is most readily apparent when adults forge an intimate and committed relationship. Although adults pursuing their reproductive interests impose a parental relationship upon children who obviously cannot give their consent or assert their own interests, they are presumably compensated by an extended period of parental care that prepares them to become autonomous adults. This does not imply that the familial relationships comprising the social family are inherently selfish. Rather, it amplifies the assumption that familial relationships are inevitably reciprocal, with varying levels of self-fulfilment attained in discrete patterns which may at differing times be immediate, delayed, and often asymmetrical. Although the social family is not necessarily comprised of selfish people, its members are self-interested, a condition not altogether removed from its natural counterpart in which an apparently altruistic act of parental care may be construed as the self-interested desire of perpetuating a genealogy. Thus decisions regarding the accumulation of wealth, and the consumption of goods and services, are made in ways which promote the reciprocity of familial relationships, thereby promoting the interests of its respective members. Some parents, for example, may sacrifice their own immediate economic interests to provide certain advantages for their children with the goal of preparing them to become autonomous adults, a goal which if achieved would presumably prove gratifying to all the concerned parties. Or other parents may determine that such a sacrificial strategy may jeopardize the development of a child's eventual autonomy, choosing instead consumption patterns resulting in more immediate forms of individual fulfilment. Consequently there is no inherent tendency within the social family regarding patterns of accumulating wealth, or consuming goods and services, because these determinations are made in respect to the interests of its individual members rather than any common familial objectives.

Second, the family is comprised of *consumers of goods and services.* Although the consumption patterns of the social family may appear similar, if not identical, to its natural counterpart, the underlying rationale differs. Unlike its natural counterpart, the social family does not consume goods and services as a unit. Rather, goods and services are consumed in line with the interests and objectives of its individual members. A family simply designates a tighter nexus of cooperative and competing interests resulting from its voluntary and dependent relationships than is the case with other affiliations of strangers. Both mandated expenditures for education and health and marketing strategies for consuming discretionary goods and services are directed towards the interests of individuals that are adjusted over time in response to the changing patterns of the voluntary and dependent relationships within families. Such a stratagem seemingly promotes the development of children into autonomous adults, because it encourages them to become wise consumers, for as such late liberal theorists as Rawls and Okin contend, such autonomy is achieved only by being able to calculate one's interest and act accordingly.

Third, the *private domain denotes a temporary locus of mutual welfare*. Since a family exists to enable the fulfilment of its respective members, it must have the ability to forge its internal voluntary and dependent relationships free from unwarranted public regulation and scrutiny. Without this requisite privacy, a family cannot provide the emotional intimacy or support, especially in respect to promoting the self-esteem of children, which justifies its continued existence in late liberal regimes. In short, members of a family implement certain strategies for accumulating wealth and consuming goods and services to preserve Lasch's haven in a heartless world. It must be stressed, however, that there is no normative structure for this haven since a wide variety of models is needed to fit widely varying needs and interests. More importantly, the social family is a temporary and flexible affiliation given the changing nature of its voluntary and dependent relationships. Both of these factors must be taken into account regarding the ordering of familial relationships within the larger public domain.

Fourth, given the wide variation of familial models and their temporary character, the *public domain is a regulated space* in which individuals conduct economic exchanges to support familial relationships. The purpose of political ordering is not to empower households as institutions mediating the relationship between citizens and the state, but to ensconce a direct relationship between the state and its citizens in which voluntary and dependent familial relationships play an incidental role. Within this scheme, parents are agents of the state and their authority is attenuated and apportioned to other social spheres with regard to the education, health, and welfare of their dependants. Or phrased differently, all adults share the responsibility and burden for ensuring the development of a subsequent generation of autonomous citizens. Consequently, there is presumably a compelling political interest for levelling the public field in which individuals compete in acquiring wealth, and consuming goods and services, a goal which may be achieved through a combination of market regulation, taxation, and policies promoting preferential treatment.

The purpose of this brief exercise in comparing the economic interests of the natural and social families is *not* to suggest that there are two (and only two) ideal and competing typologies from which we must choose, nor do the preceding summaries imply any normative endorsement. The families and economies as portrayed obviously do not exist, or have ever existed, in the pristine manner used to describe them. Rather, they demonstrate contrasting tendencies for economic ordering that the heuristic models of the natural and social families may inspire. Nor is the purpose of this exercise to imply that the natural family inevitably inspires a capitalist form of economic ordering, whereas the social family is more inclined towards promoting a socialist economy, and that the subsequent task for Christian moral deliberation is to determine which option is most compatible with the church's theological convictions and ethical principles. In this respect, it is not inconceivable to envision a socialist economy comprised of natural families or a capitalist economy consisting of social families.

The purpose of this brief exercise is to demonstrate that both of these contending familial models inspire tendencies for economic ordering that are *accidental rather than inherent to* their respective accounts of the household. For the natural family, the economic sphere is, at best, a network of necessity enabling a series of exchanges intended to promote the respective interests of various households. The economic sphere is thereby only tangentially related to the familial sphere in which the former is a means for the latter to attain its inherent goods, and households have nothing to contribute to economic ordering other than financial resources used in various exchanges. Thus we cannot speak meaningfully about sovereign familial and economic spheres that are integrally ordered, for economic ordering is premised on a series of mutually parasitic relationships among households channelling their economic resources and exchanges through various social and commercial institutions. Ironically, for households to develop rich social lives any conception of civil society must be dismissed as a distracting fiction. The only task that should command public attention is that of ordering the relationship between the state and its individual citizens, and presumably it should be such an order that greatly restricts the authority of the state to interfere in the legitimate private pursuits of its citizens. A minimalist state best promotes the flourishing of the natural family, because it provides the necessary economic freedom and opportunity for it to pursue its interest of preserving a lineage. This strategy, however, strips the family of any theological significance. If civil society is a fabrication, and the state and its citizens are the only public categories one can admit, then it is hard to imagine what providential witness the family can bear or what eschatological destiny it can intimate. How indeed can the family be integrally ordered to broader spheres of human association when its only options are citizenship and the state? Moreover, confining the tasks of public ordering to these two categories discloses a curious strategy: the really important private associations, such as the family, are omitted from the public agenda in order to protect them. Even if such a strategy would prove efficacious, it nonetheless creates a dilemma, namely, how is the family to be ordered to citizenship and the state when presumably these are the very forces that threaten its wellbeing? The natural family emerges as a free-floating and unhistorical phenomenon, neither situated in, nor contributing to, any particular social setting or providential trajectory.

By way of contrast, the social family also presupposes a liberal economic network of exchange, but it is not a nexus of necessity, merely an instrument to achieve larger social goals. Some of the individuals participating in these exchanges may be attached to families while others may not, and given these larger goals such an affiliation (or lack of one) is an irrelevant consideration. The principal public task is to enact a form of political ordering that enables individuals to achieve collectively certain social goals. Thus the family, *as a social sphere*, is effectively rendered invisible. Although promoting strong families may ostensibly be a social goal such ordering is seeking to achieve, its ultimate objective is the welfare of children rather than families *per se*. It is not inconceivable that something like the natural family could be deemed inimical to achieving what is thought to be an important social goal, and replaced with alternative arrangements for ordering procreation and childrearing. In this respect, the family is omitted from the public agenda not to protect it, but because it has no inherent political significance. Despite this omission, it may appear, at first glance, that the social family at least potentially enables a richer account of civil society than that afforded by the natural family. This appearance, however, is illusory, for the ensuing civil society is not the result of an integral ordering of sovereign social spheres, but a consequence of an assertive political will. Such a civil society is a regulated pattern of behaviour defining the relationship between the state and its nebulous people. Thus the same theological objections that were raised against the social and political ordering inspired by the natural family can also be raised against that inspired by the social family, namely, that no providential witness can be borne nor eschatological witness intimated by this ghostly spectre, for it again has no social setting in which it is situated and to which it contributes in turn.

McCarthy's account of households lodged in a neighbourhood economy offers a promising avenue for overcoming some of the deficient tendencies of the natural and social families discussed above. As he contends, it is through families that 'consumer capitalism and nation-state individualism are reproduced'.[17] The ideal family is a closed, suburban household that aspires to be as free and independent as possible. In contrast to this model, McCarthy argues that the family should be open and dependent upon a network of households. It is within this network that certain vocations and practices are undertaken as a form of social formation. The practical locus for this formation is the neighbourhood, which produces an economy of gift exchange: a neighbour, for example, removes the snow from the pavement of my house and I reciprocate by repairing his garage door. The inherent reciprocity of a neighbourhood economy reinforces the open family's dependence on a larger social setting. Moreover, such informal reciprocity and interdependence means that all adults in a neighbourhood play a parenting role in respect to their neighbours' children. This more expansive, albeit informal, parenting network is crucial, because the 'procreative family is a heavier load than marriage can bear'.[18] Consequently,

---

[17] See David Matzko McCarthy, *Sex and Love in the Home* (2001), 3.
[18] Ibid. 210.

marriage is not the foundation of the family, but is at the centre of a neighbourhood economy.

McCarthy's account of the household enables a vision of the family that moves beyond the artificial dichotomy of the natural and social families. By situating the family within a neighbourhood economy, we may identify a series of vocations and practices that both necessarily and integrally relate households to a larger sphere of human association. The family is rescued from being consigned to private oblivion (in the case of the natural family to protect it, and in the case of the social family to render it irrelevant) and placed where it may inform broader questions of social and political ordering in an intelligible manner. In this respect, his theology of the household points us generally in the right direction. McCarthy's programme ultimately fails, however, because he places more weight on the so-called neighbourhood economy than it can bear. There are two reasons, one structural and the other theological, why this is the case.

Structurally, McCarthy places too much confidence in geographic proximity as a principal feature of his gift exchange economy. He consistently lifts up the virtues of densely populated neighbourhoods of flats and attached houses as opposed to dreary, sparsely populated suburbs. Yet it is not inconceivable that the kinds of gift exchanges he envisions could occur in suburban neighbourhoods, nor does he explain why these exchanges seemingly require intense, daily, face-to-face relationships among neighbours to be efficacious. It remains unclear if repairing my neighbour's garage door in exchange for his removing snow from my pavement, for instance, is categorically any different from an accountant living in a Chicago suburb preparing tax returns for a lawyer living in Los Angeles who reciprocates with free estate planning. It may be granted that neighbours living in close proximity with each other may have more frequent exchanges, but these may very well prove to be trivial or banal in character. The less frequent contact between two individuals separated by a continent may in fact prove to be more mutually enriching given their shared interest and friendship over time. Moreover, the alienating or otherwise corrosive influence of monetary exchanges for goods and services within various markets is asserted but never argued. Consequently, it also remains unclear why the gift exchange economy he champions is thereby superior or preferable to so-called consumer capitalism. What is lacking in McCarthy's account is a richer and deeper description of the vocations and practices of the household and neighbourhood that would enable him to demonstrate their necessity in regard to more distant neighbours and unknown strangers with whom we also share bonds of civil association.

Theologically, McCarthy's portrayal of the family is rather vaporous. For all of his rich and informative description of daily life in a household and neighbourhood, what exactly constitutes a family remains vague. Is a family simply constituted by a group of adults and children who happen to spend more time with each other than with other adults and children in a neighbourhood, or is there some other biological, relational, or normative quality that McCarthy either refuses or is unable to name? At the end of the day what is portrayed is not so much a network of households within the social setting of the neighbourhood, but a loose confederation of parents and children who live in close proximity to each other. He wishes to affirm the open family, but for it to be genuinely open it must also be closed at some point, otherwise it is little more than a misty and temporary affiliation. The closure he lacks is his refusal to base the familial association on marriage. Contrary to his worry that marriage is too fragile a foundation for the family, it is the one vocation that is uniquely equipped to bear the weight he wishes to transfer. But transfer where? Presumably the neighbourhood and the church. Yet by refusing to base the family on marriage, how is the vocation of parenthood, in contrast to a loose network of parenting, to be affirmed, instituted, and practised? Particularly within the church, is it not marriage, in contrast to singleness, that enables the blessing of parenthood as a vocation? In this respect, it must be remembered that, at baptism, children are entrusted by God to the care of parents and *not* the church or the neighbourhood. By failing to provide the closure of marriage, McCarthy cannot differentiate the familial association with much precision, and thereby nor can he explicate its integral ordering to other forms of human association other than by being absorbed by them.

Despite these weaknesses, McCarthy has nevertheless pointed clearly towards the two remaining tasks of this book. One is to inquire more fully into the integral ordering of familial vocations and practices toward broader forms of social and political association, a task that will be undertaken in the final chapter. The other, more immediate issue as suggested by the preceding paragraph is to examine the relationship between the family and the church, particularly in regard to the distinct, but complementary, vocations of marriage and singleness.

7

The Church and the Family

When the centrifugal and centripetal poles of the family are held in their proper tension, familial affinity is oriented towards more expansive forms of human association. This tension is maintained by the family's normative relationships with strangers and singleness. The former is needed to differentiate the family from other social spheres in the historical and providential unfolding of a vindicated creation, while the latter is required to direct creation towards its *telos* in Christ. These relationships have been eroded with the rise of late liberalism, precipitating structural changes in the family which reflect its now problematic role in the tasks of social and political ordering. The normative status of these relationships needs to be re-established in order to recover the family as a sovereign social sphere that is integrally related to other forms of civil and ecclesial association. This recovery was initiated in Chapter 6 by examining the relationship with strangers, and the focus of our inquiry now shifts to the relationship with the church.

THE ESCHATOLOGICAL WITNESS OF THE CHURCH

The church is the *eschatological community*, the herald of God's new creation. It awaits and points towards that end when all is made one in Christ, but also remembers that at present its ministry is conducted within a created order that has been vindicated by its Lord. In respect to the family, the church affirms that its temporal ordering and providential witness entails the roles of spouse, parent, child, and sibling, but they are tempered, though not negated, by their eschatological fellowship as sisters and brothers in Christ.

Two images of the church are especially pertinent. The first is the church as the *body of Christ*.[1] Each part of the body possesses an inherent integrity which is integrally ordered to the other parts. The separate callings and vocations of Christians are made one, functioning as a whole in Christ. There is a pluriform ordering of the body that incorporates familial qualities, for the family is also a kind of body, composed of, yet greater than, its parts. The analogy cannot be pushed too far, however, because the church is not an eschatological family, nor is the family an eschatological community. Both concepts entail a contradiction in terms. Incorporation into the body of Christ is accomplished through election in the fullness of time, whereas the family embodies a timely ordering of imposed affinities. The family bears a direct witness to the providential ordering of creation, intimating the end of that order, whereas the church bears an eschatological witness, enfolding its temporal antecedents.

The second image is the church as the *household of faith*.[2] The household of faith may be construed as an eschatological space in which the familial qualities of the body of Christ are expressed; the place in which the church lives as Christ's adopted heir. Yet the ordering of this household remains pluriform this side of the eschaton. Deploying the church's various gifts, callings, and vocations requires a functional division of roles, entailing the disciplined giving and receiving of commands. These functional roles, however, are based on loving and mutual servitude rather than patriarchal discrimination or conditional reciprocity, for these roles also bear witness to unity and equality in Christ. There is neither male nor female, Jew nor Greek, slave nor free in the body of Christ,[3] but these distinctions are not eliminated in the temporal ordering of the household of faith or the familial household. Following O'Donovan, the church embodies radical equality, but this ontological status does not entail functional relationships that are 'strictly reciprocal'. The 'structures of community' require 'non-reciprocal roles' if they are to

---

[1] See 1 Cor. 12 and Eph. 4: 4–13.
[2] See Eph. 2: 19–22; 1 Tim. 3: 15; 1 Pet. 4: 17.
[3] See Gal. 3: 28 and Col. 3: 11; cf. Rom. 10: 12–13.

flourish. The prime example is the family, 'where one cannot be parent, child, and spouse to the same person, nor parent to the person who is parent to oneself'.[4] In both the family and the church, equality in Christ does not imply a corresponding functional equality of roles, but their difference is based on the gifts of the Spirit instead of sex, nationality, or social status. Contrary to Cahill, overcoming 'every inequality of race, class, or gender' is a proper task that should be undertaken by Christians, but it does not 'begin by transforming the family' as the application of the 'Christian social message of reciprocity and inclusion'.[5] In relation to the church, the family may be characterized as reflecting a distinct, though complementary, structure of household ordering. Household roles are ordered to each other along the natural patterns (which are *not* inherently or naturally patriarchal) of the relationships which define them, but their faithful performance prefigures loving and mutual servitude intimating unity and equality in Christ. In bearing its providential witness, the family also points towards an end transcending and transforming its distinctive roles and relationships.

The quality of the church's eschatological witness is most pointedly disclosed in the sacraments. In *baptism*, a person shares in the death and resurrection of Jesus Christ, enacting the passing of the old creation and its raising into the new. In baptism, there is a correspondence between the believer, church, and creation in respect to the redemptive and eschatological significance of the rite: in Christ, they are brought together into the singular presence of Christ, and thereby share his destiny. It is also through baptism that one is incorporated into the body of Christ, sharing its life in expectation of that day when its work is finished. The *Eucharist* in turn shapes the pattern of the church's life and expectation. The body of Christ gathers in its household of faith to share a meal prefiguring a banquet in the new creation. It is at the Lord's Table that the radical equality among believers is most vividly portrayed, for all temporal roles are set aside in favour of eschatological unity. The sharing of bread and wine is a communion of saints, gathered and invited by Christ to partake of the new life which has claimed them.

---

[4] See Oliver O'Donovan, *The Desire of the Nations* (1996), 265–6.
[5] Lisa Sowle Cahill, *Sex, Gender, and Christian Ethics* (1996), 215.

Although the sacraments are eschatological signs, their enactment displays familial qualities. In baptism, there is a rebirth; a passing on of the church's faith, hope, and love from one generation to the next. Baptism also entails what may be characterized as a grafting of believers onto the church's lineage of divine mercy and grace, so the household of faith may be conceived as embodying kinship in Christ. The Eucharist resembles a family meal, for at the Lord's Table the household of faith becomes the body of Christ, in a manner not unlike family members gathering at an appointed time to prepare and share a meal, instead of individuals who happen to be eating in the same place at the same time.

Given this resemblance, the family's witness is imprinted by what may be characterized as a *sacramental inlay*. Baptism reminds parents that the children they are with are gifts from God entrusted to their care. When parents present children to be baptized they consent to receiving these gifts, acknowledging the adoptive element inherent in their role. Baptism is a public act, conducted in the church's public space, in which parents declare certain pledges regarding their rearing of children. Hauerwas is correct in asserting that 'if being a parent is first of all an office of a community, rather than a description of a biological process, even those without immediate children still have "parental responsibilities"'.[6] The principal tasks of the presenting parents is to provide a place of mutual and timely belonging, in turn intimating a more expansive belonging in the fullness of time. In baptism, parents also entrust the children they are with back to the care of God.[7] Although a familial lineage serves to situate humans within creation it has no redemptive import, for as Augustine recognized, it is one's second, as opposed to first, birth that seals fellowship with God. Baptism acknowledges divine 'regeneration' rather than confirming parental 'generation'.[8] Although we may speak of a 'lineage of faith' which situates believers in the unfolding history of creation's salvation, it is transmitted, contrary to Bushnell, through the ministry and sacraments of the church, not the 'godly

---

[6] Stanley Hauerwas, *Suffering Presence* (1986), 149.

[7] See Brent Waters, 'Welcoming Children into our Homes', *Scottish Journal of Theology*, 55/4 (2002).

[8] See Augustine, *Marriage and Concupiscence* 1. 15, pp. 269–70.

seed' of the faithful. What occurs at the baptismal font extends back into the family, reinforcing a sense of sojourning within a vindicated creation being drawn towards its appointed end in Christ.

The Eucharist also accentuates the pivotal, though provisional, character of familial belonging. When a family receives the sacrament they do so as members of the body of Christ. They approach the Lord's Table not as wife and husband, mother and father, daughter and son, but as sisters and brothers in Christ. Their familial roles are decentred in sharing this eschatological meal. What transpires is again extended back into the family, assisting an unfolding of the spousal, parental, filial, and fraternal forms of love into an enfolding and more expansive familial love. The most vivid allusion is the family meal, where the Lord's Table is intimated in the household's table. The proper preparation and serving of a meal requires that a family gather at an appointed hour, cooperatively giving and receiving commands in accordance with their respective roles. When the meal is under way these roles do not disappear but become blurred, for they dine together *as a family*. The purpose of such dining is not merely to consume food, but to enable fellowship; it is a focal thing facilitating cooperation and mutuality. According to Borgmann, the Latin *focus* means 'hearth'. In ancient households the hearth was the family's central focal point where it gathered for warmth, meals, and fellowship, and its maintenance required cooperation among the members of a household.[9] A family meal is a particular focal thing, entailing corresponding focal practices. Family dining has an 'order and discipline that challenges and ennobles the participants. The great meal has its structure. It begins with a moment of reflection in which we place ourselves in the presence of the first and last things.'[10] The distinct, but cooperative, focal practices required for preparing and eating a meal also enable a larger table fellowship, enriching the life of a family.

Moreover, such dining discloses the family as an association that is greater than the sum of its parts, so it is not coincidental that extending hospitality to strangers often occurs at a household table. Again as Borgmann notes:

[9] See Albert Borgmann, *Technology and the Character of Contemporary Life* (1984), 196–7.
[10] Ibid. 205.

Especially when we are guests, much of the meal's deeper context is socially and conversationally mediated. But that mediation has translucence and intelligibility because it extends into the farther and deeper recesses without break and with a bodily immediacy that we too have enacted or at least witnessed firsthand. And what seems to be a mere receiving and consuming of food is in fact the enactment of generosity and gratitude, the affirmation of mutual and perhaps religious obligations.[11]

As Borgmann contends, for Christians, it is not a long step from the fellowship of the household table to that of the Lord's Table.[12] The significance of family dining should not be overestimated, but nor should it be underestimated, for as a focal point it serves as a modest reminder that the church's eschatological witness is not cut off from its providential antecedents, for they too anticipate the fellowship and communion of Christ's new creation.

Although the sacramental inlays of baptism and Eucharist link the family and church together, they also heighten the tension between them. For many Christians, birth and baptism have become too closely associated with their respective emphases on such similar themes as the beginning of a new life and promise of ongoing care. Yet they remain, properly, distinguishable events. Birth has an unconditional character. Despite the best family planning, birth retains a given and indeterminate character. Birth is a providential sign of hope in an unfulfilled eschatological promise. According to Hauerwas, for example, 'having children must be placed in the context of some very substantive claims about the nature of the world and God's relation to it'.[13] Given the sinful condition of the world, children embody a faith that 'hope is stronger than despair'. There is an integral relation between redemption, providence, and eschatological fulfilment symbolized in childbirth.

Through our obligation to have children Christians are bound in time as they form communities that make clear their conviction that God is working in the world to form a kingdom of peace and justice. Thus our commitment, indeed obligation to have children is our pledge that our salvation is not ahistorical but takes place through the contingencies of history.[14]

---

[11] Ibid. 205.   [12] See Albert Borgmann, *Power Failure* (2003), 125–6.
[13] Hauerwas, *Suffering Presence*, 147.   [14] Ibid. 148.

Baptism as an act of faith, however, tempers and redirects the hope embodied by a child, for childbirth *per se* has no salvific significance. It is baptism, not the child to be baptized, that is the proper object of parental hope and expectation; God, not offspring, holds the promise of redemption. In this respect, the second birth of baptism is a judgement on the limits of the first birth.

A similar tension exists between the hospitality of the family meal and the exclusivity of the Eucharist. Extending the hospitality of the household table to strangers denotes that the proper ordering of the family is oriented towards broader spheres of association. A place of timely belonging secures the necessary boundaries for offering a hospitable space, suggesting that household members and strangers belong together in the fullness of time. Familial hospitality is a providential sign of hope in Christ's kingdom when the need for hospitality has come to an end. This is also why the hospitality of the Lord's Table is *not* extended to strangers, because the Eucharist prefigures an eschatological banquet where there are no strangers to exclude, for all are one in Christ.

The heightened tensions resulting from the sacramental inlays emphasize, along with Augustine and Baxter, the superiority of the church over the family, without attempting to shape the latter in the image of the former. Thus, we may say that the family *draws upon and is drawn into the church* in ordering its private and public poles. The family draws upon the church in providing the normative content of its particular vocations, virtues, and practices that are foundational to the ordering of its inherent affinities. The resulting structure is not patriarchal or paternalistic lordship, but loving and mutual service in obedience to Christ. Familial privacy is thereby ordered to a redemptive and unconditional love that is reciprocal, sympathetic, and forgiving, in character. In being drawn into the church, the family acknowledges that its privacy is not synonymous with isolation, or the autonomy of its individual members. The internal *and* external ordering of the family is always relational, for the family is one *social* sphere among the many constituting civil society. In drawing upon and being drawn into the church, the family finds its timely belonging in the providential ordering of a vindicated creation, as well as its ultimate belonging in the fullness of time.

These sacramental inlays also imply how drawing upon and being drawn into the church help demarcate the family's private and public dimensions. Familial privacy entails unconditional qualities derived by birth, whereas its public ordering emphasizes the opening of familial affinity to strangers. These providential tasks, however, are tempered by the eschatological signs of the sacraments. Baptism, for instance, serves as a reminder that parenthood is a trusteeship, and the Eucharist stresses the need for given boundaries if the family is to extend hospitality to strangers. The private and public ordering of the family are mutually dependent tasks, one defining and enriching the other. This is why the church is not a family, nor the family a church, because confusing their witness distorts the family's private and public poles. For example, if children were baptized into a family or familial hospitality was withheld from strangers, the resulting 'family' would be something other than a timely place of belonging. The privacy of unconditional belonging would become a public act of judging who qualifies for membership, and a household would turn in upon itself in the name eschatological exclusivity. In exchanging the direct providential witness borne by the family for the indirect eschatological witness it intimates, the very understanding of what constitutes the family's private and public poles is transposed, disfiguring its normative structure.

A creative tension needs to be maintained between these poles if the family is to bear faithfully its providential witness; one which simultaneously embodies the affirmation of *and* judgement upon the inherent limitations of its affinities. To maintain this tension, the family requires the *complementary yet contrasting witness of singleness*. Singleness affirms the family, because it is a vocation that is not structured or oriented towards its own perpetuation. Every single person comes from a family, affirming its temporal ordering of a vindicated creation. Given its dependence on the family, Augustine and John Paul II are correct in condemning any spiritual pride that might accompany celibacy or virginity. Singleness, however, also embodies a judgement against the limitations of familial affinities, and the incomplete nature of its association as a sovereign sphere. Although the core of familial love and belonging is the seed of creation's providential ordering over time, its *telos* is eschatological communion with Christ. Without the witness of singleness the family becomes an end in itself, diminishing its destiny to a lineage rather than the transformation of its roles and relationships. The new creation, contrary to Bushnell, will not be the outcome of superior breeding, so that singleness negates the pretentious claim that genetic inheritance holds any redemptive significance. Clapp is thereby correct in emphasizing the vocational equality of singleness and marriage, for neither bears a complete witness in their own right. In the absence of any tension between them, these two mutually exclusive ways of life cannot disclose, by way of contrast, both the structure *and* end of creation's temporal ordering. Without this tension singleness is either reduced to an anomaly or elevated to an ideal autonomy, resulting in the rather odd caricature of singles as merely persons who are not presently married, or marriage as a contract between two single persons.

In addition, the family requires the complementary and contrasting witness of singleness to affirm the *familiarity* of timely belonging, while also acknowledging the *unfamiliar* destiny towards which it is being drawn; a destiny in which the limitations of all temporal associations are displaced by an eternal mode of being. This tension is amplified in the familial and ecclesial spheres where what is familiar and unfamiliar are contextually reinterpreted. At the household table, for example, it is the familial roles that are familiar, while sisterhood and brotherhood in Christ appear out of place, whereas at the Lord's Table it is the former relationships that seem strange in comparison to the latter. It would be odd if while dining as a family a father and daughter regarded each other as sister and brother, yet this is precisely the relationship they share at the Lord's Table. It is in the tension present in these two contexts that the family and singleness *together* bear a complete witness to God's providential ordering of creation towards its eschatological end. In short, the vocational and contrasting witness of singleness helps safeguard the nature of marriage in order that it might evoke a familial history.

Late liberalism has largely rejected the premise that there is any nature to safeguard or history to evoke. Rather, the former is a barrier to be overcome, or a resource to be exploited, in constructing the latter through wilful force. Yet it is precisely these categories that must be recovered if Christian social and political discourse is to be offered as an alternative to that of late liberalism. Before I sketch out what the rudiments of such an alternative form of discourse might entail—in the next chapter—the relationship between the church and the family requires further scrutiny and clarity.

THE CHURCH IS NOT A FAMILY

Although the vocations, virtues, and practices pertaining to the family are blessed and upheld by the church, none of the familial roles are an ecclesial office, nor is the family *per se* a peculiarly Christian institution. The church's eschatological space supplants a place of timely belonging, drawing family members towards where they belong in the fullness of time. The new creation, prefigured imperfectly in the church, marks a new ordering of relationships in Christ instead of a heavenly family reunion. In this respect, the church satisfies the family's natural orientation towards broader association without negating the structuring of its particular affinities.

Maurice recognized that the family cannot sustain itself in isolation from other spheres of human association, and thereby has a natural longing for larger spheres of human association. He proposes that the church as universal family is the satisfaction of this desire. But in doing so he commits three crucial errors. First, he fails to preserve the particularity of familial bonds which he purportedly wants to use as the bedrock of his proposal. The fact that every person is born within a given network of relationships provides the basis for a universal social and political order; all are ultimately sisters and brothers. Consequently, the family and the church are simply smaller and larger versions of a common familial and civil order. Yet if this is the case it is difficult to see why particular spousal, parental, and filial bonds are of any importance since everyone is already a sibling to everyone else in the universal family. Moreover, collapsing the social and political order into a universal family effectively removes strangers against whom particular families differentiate and define themselves.

Second, portraying the church as universal family effectively removes its eschatological witness. The church points to itself as satisfying the desire for greater affinity and association. It may be objected that Maurice is cognizant of the fact that universal association is not yet complete, thereby preserving an eschatological expectation of its completion. In the meantime the church points towards a time of universal familial belonging. Such expectation, however, is arguably not a Christian hope. Christians hope for a reign in the fullness of time that transforms and negates the church and family as institutions belonging to a temporal, but not, eternal realm. Hence, the complete and necessary absence of singleness in Maurice's universal family/church, for such a vocation has no witness to bear. Christians properly place their hope in Christ's kingdom, not his church or family.

Third, Maurice contends that the church as universal family is needed to resist evil pretensions and tendencies towards universal empire. In this respect, he is correctly asserting the principle that the social must resist being subsumed into the political. But in portraying the church as a family rather than a society, it can only resist but never govern. Perhaps unwittingly, Maurice transforms the church into a sectarian enclave through its very attempt at becoming *the* universal social order, for by definition virtually *any* regime outside the universal family is an imperial pretension that should be resisted. The church/family becomes a kind of haven in a heartless political world, isolated and unrelated to any social sphere beyond itself. The price of this isolation, however, is dear for it means that the church has little, if any, constructive role to play in broader arenas of civil ordering, a curious consequence since creation's destiny is God's city, again not his church or family.

Maurice's intuition that strong social bonds, such as those provided by the family, offer the best bulwark against imperial pretensions is certainly correct.[15] Yet in transforming the church into the universal family as the foundation of social interaction, he fails to take into account the historical process of social differentiation which the family has inspired. Maurice thereby fails to recognize that the universal familial loyalty he is championing can become every bit as totalizing and tyrannous as the imperial pretensions he

---

[15] A similar observation is made by Bertrand Russell, *Marriage and Morals* (1929), 162–74.

wishes to obliterate. He simply offers no insight into how social exchange should be conducted by individuals who do not share the kind of expansive familial bonds he imagines. What remains unaddressed is how the social and political lives of individuals should be properly governed when they are seemingly linked by few, if any, common natural or historical affinities.

Critical familism is presumably in a better position to address this question, given its greater comfort with late liberal principles of social and political ordering. As Browning and his co-authors demonstrate, the family is a complex association which various descriptions and depictions lend important, but only partial, information. They take for granted the context of a differentiated society that Maurice ignores. They also demonstrate how historic Christian teaching on the family may be applied to contemporary circumstances in a more salutary manner. The family can be affirmed, for example, without recourse to patriarchal structures as seen in their engagement with feminist, therapeutic, and economic voices. More importantly, their proposed theological framework comprised of elements of Thomistic categories, the principle of subsidiarity, and orders of creation offer a potentially fruitful entrance into the arena of public moral discourse. The relation between the family and the church, as well as the state, should be mediated by a robust civil society comprised of various social spheres. Encountering strangers is, therefore, not only inevitable but necessary, so there is no need to pursue forms of interaction and exchange which presuppose familiarity. The family need not be absorbed into the church as a larger version of itself. Rather, the two need to be in critical dialogue, especially in regard to an internal ordering of the family that is compatible with both Christian faith and the late liberal context in which that faith is lived.

Yet for all its promise, critical familism fails to make a convincing case, particularly in respect to its underlying 'practical theology'. The failure is perhaps a strategic one, for Browning and his co-authors derive their chief concepts from a confessional stance that they then translate and explicate in a mode of moral discourse that is admissible to the public arena. Once this move is made, they claim, then a thicker moral account of marriage and family can be added. The opposite seems to have occurred. Critical familism is more an attempt to reformulate a Christian understanding of marriage and family in the light of a dominant late liberal ethos than to cast a light of faith upon it. In accepting the primacy of autonomous persons, as both the object and interlocutors of public discourse, an account of the family is offered that is fashioned in the image of late liberal ideology, covered with a thin veneer of covenantal rhetoric.

This is seen in a steadfast refusal to assign any *inherent* value to sacrificial love. Admittedly, an occasional sacrifice is permissible if required to restore mutuality. But if a sacrificial act is merely a restorative method, then it is also effectively reduced to a means of self-fulfilment. Hence the high degree of confidence placed in therapeutic techniques and public policies for assisting family members *as individuals* to negotiate their intersubjective relationships. Such confidence is misplaced, however, for as Lasch makes clear, they draw on the sources which have weakened the very familial bonds they purportedly wish to strengthen. Rather, it is by placing mutuality within the larger context of a familial love that is equipped for sacrifice, that care and affection are naturally extended to those who cannot contribute to one's self-fulfilment. The family is not so much a place for applying negotiating skills as practising the sacrificial virtues that give love its greatest breadth and depth. It is telling that the authors have nothing to say about how a family is empowered to love one of its members with whom no mutuality can possibly be established or restored. There are tragic circumstances when the *only* method of expressing marital fidelity, parental affection, or filial love is through self-sacrifice.

Moreover, contrary to the assertion that a healthy self-regard promotes mutuality, it again appears that the reverse is the case; mutuality is reduced to a means of expressing and strengthening a primary regard for oneself. The family is good because it helps its members achieve, respectively, their full potential as persons. Despite frequent allusions to equal regard, the family is little more than a collection of individuals pursuing reciprocal relationships, instead of an association in its own nature and right. There are few, if any, images of the family as a community greater than the sum of its parts. The good of a family is the composite of individual goods comprising it, so mutuality is valued to the extent that it promotes the wellbeing of those sharing various familial relationships. This is seen in basing a familial covenant on empathy in which family members come to value the 'ultimate worth' of each other's personal stories. But this means that nothing can be said about how the narrative identities of two spouses may become the single story of a marriage, or how the narrative identity of a family becomes the personal stories of parents and children, or how a familial narrative becomes enfolded into God's story of a vindicated creation. Although Browning and his co-authors contend rightly that the good of the family must be subordinate to the common good, they invoke a diminished understanding of the common good as a refraction of the individual goods comprising it, instead of a *telos* transcending them.

It is not surprising, then, that no mention is made of any witness that the family is called by God to bear, for it discloses nothing greater than itself. The family tells us nothing about the providential unfolding of a vindicated creation, for it is a covenant confined to the restricted purpose of enabling the respective self-fulfilment of its parties. Thus there is no calling to extend hospitality to strangers, for they have nothing to contribute to how a family negotiates its democratized relationships. In this respect, critical familism lacks a realistic concept of the differences between children and adults, levelling a relationship that should be functionally hierarchical. Although a democratized marriage is intelligible, extending the principle to the parent–child relationship begs the question: must children be treated as consenting adults before they may voluntarily undertake the task of being children? Nor in this scheme does the church bear an eschatological witness to creation's destiny, for in relation to the family it is one among many agencies assisting individuals in learning the requisite skills for constructing their respective narrative identities. Unlike in Maurice, the church is not a universal family, but a family-aid agency. Consequently, singleness can neither affirm nor judge the family, for it is an irrelevant consideration, except in those circumstances when a single parent requires assistance.

If the family is little more than the aggregate of its members, however, then the only available avenue for promoting the family in the public arena of late liberal society is to assert the substantial evidence that when it is diminished children tend to suffer. In this respect, the church also serves as a child advocacy group. But in distilling Christian principles to a plea for better childcare, we encounter not so much a common ground as an empty space, begging to be filled by substantive theological and moral discourse. It is again telling that no mention is made of the Eucharist, for by way of contrast it has nothing to disclose about how the family and the church should be related in pursuing their distinct, though complementary callings. Both may enable, but neither provides, a place of timely belonging intimating a belonging in the fullness of time. Both may only point to the narrative identities of the individuals comprising their respective and overlapping stories. A critical dialogue could help restore a proper tension between the family's providential witness and the church's eschatological witness, but such a task cannot be undertaken when interlocutors dissolve into a sea of autonomous persons seeking their fulfilment.

THE FAMILY IS NOT A CHURCH

Although a particular familial covenant of mutual love and fidelity is an evangelical witness, it is not as such a church. The ordering of familial affinities is not synonymous with the order of Christ's household of faith. The family's evangelical witness underscores its implicit eschatological objective, for it is borne by sisters and brothers in Christ, rather than embodied in familial roles and relationships. The timely nature of familial belonging also discloses that it is not the place we belong in the fullness of time. The family is not an end in itself, but a provisional and providential sign of hope in that day when the temporal and pluriform ordering of its affinities is transformed by the eternal and uniform order of Christ's reign. If the church is not a foretaste of a heavenly family reunion, then neither is the family a heaven on earth.

The family to be the family needs the church to be the church, creating an inevitable, but productive, tension between the two. John Paul II, in his apostolic exhortation, *Familiaris Consortio*, goes far in restoring this tension. This restoration is seen in his emphasis on the eschatological witness of celibacy, and the family's evangelical witness of offering hospitality to needful strangers. The conjugal core of marriage provides a foundation for a deepening and expansive familial love that is enacted in acts of such hospitality. As a unique association of natural affinities, the family promotes mutual and sacrificial fidelity, while as a community in dialogue with God it is drawn out towards ministries of evangelization and service. Safeguarding the nature of these familial affinities is also a witness to God's redemptive history. Procreation and childrearing, for example, are not the means and outcomes of reproductive projects, but the obedient ordering of marital and parental vocation authorized by God. Within the bonds of its affinities and in its embrace of strangers, the family bears witness to creation's vindicated order, while in relation to vocational singleness it intimates its own transformed destiny in Christ's new creation.

This apostolic exhortation may be characterized as an attempt to ground a theological account of the family in a dynamic relationship between providence and eschatology. Christ's new creation entails a transformation of the old instead of its negation; the new is born out of the old, preserving a degree of continuity. Spousal, parental, and filial relationships will give way to sisterhood and brotherhood in Christ, yet the expansive imagery of this analogy is drawn from a familial origin. It is nevertheless the witness of vocational singleness, not marital and parental callings, that bears the greater witness to the new life in Christ.

The many strengths of this theological framework are weakened, however, by its portrayal of the family as a *domestic church*. According to John Paul II, it is within the family where its members first encounter each other as brothers and sisters in Christ. Through the grace bestowed upon these encounters, 'the Church of the home'[16] is 'grafted' onto Christ's larger household of faith.[17] Consequently, the family is a ' "Church in miniature" (*Ecclesia domestica*)', representing the 'mystery of *the* Church'.[18] These 'small'- and 'large'-scale churches are both signs of 'unity for the world', exercising their prophetic roles in 'bearing witness to the Kingdom and peace of Christ, towards which the whole world is journeying'.[19] Differentiating the family from the church along a degree of scale, however,

---

[16] See John Paul II, *Familiaris Consortio*, 3. 38, p. 75.
[17] Ibid. 3. 49, p. 92.   [18] Ibid. 91 (emphasis added).
[19] Ibid. 3. 48, p. 90.

blunts the tension between them, exposing similar distortions that are present in Bushnell and Maurice.

Similar to Bushnell, the family in the Pope's teaching is a redemptive instrument. Since it is both a saved and saving community, parenthood is a means of bestowing grace upon children and parents. Although there is no hint of propagating godly seed, procreation and childrearing are nonetheless granted a salvific significance. In its evangelism, the family need point no further than itself, for it is a smaller representation of Christ's temporal ministry and creation's destiny. The family is not so much transformed by God's new reign as it is a prototype of Christ's new creation, so the 'Church can and ought to take on a more homelike or family dimension'.[20] It is telling that one's first encounter with sisters and brothers in Christ occurs in the family instead of the liturgical and sacramental life of the sanctuary. Yet this emphasis on the domestic church as point of first encounter is accomplished only at the expense of diminishing the witness of vocational singleness. Since both the family and the church share a common eschatological witness, singleness is reduced to a prerequisite lifestyle that enables a person to devote more time to the larger church. Consequently, singleness cannot, by way of contrast, both affirm *and* temper the providential witness of the family. More importantly, nor can singleness serve as a judgement against the limitations of familial affinities which can only be saved in the fullness of time, and not within the structures of timely belonging.

One result of this diminished eschatological witness is that the church also takes on familial qualities. Similar to in Maurice, Christ is portrayed as the founder of a 'great family', providing a home 'for everyone, especially those who "labour and are heavy laden" '.[21] This imagery presupposes a spiritual affinity that can only be granted by God in the fullness of time, thereby distorting the temporal, or better, secular, mission and ministry of the church. The family, however, is not called to kingly ministry for the sake of recruiting new sisters and brothers into an expanding household, nor is it persuading people to transpose their familial loyalties by becoming Christ's adopted

---

[20] See John Paul II, *Familiaris Consortio*, 3. 64, p. 117.
[21] Ibid. 4. 85, p. 162.

children. Rather, the family pursues a ministry to strangers in obedience to a love that both incorporates and transcends itself, bearing witness to an order of love by those who do the will of Christ's Father. This is why the Lord's Table and the familial table are not larger and smaller versions of a common meal, for the former is restricted to sisters and brothers in Christ, while at the latter hospitality is extended to strangers in Christ's name. Curiously, it is still spouses, parents, and children, rather than sisters and brothers in Christ, who gather at the Lord's Table. Blurring the distinctiveness of the two tables is symptomatic of a more ambitious attempt to ease the tension between family and church, emphasizing an unwarranted continuity between the providential unfolding of creation's history and its eschatological destiny. Yet the price paid is to suggest that the church can offer a surrogate place of timely belonging, while the family may provide a foretaste of belonging in the fullness of time, tasks which neither have been equipped by God to perform. John Paul II purportedly wants to promote a dialogue between God and families, mediated by the church. But similar to critical familism, it is difficult to imagine how such a conversation can be pursued when the mediator and human interlocutor have become fused.

Perhaps by turning to Clapp this dialogue can be rescued, for he too goes a long way in restoring a productive tension between the family and the church. Like Baxter, he subordinates the family to the church by recasting the former as a mission base of hospitality. Strangers remain integral to household ordering, for they embody the beneficiaries of its evangelical witness. His recovery of singleness as an eschatological witness and complementary vocation affirms marital fidelity while also judging its inherent limitations, for the purpose of the family's evangelical mission is to point to a social reality that transcends the natural affinities of kinship. Clapp's otherwise promising account, however, is plagued by two troubling aspects, namely, his portrayals of the church as first family, and children as strangers.

According to Clapp, 'Jesus creates a new family' that 'demands primary allegiance' over the biological family.[22] One's natural bonds should be forsaken in order to be adopted into God's family. A second

---

[22] See Rodney Clapp, *Families at the Crossroads* (1993), 77.

birth in which familial relationships are radically reconfigured is
needed, because Jesus expects the 'family of the kingdom to grow
evangelistically rather than biologically'.[23] In becoming Jesus' disciple, for instance, Mary 'has a new son, new sisters and brothers', for
those 'who do the will of God are her closest relatives'.[24] Paul
reinforces this familial imagery of the church by portraying conversion as admission into an adoptive family in which believers 'take on
new parents, new sisters and brothers, new names, new identities'.[25]

The church, however, is *not* God's family; it is the eschatological
community bearing witness *to* God's kingdom. The church does not
reconstruct familial relationships, but anticipates their transformation. One's second birth does not procure new parents or offspring,
but only new siblings, for the former roles have no meaning or place
in Christ's new reign. It is not so much that the church as first family
provides a model from which second families derive their meaning,
but that the nature of timely belonging is ordered in accordance with
God's eschatological kingdom. In caricaturing the kingdom as God's
family, Clapp undercuts the very power of the witness of singleness
and familial hospitality he wishes to affirm. If the church is the first
family, then the vocation of singleness does not entail forsaking the
way of marriage and family, but transferring one's familial identity
and loyalty to the church. Yet if this is the case, then singles do not
bear a radical witness to Christ's resurrection, but place their hope in
a spiritual, rather than biological, lineage.

Furthermore, by contending that families derive their intelligibility
from the church as first family, Clapp weakens the theological base for
the family's mission of hospitality. His description of the Eucharist is
revealing in this regard:

The church's central sacrament, the Eucharist, symbolizes a basic domestic
activity—and that is no accident. Biological family recognizes the joyful
need to solidify its union with common meals, and Paul expects the same for
the church when it eats at Eucharist (1 Cor. 11: 17–34). Christians are called
to be hospitable within both the first family of the church and the second, or
biological family... [26]

---

[23] See Clapp, *Families at the Crossroads*, 78.
[24] Ibid. 81.   [25] Ibid. 82.   [26] Ibid. 140.

The Eucharist and a household meal are not identical acts. The Lord's Table is *not* hospitable, for no strangers may be admitted to the eschatological banquet reserved for sisters and brothers in Christ. For Christians, it is a short step from the table fellowship of the familial household to the fellowship of the Lord's Table, but it is nonetheless a gap that needs to be traversed rather than filled in. The resemblances of the two tables suggests that their distinctiveness should be maintained, instead of collapsed, if they are to be mutually informative and revealing. It is the family's embodiment of timely belonging, not its anticipated transformation in the fullness of time, that enables it to extend hospitality to strangers. In virtually collapsing the familial and ecclesial households, Clapp comes perilously close to portraying the kingdom as a heavenly family reunion rather than Christ's new creation. In this respect, he engages in a dangerous move of mixing the familial with the kingdom, creating a hybrid metaphor that is totalitarian in its implications, because no differentiation can be preserved between the social and the political, or the providential and eschatological.

In addition, Clapp contends there is no natural parental instinct. In support of his claim, he cites historical evidence that child abuse and neglect has been more prevalent than affectionate care. Consequently, there is no reason why parents should assume that their 'children are automatically friends' rather than strangers.[27] There are four instances in which the role of children as strangers are disclosed: they are 'aliens' who learn how to live in their parents' world; because parents are estranged from themselves; they are related to God as well as their parents; and parents subsequently 'admit' their dependence and vulnerability. As strangers, children teach their parents about a fundamental alienation, as well as providing a means for overcoming it in the relationship that they form together. Childrearing is 'practice in hospitality, in the welcoming and support of strangers. Welcoming the strangers who are our children, we learn a little about being out of control, about the possibility of surprise (and so of hope), about how strange we ourselves are.'[28]

Although Clapp rightfully emphasizes that children are not parental possessions, and as unique beings they draw parents out

---

[27] Ibid. 140–4. [28] Ibid. 148.

towards more expansive realms of love and hospitality, it is doubtful whether his characterization of children as strangers adequately captures the full theological and moral significance of parenthood. He fails to address the possibility that the parent–child relationship bears witness to a *unique* form of covenant fidelity. Are not these 'strangers' he calls children bound together with their parents in a relationship that cannot be replicated with any other strangers? Parents do not simply will themselves to love a stranger in their midst. They are commanded by God to love the children entrusted to their care *as parents*, entailing a particular relationship which is not shared with friends, neighbours, and strangers. The family is not a company of strangers, but a community based on a core of presumed familiarity (not necessarily friendship) upon which hospitality may be extended to people sharing less natural and historical affinities. In refusing to admit any significance in the biological bond between parent and child, Clapp undercuts the embodied witness of procreation and childrearing he wishes to affirm. And in doing so, he effectively weakens the integral relationship between creation, providence, and eschatology. In short, in stressing the radically transformative power of God's kingdom he fails to acknowledge that Christ has already vindicated creation, so that parents may receive children as gifts to be cared for, instead of guests to be entertained.

The preceding discussions are the culmination of the constructive phase of this inquiry. To recapitulate, the purpose of this constructive task is to embed an essentially Augustinian account of marriage and family in a more fertile social and political setting, a field that has been neglected as symbolized by the loss of strangers and singleness in theological and moral discourse. This constructive reclamation was initiated in Chapter 5 by explicating alternative philosophical, theological, and moral themes. Chapter 6 built upon those themes, portraying the family as a timely place of mutual belonging that bears witness to the historical and providential unfolding of God's vindicated creation. In addition, a case was also made that the family required contact with strangers in order to be drawn out towards larger forms of human association, while at the same time differentiating itself as a sovereign social sphere. In this chapter the differentiation between church and family was examined as an important distinction to be maintained if their respective eschatological and providential witnesses were to retain a proper and revealing tension.

Yet even if this reclamation project has enjoyed any modest success, a crucial question remains: does this account of marriage and family inspire a form of social and political discourse that might serve as an alternative to that offered by late liberalism? This is the question that is addressed in the final chapter.

8

The Family, the Church, and Civil Ordering

This chapter addresses a question that has been anticipated in the preceding ones: does the normative account of the family developed in this book inspire a form of social and political discourse that might serve as an alternative to that offered by late liberalism? I begin answering this question by examining the bonds of human association that embody and enact a series of overlapping affinities. Following this discussion, the gift and task of social ordering is described as an expression of providential patience. This patience is in turn complemented by eschatological expectation which is explicated in an inquiry into the relationship between destiny and the common good. Finally, the challenge of political ordering is taken on by examining what the nations should desire, and how this desire is demonstrated through acts of judgement.

THE BONDS OF HUMAN ASSOCIATION

As was argued in the previous chapter, the relation between the family and the church may be characterized as one that is both *correlated* and *differentiated*. Both bear witness to God, but the former points towards creation's providential unfolding while the latter emphasizes creation's eschatological destiny. Marriage is therefore practised within the familial sphere while singleness is lodged in the ecclesial community. Although family and church are bound together by their complementary witnesses, they are distinct associations in their respective right, and their relation must strive to preserve rather than weaken their appropriate differences. The family cannot be the church, nor should the church endeavour to become a family, if they are to faithfully perform the tasks that God has assigned them to undertake. Parenthood is properly not an ecclesiastical office, nor is singleness *the* normative foundation of parenthood.[1]

The same principle applies to social and political spheres, whose relation also entails differentiation and correlation.[2] Like the family, social and political institutions bear a providential witness. To properly enact this witness, institutions and offices must maintain their distinctiveness in relation to both the family and the church, as well as other social spheres. A Chief Executive Officer of a corporation, for example, is not authorized in virtue of that office to regard her workers as her children, nor does a mother have the authority to treat her children as her employees. Likewise, the office of commander-in-chief has no ecclesiastical standing, and the office of bishop does not authorize its holder to command a nation's armed forces. In addition, the office of director of a corporate board has no political standing, and a magistrate in virtue of his office cannot claim the right to a seat on a corporation's board of directors.[3]

Although the ecclesial, familial, social, and political spheres are properly differentiated with regard to their respective tasks, they are also correlated in their common purpose of ordering the providential unfolding of creation towards its eschatological destiny. The family, for instance, must associate or communicate with economic institutions in order to generate income and satisfy its wants and needs, and economic institutions in turn offer employment and produce goods and services that are consumed by families. The church interacts with government by taking advantage of various services that enable it to perform its ministries, while government should at least not impede

---

[1] Although single persons may, for a variety of reasons, be parents.

[2] For the purpose of this inquiry I adapt Dietrich Bonhoeffer's four mandates: church, marriage, labour, and government (see *Ethics* (1955), 179–83). Rather than marriage I refer to family, and labour is expanded more broadly to economic exchanges and relationships. Cf. D. Stephen Long's categories of *ecclesia, oikos, agora,* and *polis* (*The Goodness of God* (2001), 155–299).

[3] Provided we are not dealing with a hybrid entity that is owned by both the government and private shareholders.

the church's charitable work. Corporations depend upon government to provide police protection and enforce legal contracts, while government in turn needs corporations or other business ventures to generate employment and tax revenue.

Such correlation and differentiation are needed to define and perform the roles and tasks appropriate to each sphere. In this respect, social and political associations bear with the family a providential witness that is distinct from but also complementary to the church's eschatological witness. This witnessing, however, does not point towards abstract ideals, but is embodied in particular acts and practices. It is through these acts and practices that humans participate and communicate in a series of distinct but related associations that bind them together. Moreover, these associations are formed and maintained within what may be characterized as a specific *space, time, and location,* and this characterization may be further elaborated by examining three corresponding relationships.

First, the relation between the *finite* and *infinite* creates a space for human association. Finitude, as a prominent feature of human life, is unintelligible in the absence of the infinite, for the latter defines the former. It is simply false to claim that human life entails infinite possibilities. Humans, for example, cannot be or become amoebas. The same limitation applies to the possibilities of human association, for the roles and relationships inherent within each association are defined largely by foreclosing the possibility of other roles and relationships. In this respect, the church bears witness to the infinite life of the triune God, but it does not point to itself as the embodiment of that infinite life. Consequently, the church itself does not exhaust the possibilities of human association, and indeed cannot, since it is part of a finite creation. It is precisely because of the object of the church's witness that no single sphere may properly claim to embody all possibilities of association, or command an exclusive loyalty. To insist that ecclesial, familial, economic, or political association is *the* only genuine one, and all others are false, or misleading distractions, is to deny the vindication of created order. Each of these associations can, and does, make false claims upon our attention and loyalty, but this does not negate the validity of their proper tasks of exercising dominion over creation as established by God in Christ.

Second, the relation between the *temporal* and the *eternal* creates a time for human association. Eternity enframes temporality, and without this framing the forms of human association could not provide a place of timely belonging, or intimate a belonging in the fullness of time. In this respect, the witness of all associations is properly secular,[4] for none can point to itself as the *telos* of its witness; none embody their own destiny. In bearing its eschatological witness, for instance, the church does not refer to itself but to creation's destiny in Christ. There is no cathedral in the New Jerusalem, for none is needed. All ecclesial, familial, economic, and political associations must expect their own demise in the fullness of time, for creation's destiny is not an eternal church, family, market, or nation-state. This expectation does not diminish the significance of the temporal, but brackets it so that humans can faithfully and properly perform their calling to stewardship. Any attempt to displace the eternal as creation's *telos* with the temporal is to deny creation's redemption by and for Christ.

Third, the relation between the *penultimate* and the *ultimate* creates the location of human association. It is God's act of grace in the Incarnation that is the final act; it is the final, eternal, and singular Word which orders and consummates the provisional, temporal, and discordant words preceding it. Consequently, it is the ultimate which authorizes the penultimate by imposing limits on what is and what is not within the given venue of a particular sphere. Or in Bonhoeffer's words, the 'penultimate... does not determine the ultimate; it is the ultimate which determines the penultimate'.[5] Every association is located in the penultimate, for the acts each is authorized to perform have no ultimate import except in their transformation in creation's redemption in the fullness of time. This does not diminish the importance of penultimate acts, but makes them effectual by defining and delimiting their scope. Penultimate acts may prove to be ill-judged or simply wrong, but this does not invalidate both the need and authority to act as demanded by penultimate locations of

---

[4] See Bernd Wannenwetsch, *Political Worship* (2004), 251–5, and Oliver O'Donovan, *The Desire of the Nations* (1996), 246–7; cf. John Milbank, *Theology and Social Theory* (1990), 9.

[5] Bonhoeffer, *Ethics*, 110–11.

authority. In this respect, the church bears witness to the ultimate, but its acts are not thereby granted an ultimate authority. A church council may prohibit the ordination of women, but it cannot forbid them entrance into the kingdom of God. Likewise, a parent may disown a child, and an employer may dismiss an employee, but neither act has any bearing on who is included or excluded from Christ's fellowship. A magistrate may pronounce a verdict against a criminal, but the pronouncement has no standing in the New Jerusalem. Any attempt to claim ultimacy for penultimate acts is to deny Christ's lordship over the creation he has vindicated and redeemed.

A series of what may be designated as *affinities* shapes the specific texture of the space, time, and location of human associations. If these affinities are removed or weakened, an association loses its particularity and normative grounding, for the correlation and differentiation that defines and delimits an association is rendered, at least functionally, inoperative. Any association is admittedly a social or political construct. But it is constructed in accordance with a particular tradition and *telos* that is inherent to its nature and history. Otherwise the construct becomes an abstraction that has little real or practical import, for it can neither define nor delimit because it cannot sufficiently correlate *and* differentiate. To speak of ecclesial, familial, social, and political associations in general helps us to correlate or classify similar types, and to differentiate typologies; a church, for instance, is not a family. But such generalizations tend to obscure important differences within each classification. To identify these differences we must speak, for example, about such particular associations as the Church of England, the Smith family, Royal Bank of Scotland, or the British Parliament. Such discourse requires an ascription of the affinities of tradition and aspirations embodied in these concrete expressions, respectively of ecclesial, familial, social, and political association. And such ascriptive discourse in turn enables us to both differentiate and correlate *within* each form of association. The Church of England is not the Church of Scotland, but they share the affinity of Christian mission and ministry. The Smith family is not the Wong family, but they hold in common the affinity of childrearing. The Royal Bank of Scotland is not the

Bank of America, but both lend and invest capital. The British Parliament is not the United States Congress, but they share the affinity to legislate. These ascribed affinities permit a form of normative assessment that honours both general and particular qualities which are often assumed to be incompatible. We need not run roughshod over particular histories and customs in articulating universal goods, nor must we invoke relativism to protect particularity. Rather, criteria can be employed that enable an assessment of an act, or proposed act, in respect to the affinities that are inherent to a form of human association, and that are also applicable to the particular expressions of those affinities within different cultures and civil communities.

Let us suppose, for example, that Parliament and Congress are both debating proposed legislation that would either permit or forbid same-sex marriage. The proposals may be debated both in terms of moral claims regarding what constitutes marriage, and to what extent government has the authority to amend traditional custom and practice within its jurisdiction. The end result may very well be the enactment of diametrically opposed laws—one permitting, the other forbidding—given their particular legislative traditions and sentiments of their respective citizens. In this respect, we may say that inherent affinities enable a form of moral discourse that allows us to make, assess, and amend certain normative claims about the nature of human association that take into account the pluriform expression and ordering of the space, time, and location of particular associations in their historical unfolding. With the preceding discussion in mind, here are five affinities that are especially pertinent to this inquiry.

First, we may speak of an affinity that is *created*. Humans are part of a creation, and as creatures seek fellowship with their creator. This fellowship is made possible through the incarnation which mediates the gulf separating the finite from the infinite, and the temporal from the eternal. Moreover, in his resurrection from the dead, Christ has given humans the *freedom of a vindicated order*. All other affinities, and the freedoms they offer, are derived from this creational affinity. In the absence of order there can be no freedom, and in the absence of freedom there can be no fellowship with God, for humans cannot be the creatures God created them to be when they resist conforming themselves to creation's order. Such resistance debases created

affinity into fabricated relationships that enslave rather than liber-
ate, for they displace a common quest for fellowship with God with
assertions of personal power instead of performing acts which
promote fellowship. Bishops, for instance, may use their power of
appointment to reward cronies and punish critics. Parents might
stoop to ridicule in silencing precocious children. Supervisors may
bully employees to gain larger bonuses by surpassing productivity
goals. Police officers might beat criminals to extract a confession. In
each of these instances there is admittedly a semblance of authorized acts, for each of these roles must have the power to exercise
discipline, and coercive force in the case of policing, in establishing
an orderly freedom within their respective spheres. The issue at
stake, then, is not power *per se*—for power is simply the capability
to accomplish something[6]—but the purpose to which it is
employed. In each of these instances individuals are called to use
the power of their respective offices to maintain peace and concord
within ecclesial, familial, and civil communities, because it is in a
peaceable and concordant order that humans are free to receive the
gifts of the Spirit, and practise their associated virtues. When
bishops, parents, supervisors, and constables assert a power which
merely compels the kind of behaviour they prefer, it abuses the
authority of the offices they represent, for within the vindicated
order of creation the bonds of human association are those which
unify in love and freedom, rather than divide through threat and
intimidation. It is in the freedom of created order that the space
and location enabling the created affinity for fellowship unfolds
over time.

Although this created affinity for fellowship with the creator binds
humans together, they also share what may be described as a *natural*
affinity for *association*. As the Christian theological tradition has
recognized and affirmed, humans are by nature social creatures.[7] As
humans are drawn towards greater fellowship with their creator, so
too are they drawn towards one another. Humans cannot be human
in isolation from each other, for they must cooperate in order to

---

[6] See Oliver O'Donovan, *The Ways of Judgment* (2005), 130.

[7] It is also a belief, based on similar theological presuppositions, shared by such
early liberal theorists as Althusius and Grotius.

perpetuate themselves. It is in this need and desire for association that humans find their *freedom in relationship*, for in the absence of being related humans are not free to be human, but remain enslaved to the basest demands of natural necessity.[8] This freedom is seen most prominently in the procreation and education of children, for these closely related acts are not solely responses to the species instinct for survival, but are also divinely ordained ways for humans to obey God's command to assert their dominion over creation. It is, at least partly, through ordering the cooperative tasks of procreation and childrearing that humans are free to be God's stewards of creation. The differentiated spheres comprising creation recognize and support these tasks in a variety of ways. Through marriage, for instance, the church validates that a woman and man have become one-flesh, and in baptism it pledges its support of parents in performing their parental duties. In publicly declaring their mutual support and fidelity, a couple also avows their dependence upon and responsibility to broader spheres of association in following their marital and parental callings. Employment opportunities, markets, and financial institutions provide a network of economic exchanges that enable parents to meet the material needs of their children. Government supports parents through the provision of schools, healthcare, and taxation policies. The overlapping qualities of the various associations that are related to procreation and childrearing are paradigmatic of the natural affinities binding humans together: no one participating in the ecclesial, social, and political spheres can be said to be isolated from any contact with or dependence upon the familial sphere. Through this freedom gained by being related, a space, time, and location are created that satisfy the natural need and desire for association.

The members of an association, however, are not free to form and maintain their relationships in any manner they please, nor are they necessarily at liberty to include and exclude whom they will. Rather, the spaces, times, and locations of particular associations are, more often than not, given, and the people with whom one is associated are often not of one's choosing. The created and natural affinities which bind humans together require corporate and cooperative structures if

---

[8] See Karl Barth, *Church Dogmatics* (1961), iii/4. 116–323.

they are to be properly enacted, requiring in turn relationships that are involuntary in character. Consequently, we must speak about *imposed affinities* that *define the freedom* of particular associations. A bishop, for example, may impose an unpopular priest upon a wary parish. A parent may restrict the activities and movements of an unruly teenager. A corporate manager may transfer a disagreeable, but otherwise competent, employee to a different city. A government may conscript unwilling citizens into the military. Impositions that define freedom, however, are not arbitrary acts of force or compulsion, but stem from the authority that is germane to a particular association, and exercised by the appropriate office. Bishops have the authority to appoint priests irrespective of their personal preferences or those of the parish. Likewise, parents have the authority to restrict the activities of their children, managers to transfer employees, and governments to impose conscription, and the wishes of children, employees, and conscripts may at times prove irrelevant in exercising such authority. This does not suggest that those in authority always exercise good judgement, only that in virtue of their respective offices they may impose certain commands upon those who are properly under their authority. Moreover, although an office authorizes certain types of impositions, the authority of the office also limits what its holder can command or forbid given the affinities which bind an association together. Bishops are not authorized to appoint priests to parishes outside their jurisdiction. Parents do not have the authority to abuse or abandon raucous adolescents. Managers cannot transfer unlikable employees to other corporations. Governments may not conscript citizens to serve in the armies of other nations. Again, this does not imply that the kinds of acts, or similar ones, noted above have not or could not be performed, but they would serve to exemplify abusing, rather than exercising, proper authority by failing to honour the limits inherent to an association's office. It is in honouring both the assertion *and* limits of authority that the space, time, and location demarcated by the imposed affinities of an association define, rather than eviscerate, freedom as something more than a mere gesture of power. It is only in embracing an office's power *and* its restraints that bishops are free to be bishops, parents are free to be parents, managers are free to be managers, and governments are freed to govern. And in this embrace, priests are freed to be priests, children are freed to be children, employees are freed to be employees, and citizens are freed to be governed, for they are thereby given the space, time, and location that, by respecting the authority and limits of imposed affinities, define the freedom of their respective associations.

Although the imposed affinities of particular associations define freedom, their expression is not self-contained. There are not four different species of freedoms corresponding to the ecclesial, familial, social, and political spheres that are isolated from each other. Rather, given humankind's social nature, we may also speak of an affinity towards broader forms of association which constrain how the freedom defined is thereby expressed. Consequently, we must also speak about how *social affinities constrain the expression of freedom*. Civil society may be said to be comprised of social spheres within which various associations are established and maintained. Over time, the interactions of these associations form a history and tradition that is formative for a particular society or culture. The customs and practices derived from this formative tradition set certain expectations and limits for how the offices within the various associations exercise their authority. Bishops, parents, managers, and government officials, for instance, do not create their roles *ex nihilo* or as abstractions, but inherit customs and expectations that serve to constrain their acts and commands. Contrary to Kant and Rawls, we cannot order society by transcending actual social histories and associations. These constraints, however, do not ensure that particular acts are necessarily good or just. Some churches, for example, forbid the ordination of women. A number of societies permit individuals to purchase sperm, eggs, and the services of surrogates to obtain a baby. Many managers are forbidden from hiring children to work in factories. Some regimes permit (or at least tolerate) seizing private property for public use. The issue at stake in each of these instances is not to determine whether or not they embody good or just practices, but to illustrate that other social spheres impinge upon or constrain the internal ordering of each particular sphere. Forbidding the ordination of women may reflect cultural perceptions regarding their role and status. Permitting the purchasing of reproductive services or forbidding the employment of children may incorporate, respectively, the value placed on free or regulated markets. Permitting seizure of private property may embody a tradition of the state promoting the common good. To what extent each of these practices serves to strengthen or weaken the respective ecclesial, familial, economic, and political spheres is properly a subject of moral and political debate, but these are debates that cannot be conducted in isolation from broader strands of social affinities. Any attempt to determine whether or not it is good to ordain women, regulate assisted reproduction, forbid child labour, or seize private property as isolated and unrelated issues is simply to ignore the complex and overlapping spheres of a created and vindicated order.

Moreover, each of these instances helps us to account for variation and change over time; two factors which are problematic only if we fail to acknowledge the pluriform and differentiated character of a vindicated created order. Differing and changing expectations and mores influence, for good or ill, practices within the various spheres. Some churches have always ordained women, while others which once forbade now permit this. Some societies have always regulated assisted reproduction, while others which once permitted virtually unrestricted access now impose strict limitations. Some corporations employ children (or are supplied by businesses employing children), while others which once did no longer do so. Some governments have always forbidden, or greatly restricted, the seizure of private property, while others that once forbade now seize aggressively. Again, the issue at stake is not to determine which of these various options is right or wrong, or judge whether changes in practice over time are progressive or regressive. Rather, these instances serve as a reminder that such variability and change is necessarily a salient feature of ordering a temporal and finite creation. Consequently, the ordering of social affinities is also comprised of a series of proximate, provisional, and constrained judgements which are subject to review, repentance, and amendment. Any presumption that these judgements can be somehow final is to move beyond a penultimate boundary and enter a realm of ultimacy that belongs only to God as the final judge. This does not imply, however, that such penultimate judgement is relativistic, but that in acknowledging the deficient and tentative nature of such judgement we express the freedom that is granted through constraint. This is why moral deliberation does not begin with form, but rather, is the deliberative and provisional end point. We do not begin such deliberation with a priori convictions that it is either right or wrong to ordain women, use reproductive technology, employ children, or seize private property, for such prior convictions mean one has already passed an ultimate judgement. To use an end point as starting point is to bypass the very constraints which make the expression of freedom possible, for it is only through such constraints that we are freed to create the space, time, and location in which penultimate ecclesial, familial, social, and political structures may be established to order the finite and temporal affinities of human association.

Since freedom is expressed within social constraints, then we must also speak about the power to order human associations in ways which both protect their internal goods and promote the common good. Consequently, we may also speak about a *political affinity* which binds a civil community together in *obedient freedom*. In the absence of lawful government, humans are not free to participate in the differentiated spheres and associations made possible by Christ's vindication of created order. Government is thereby the body authorized by God to perform acts of judgement,[9] which members of a civil community are called to freely obey, for freedom is the direct correlate of authority.[10] Most importantly, government has been granted this authority to judge, because it has already been subjected to the rule of Jesus Christ; all governments assert their authority because they are first under authority. If a particular regime lacks or ignores such limited authority the judgements it enacts are arbitrary, destroying, rather than enabling, the freedom of its citizens. According to O'Donovan, 'judgment is *an act of moral discrimination that pronounces upon a preceding act or existing state of affairs to establish a new public context*'.[11] Such judgement entails discriminating acts that separate right from wrong, and through legislative, judicial, and executive pronouncements, government creates a public space in which human associations may conduct their affairs in an orderly and peaceful manner. If these judgements are to be effectual, however, then government must have the power to assert its authority. Such power is neither mysterious nor nefarious, but is simply the practical ability to get things done.

---

[9] See Rom. 13; see also O'Donovan, *Ways of Judgment*.
[10] See Oliver O'Donovan, *Resurrection and Moral Order* (1986), 122.
[11] O'Donovan, *Ways of Judgment*, 7 (emphasis original).

In short, there is nothing inherently wrong or evil with possessing power, so long as it is asserted within the constraints of properly delineated authority. Congress, for example, has the authority to declare war, but not to judge the adequacy of the Nicene Creed. Moreover, power is not a generic or neutral property that can be seized and utilized by any form of human association. As Augustine recognized, there is a difference in kind, rather than degree, of the power asserted by brigands as opposed to the police, for the latter possess the authority which the former lack.[12] Consequently, power asserted with political authority is not coercive *per se*, for what is at stake is not the interests of the state, but the welfare of the people. Brigands may be obeyed due to the fear they engender, but the lawful commands of police officers are obeyed freely because the authority they represent is respected. This is not to say that police forces or individual officers cannot be corrupt and degenerate into little more than brigands in uniform. Rather, it is to emphasize that, in the absence of authorized power, good judgements cannot be rendered on behalf of a civil community. Deliberative, judicial, and executive representatives of the community must have the authority and power to judge, on behalf of the community, whether or not a particular church shall be established; who is and who is not eligible to marry; whether or not to impose tariffs on imported goods; if capital punishment can or cannot be used to punish criminals. Through acts of political judgement, government seeks to balance the various social constraints in which freedom is expressed. And in seeking a proper balance government must resist two temptations in exercising its authority, which may be simply noted at this juncture since they are more fully addressed in the following sections: (1) refusing to accept authority resulting in withheld obedience; and (2) claiming unwarranted authority resulting in coerced obedience.

The preceding discussion has served to place the family within a broader matrix of social spheres and associations comprising a civil community, a process that was initiated in the preceding chapter regarding the family's relationship with the church. Although this discussion is admittedly cursory, it demonstrates that created, natural, imposed, social, and political affinities are ordered both internally

---

[12] See Augustine, *City of God* 4. 4, p. 139.

within particular social spheres and associations, and these spheres and associations are in turn integrally related and ordered to each other. One cannot examine the space, time, and location of ecclesial, familial, social, and political ordering as isolated or autonomous spheres. Civil community is not simply the sum total of the roles and offices of each respective sphere; rather, these roles and offices are already embedded within the traditions, practices, and virtues of a particular civil community. Attention will be focused more directly back to the family in the following sections in order to examine how its internal ordering affects broader issues of social and political ordering, and conversely, how these broader issues influence internal familial ordering.

THE GIFT OF SOCIAL ORDERING

For late liberalism, social ordering is a *project*. This orientation was exhibited generally in Rawls's assertion that a well-ordered society is one which accords with abstract principles discerned behind a veil of ignorance. Based on these principles, the task of social ordering is to construct institutions which enable individuals to pursue their respective life-plans. Hence, his emphasis on equality and fair opportunity since no one can know in advance what her or his social status might be. In respect of marriage and family, these emphases are incorporated in structures which instantiate reciprocity and mutuality. The former is seen in Okin's insistence that homes must be structured in such a way that remunerative and household labour are divided evenly between spouses. Governmental regulation is needed to enforce these reciprocal relationships, especially in distributing equitable shares of income, for households should model the value of gender equality. Furthermore, Okin agrees with Rawls that children require extensive exposure to other social institutions (e.g. schools) that will instil equalitarian values to counter any lingering vestiges of household patriarchy. To a limited extent, Browning and his co-authors propound similar late liberal principles, with their emphasis on the mutuality of various family roles. Their principal difference is one of emphasis. They allow greater latitude in how gender equality may be expressed, as seen in their sixty-hour employment cap which may be divided in varying allotments as negotiated by spouses, and they are seemingly less open to governmental regulation except to protect the welfare of dependent children. Consequently, the authors recommend that spouses should be in conversation with the church concerning how they can best be supported in constructing their marriages and families.

In contrast, social ordering may be regarded as a *gift* to be cared for rather than a project to be undertaken. Marriage and family are not relational patterns that are constructed to enable the pursuits of its respective members, but are forms of association that order marital and familial affinities. In this respect, reciprocity and mutuality are not external values that should be used to reform the institutions of marriage and family, but are inherent qualities which unfold in the proper ordering of the household. This inherency is seen in Augustine's goods of marriage in which *proles*, fidelity, and friendship enable a couple to accomplish the cooperative tasks entailed in their vocations as spouses and parents. It is in faithfully following these vocations that reciprocity and mutuality emerge out of their cooperation instead of being the end products of constructed marital and familial projects. This underlying cooperative principle is incorporated in Baxter's structural account of the family which is governed through a three-part series of relationships, as propounded in the New Testament's household codes. These normative relationships not only shape the internal ordering of the household, but also prepare its members for more expansive forms of social and political association. Contrary to late liberal dogma, external values are not needed to counteract those learnt in the family; rather, it is through mutually ordered constraints among the family and other social spheres that the former is oriented towards broader association. This principle is reinforced in McCarthy's observation that familial roles and responsibilities are prior to any particular family, and which in turn are embedded in given social and political economies. To assert that a family is a project that can be constructed is to simply ignore the existing conditions which make it intelligible.

The contrast can be further elaborated by revisiting the affinities and their corresponding freedoms, examined in the previous section, which are either absent or operative in the notion of social ordering as project. Late liberals presuppose there is no created affinity (Rawls and Okin), or that it is ill-defined and incomplete (Browning *et al.*). There is no (or at least no strong sense of) creational order that can be discerned through reason or revelation, and thus no freedom can be derived from it. Whatever order exists is an artefact of the human will which is imposed upon creation over time. A person, for example, simply chooses, for a variety of reasons, to marry, and is not responding to a calling or vocation that would limit the parameters of freely choosing. Although humans may share a natural desire for association, the inclination is instrumental instead of definitive. Freedom is not found in being related to others; rather, relationships are constructed to enable its parties to express their freedom as autonomous persons. A person requires the assistance of another in exercising the free choice to become a parent. In this respect, freedom is not defined through imposed roles and institutions, but identity is formed in being freed from these impositions against the will. A person decides that becoming a parent is crucial to her or his identity, but finds marriage undesirable. Consequently, freedom is not expressed in a matrix of social constraints, but in overcoming them. A single person obtains a child either through adoption or collaborative reproduction. The political project, then, is to construct legislation and policies that enable persons to freely pursue the construction of their life-plans. Freedom is not, therefore, derived from obedience, but in consenting to whatever structures are needed to promote a fair pursuit of one's interests. No restrictions should be placed on access to assisted reproduction, for example, but this does not entitle one to abuse or neglect the child that is obtained.

Leaving aside the absence or muted status of created affinity, it would appear that the principal difference between a late liberal account of marriage and family and the Christian counter-proposal being developed in this book is over natural affinity. According to late liberals, there is no inherent nature of the familial association that should be honoured and supported, both in respect to its internal ordering and its ordering to broader associations, for it is a means that enables individuals to pursue their respective interests. Consequently, freedom is not found in familial relationships, defined through imposed roles, expressed within social constraints, and enacted in obedience. Rather, freedom is constructed in overcoming these limitations by subjecting the structures and institutions of various associations to wilful control. The freedom propounded by late liberalism, however, is more apparent than real, for in rejecting any nature of the familial association they have merely exchanged teleological restraints for a more ruthless assertion of wilful power. Spouses and parents are not free to construct their roles in any manner they choose, for specific practices must conform to imposed ideological commitments to an egalitarian household (Rawls and Okin) or interpersonal intimacy stressing reciprocity and mutuality (Browning *et al.*). In addition, since children must be instilled with liberal values to counteract those of their families, parental acts are constrained by other social institutions which assume a greater role in childrearing. Moreover, in appealing to governmental regulation to ensure both the efficacy of these social constraints and the egalitarian ordering of households, late liberals are also presumably sanctioning the coercive power of the state to enforce compliance. Consequently, families failing to comply with ideological expectations that civil community deems at present to be correct are subject to stigma, sanctions, and in some cases punishment. Ironically, these acts are justified by the necessity to protect the autonomy of individual citizens.

Herein lies the fundamental deception and contradiction of late liberal social and political theory. Denying any inherent nature of the familial association is deceptive because it does not promote freedom, but creates a vacuum that is filled by an ideological commitment to autonomy. Consequently, individuals are given great latitude in regard to sexual conduct, and with whom and how they will cooperate in forming families. So long as no one is harmed, individuals are free to pursue their interpersonal and reproductive interests with minimal social and political restraints. Yet to preserve this autonomy, a contradiction must be invoked, namely, that childrearing be subjected to extensive social constraint and political regulation. To promote the good of a late liberal civil community, parental authority, and thereby freedom, must be curtailed. Children will not learn how to be autonomous individuals unless they are properly taught, both within the household and other social institutions. Parents, in short, are not free to raise children in any manner they please or deem to be right. If the contradiction is to successfully defend the deception, then late liberal civil community must at one level refuse to accept rightful authority resulting in withheld obedience, while at another level claim unwarranted authority resulting in coerced obedience. Rejecting the moral authority to order and promote how and with whom families are formed means that individuals are free to withhold their obedience to conform to the normative roles, relationships, and offices which are inherent in the familial association, while claiming an unwarranted political authority to control childrearing compels parents to obey regulations that corrode the practices and virtues that make the parental vocation intelligible.

The troubling character of withheld obedience can be seen in Nelson's defence of adultery. According to Nelson, 'Self-love is basic to personal fulfilment'[13] and failing to become self-fulfilled is tantamount to committing a sin. In order to avoid sinning, we must form loving relationships with others, otherwise our self-love, and thereby self-fulfilment, is incomplete. Sexual intimacy is one of the most basic ways of expressing love, both of ourselves and of others, for sexuality is the foundation of one's identity. Consequently, every human relationship is sexual in nature, and every person therefore has a right to be sexually fulfilled. Nelson admits that traditionally marriage has been the principal channel for seeking sexual self-fulfilment, but the primacy of this route is now being radically challenged by rapidly changing values and mores. There is no longer any single normative family structure, particularly in respect of monogamous marriage. These changes need to be affirmed and embraced by the church, as well as the larger culture, for they offer more diverse and promising ways for individuals to achieve their sexual self-fulfilment, a goal, Nelson claims, that is blessed by the gospel. Marriage should now be perceived as an 'open-ended' relationship that is enriched by a wide array of 'secondary relationships', some of which may include sexual intimacy.[14]

With this fulfilment motif in mind, Nelson draws a distinction between adultery and infidelity. The former is sexual intercourse with a person who is not one's spouse, whereas the latter is the 'rupture of faithfulness, honesty, trust, and commitment'.[15] Marriage is not an

---

[13] James B. Nelson, *Embodiment* (1978), 115.   [14] Ibid. 140–1.
[15] Ibid. 143.

exclusive devotion, for there can be supportive and compatible 'secondary relationships of some emotional and sensual depth, possibly including genital intercourse'.[16] Presumably one can commit adultery while remaining faithful to one's spouse. This conclusion is not as contradictory as it appears to be, for Nelson contends that it is 'both unrealistic and unfair to expect that one person can always meet the partner's companionate needs—needs which are legitimate and not merely individualistic, hedonistic, and egocentric'.[17] Interpersonal intimacy with a variety of individuals should not exclude the possibility of sexual intimacy as well for the sake of personal growth since humans are sexual beings, and all relationships are thereby sexual in nature. Friendship, by definition then, must *always* be open to the possibility of sexual intimacy. Moreover, secondary relationships strengthen marriage. Only immature persons will not be open to the possibility of sexual intimacy with another person other than one's spouse, and immaturity, which retards self-fulfilment, is more of a threat to a marriage than an adulterous act. Given the gospel's message of self-fulfilment, the church, and by extension civil society, must also be open to the possibility of secondary relationships that include sexual intimacy. Consequently, adultery is justified when 'sexual sharing realistically promises to enhance and not damage the capacity for interpersonal fidelity and wholeness'.[18]

Nelson's defence of adultery is based on a series of fundamental and curious dualisms. The first dualism is separating adultery and fidelity. One can remain faithful to one's spouse while committing adultery. Since the goal is sexual self-fulfilment the adulterous act will strengthen a marriage, or at least those of mature couples. Out of marital fidelity, a non-adulterous spouse should take delight in how fulfilled the adulterous partner has become. This claim, however, is intelligible only by invoking a second dualism, namely, dividing the will from the body. Fidelity is presumably a state of mind; one can remain faithful in mind while being adulterous in body. The body is a secondary consideration, for it is a means of achieving self-fulfilment. We may do with our bodies what we will so long as what is willed is self-fulfilling. Both spouses should take delight in each other's act of adultery, for as each partner becomes more

---

[16] Nelson, *Embodiment*, 144.   [17] Ibid. 146.   [18] Ibid. 151.

sexual-self-fulfilled their interpersonal bond of fidelity is strengthened. Separating mind and body is, to say the least, a puzzling move to make in a book that is purportedly dedicated to recovering the embodied character of Christian faith. Yet Nelson is forced to make this move because of the late liberal notion of agency he uncritically presupposes. Self-fulfilment can only be attained by what is willed, and the body is as much an impediment as a means in obtaining what the self wills. Resolving this dilemma leads to a third dualism between primary and secondary relationships. A primary relationship is presumably one that is willed as such and thereby the object of a spouse's principal fidelity, while a secondary relationship is also one (or more) that is willed as such and the object of less significant fidelity. It is difficult, however, to imagine how such a dichotomy can produce the kind of wholeness Nelson envisions. If a secondary relationship is to produce self-fulfilment must not the self be, at least for a time, fully attentive to the other? And if such a self-fulfilling relationship includes sexual intimacy, must not the self be, at least for a time, fully present in mind and body? And in those times of mindful attentiveness and bodily presence, does not the adulterous act become the primary relationship and the marriage a secondary one? What Nelson describes is not a relation between so-called primary and secondary relationships, but an episodic sequence of events in which the 'spouse' is identified as such because of the frequency of her or his appearances in these episodes. But this effectively strips marital fidelity of any normative meaning, for a spouse is simply the lead character surrounded by a supporting cast. Following Nelson's schema, a happily married couple could refrain from any sexual intimacy with each other while voraciously seeking their sexual self-fulfilment with a host of other individuals. The couple might delight in each other's sexual exploits, but in what sense, other than a legal contract, can they be said to be 'married', since their sexual fulfilment is achieved through entirely vicarious means? How exactly are they being faithful to each other?

The net effect of these dualisms is that it prevents Nelson from making the most crucial dualist distinction at stake, namely, who is and who is not married. His open marriage is little more than a shifting pattern of so-called primary and secondary relationships which blur the lines that define marriage as such. Marriage is simply a designated and variable relationship promoting the self-fulfilment of its parties within a larger matrix of subsidiary relationships. Nelson cannot differentiate between the ways of singleness and marriage, and therefore judge the morality or immorality of any acts, such as adultery, other than in terms of enabling or disabling self-fulfilment, because he is unwilling to invoke any normative understanding of marriage that entails exclusivity. Marriage is by definition an exclusive association between wife and husband, otherwise their bond is simply a peculiar arrangement between two (or more) singles. Marriage entails a mutual and exclusive fidelity between a couple in both mind *and* body, for it is not a designated primary relationship but a binding covenant grounded in their one-flesh unity. There are no so-called primary and secondary relationships that constitute this union; rather, there is a marital covenant that encounters other relationships that either support or weaken it; hence, the need for discrimination and judgement.

Nelson's defence of adultery is intelligible only if the veracity of his late liberal ideological commitment to self-fulfilment is accepted. His commitment, however, is enslaving rather than liberating. When individuals are devoted ultimately to their respective self-fulfilment, they are not free to obey the normative and exclusive terms of the covenant that make them wife and husband. In the absence of any authority commanding mutual fidelity—a fidelity it must be emphasized that does not separate mind from body—a woman and man are not free to be married. The communication that is inherent to the marital covenant cannot be extended to others if that covenant is to remain genuinely marital in practice; an 'open marriage' is in fact no marriage at all. What Nelson has done is to reshape marriage in the light of late liberal social theory that reduces all human interaction to contractual exchanges, recasting it as a contract of allied consumers. Presumably, a larger market of emotional and sexual intimacy can only benefit these consumers in comparison with what they can offer each other. Moreover, a similar pattern is extended to parenthood in which individuals enter a market where they may select from among various methods such as procreation, collaborative reproduction, or adoption to obtain a child. Yet if marriage and family, following Grant's analogy, is a package deal that must be purchased in total in order to provide a mutual place of timely belonging, then Nelson's 'open marriage' destroys the very foundation which enables broader and mutually enriching forms of human association. It is through the exclusive nature of marriage that a couple may open the fellowship of their household to include children, and it is in turn through these exclusive familial relationships that the household is properly oriented to a more expansive range of association. Moreover, if marriage and family is a package deal, then there are accompanying normative demands that must be obeyed if these institutions are to make their rightful contribution to the good of civil community, and if this obedience is withheld, then marriage and family are effectively reduced to units consuming not only material goods, but sexual and emotional intimacy. This reduction, as well as its ill effects, is admitted implicitly by late liberal social and political practice. Although marriage (broadly construed) and the formation of families is given great licence in most late liberal regimes, this libertarian indulgence is compensated by relatively tight regulation of childrearing. As argued in the next section, this compensatory move requires the state to claim an unwarranted authority, resulting in coerced obedience.

DESTINY AND THE COMMON GOOD

Late liberal regimes must overcompensate with regulated childcare, because the civil community could not survive if the libertine policies governing marriage and forming families were expanded to include childrearing. Liberal civil communities could very well implode or dissipate if parents were simply left to their own devices, for there is no guarantee that they will instil in their children the liberal values needed to perpetuate the community from one generation to the next. The state and civil society need to protect themselves from idiosyncratic parents. Late liberal regimes, then, face a perplexing dilemma: they must simultaneously promote individual liberty, as exemplified in libertine attitudes towards marriage and family formation, while reproducing liberal values in each generation, a vital task that cannot be entrusted to parents. Bertrand Russell recognized the threatening nature of this dilemma, and proposed that it could be resolved by making the state the father of all children. Some women would be paid by the state to bear children, while other women would be employed to rear them, with or without the assistance of a husband. The only glitch preventing Russell from fully endorsing his own proposal was the rampant nationalism and militarism of his day. Yet he was guardedly hopeful that the pace of growing internationalism would quicken to not only counter the threat of nationalistic and militaristic regimes, but also fill the void left by rapidly decaying families.[19]

Less ambitiously, most late liberal regimes are content to restrict and assist, but not assume, parental roles. The state need not be the father of all children, but only the godfather of all parents. This role is performed through laws and policies that both command and forbid certain parental acts. Parents, for example, may be required to enrol their children in approved schools or employ certified tutors to satisfy compulsory education statutes. Children may also, in some instances, be inoculated or receive medical care with or without parental consent. The state may also intervene to remove endangered children from homes where they are neglected or abused. The state, however, does not limit itself to imperious directives and prohibitions, but also provides assistance. Social services, for instance, may provide financial support for dependent children, counselling for troubled families, and courses on parenting skills. In addition, a wide range of voluntary and commercial activities reinforce these constrictions upon parental prerogatives by reducing time spent pursuing common household activities. The net effect of these laws and social interactions is to reduce the family's primary role to providing interpersonal intimacy, and consuming goods and services. As both Lasch and McCarthy contend, however, such a reduced role erodes, if not destroys, the inherent moral fabric of the family, because the most formative virtues and practices are performed outside it.

It may be objected that the preceding criticism of the state's regulation of childrearing and subsequent reduction of the family to a unit of economic consumption is unwarranted. As such early liberals as Grotius, Althusius, and Baxter had argued, the family, church, and

---

[19] See Bertrand Russell, *Marriage and Morals* (1929), 162–74.

state should work together in preparing children to learn the appropriate values and skills in order that they might make useful contributions to civil society when they become adults. Given the greater complexity of post-industrial societies, traditional parental responsibilities and prerogatives must be reassigned to other social institutions better equipped to teach these crucial values and skills, and the state is required to make these reassignments effectual, for it alone possesses sufficient power to compel the obedience of reluctant parents. In order to promote the common good of the civil community, the state must ensure that its citizens have every opportunity to develop as autonomous persons, thereby justifying a more extensive regulation of childrearing. Reducing the family to a unit of economic consumption is a necessary outcome of this promotion, but it is not necessarily an ill consequence, because it liberates individuals to construct richer personal lives through a wider matrix of possible relationships beyond the narrow confines of families.

This objection, however, fails to acknowledge the antithetical presuppositions separating early and late liberalism. The former presupposed that family, church, and state should work together because they shared a common set of convictions and aspirations. They were integrally related and mutually reinforcing institutions which cooperatively promoted the common good. There was no need for the state to extensively regulate childrearing, other than to intervene in specific cases when parents were either unable or refused to perform their duties properly, for such intervention would have proved redundant. Consequently, the family was more integrated into the economy as a unit of both production and consumption. Late liberalism on the contrary presupposes that families, religious communities, and the state hold conflicting values and goals. They are antagonistic institutions, and the state is thereby justified in sequestering the public influence of families and religious bodies in promoting the peace and order of the civil community. Thus the rationale of some regimes, for example, of requiring parents to enrol their children in some type of government-sanctioned educational scheme, and prohibiting the wearing of religious symbols or garb in publicly financed schools. Consequently, extensive regulation of childrearing is a significant, as well as ironic, component in the state's strategy for protecting the civil community against its own predominant value of autonomous personhood.

We may also say, then, that late liberalism is premised upon an inarticulate, but nonetheless prevalent, eschatology of survival derived from historicist dogma. Civil community is an artefact of wilful human construction. Its component parts are thereby all works in process: personal relationships, social, and political institutions are all subject to endless deconstruction and reconstruction. Consequently, there is nothing unnatural or troubling about dividing marriage and family formation from childrearing, for there is no marital, parental, or familial nature to protect, only contracts to be negotiated and renegotiated. The end of personal, social, and political construction is what their builders will it to be. Late liberal civil community is thereby justified in resorting to illiberal measures to ensure its survival, for death negates the possibility of willing a future. What this historicist eschatology fails to recognize is that personal, social, and political construction is not *ex nihilo*. Personal identities, social relationships, and political institutions are admittedly constructs, but they are assemblages that are comprised of given and limited material. Moreover, it is the material of a created order that has been vindicated by Jesus Christ, so that its end is not what we will it to be but what is willed by God. Consequently, the forms that human associations might take are not limitless, for they embody a created order, and thereby an inherent nature providentially unfolding over time, drawn by their destiny in Christ. The integral affinities of marriage, procreation, and childrearing must therefore be protected, for their haphazard separation not only distorts the internal order of the familial association, but strips singleness of its eschatological witness, in turn depriving all other temporal associations of an ultimate reference point which properly delineates their penultimate ordering. In this respect, late liberalism turns the relation between providence and eschatology upside down. Singleness does not bear witness to the family's destiny; rather, personal, social, and political relationships comprise the future constructed by autonomous individuals.

Thatcher's attempted recovery of betrothal offers a revealing venue for examining this contrast in greater detail. He contends that the church has not paid sufficient attention to its own changing tradition of marriage, and is thereby ill equipped to provide adequate pastoral care in the light of changing sexual mores and practices. To simply reassert the traditional prohibition against sexual intercourse outside of marriage is to bury its head in the sand, further alienating people from its ministry. This is especially the case in respect of cohabitation, which is now widely practised in Western societies. Although many cohabitating relationships are of short duration and casual in nature, a substantial number of couples go on to marry, so their cohabitation serves as preparation for marriage. The church needs to seize this preparatory potential to rethink its teaching on marriage in the light of the postmodern times in which it now performs its ministry. Consequently, Thatcher commends the recommendation of the Church of England's report, *Something to Celebrate*, that 'cohabitation is, for many people, a step along the way towards that fuller and more complete commitment'.[20] He admits, however, that the report's lack of 'sufficiently detailed historical and theological foundations' lays it open to the scorn of reactionary critics.[21]

Thatcher attempts to correct this deficiency by arguing that a so-called defence of traditional marriage is itself a modern construct. He argues that Christian teaching on marriage has undergone radical, and often contradictory, changes over time. He notes that at various times the church has recognized clandestine marriages and other informal exchanges of consent, and often permitted sexual intercourse during courtship or betrothal periods in accordance with local custom. It is not until the state began registering marriages in the eighteenth century that it was generally presumed that a marriage began with a wedding. The church was not the driving force behind such governmental regulation, but conformed its practices to this secular initiative. The growing popularity of cohabitation is, therefore, a rebellion against bourgeois marriage rather than Christian marriage.

Instead of decrying this rebellion, Thatcher contends that it provides an opportunity for the church to reclaim and reinstate its premodern practice of betrothal. There are striking similarities between cohabitation and betrothal which the church can exploit in making the latter a more formal entry into marriage. The chief

---

[20] Adrian Thatcher, *Marriage after Modernity*, 105.   [21] Ibid. 107–8.

liability of cohabitation is that it is a private agreement to live together without any necessary intention to marry. Thatcher would remove this weakness by making betrothal contingent upon a mutual declaration of intent to marry, which would be publicly recognized through liturgical ceremony and governmental registration. A betrothed couple would be permitted to engage in sexual intercourse, but should refrain from becoming parents until they are married. Moreover, the couple would receive the church's pastoral support in their move towards becoming married. Thatcher is confident that recovering the premodern 'practice of betrothal' would provide the groundwork for constructing a 'postmodern theology of entry into marriage which would have considerable value at the present moment'.[22]

It may first appear that Thatcher's recovery of betrothal goes far in addressing the concerns raised in this section. A declared intention to marry and refraining from parenthood until marriage has occurred would surely help to resist the libertine practices that have been decried. The appearance, however, is misleading, for Thatcher has reconfigured marriage into a relatively safer process of relational construction which serves to reinforce, rather than challenge, the divide separating marital and family formation from childrearing. At each significant stage in the process a safety net is provided: the intent to marry within the betrothal stage is non-binding, and despite the vows of lifelong marriage there are virtually no restrictions preventing a married couple without children from divorcing. It is only when the welfare of dependent children is at stake that some implied limits are invoked that might impede an unhappy couple from separating.[23] Yet it is also at this point that late liberal regimes intervene with stricter regulation. Thatcher merely overlays a thin veneer of theological rhetoric regarding a revocable intent to marry and remain married upon late liberalism's eschatology of survival. The marital process is always premised by a tentative commitment which only becomes more binding with the presence of children. Ironically, it is children that keep a marriage together, rather than marriage providing a firm foundation in which parents and children belong together in a family.

---

[22] Thatcher, *Marriage after Modernity*, 120.
[23] Cf. similar arguments in Don S. Browning *et al.*, *From Culture Wars to Common Ground* (1997), 332–3, and Russell, *Marriage and Morals*, 175–88.

Thatcher cannot effectively bridge the gulf separating marital and family formation from childrearing, because, contrary to his frequent invocations of Christian tradition, he remains too deeply embedded in late liberal eschatology. Marriage and family are not normative forms of human association ordained by God, which by their nature must look beyond themselves to see their destiny embodied in the witness of singleness, but the end products of singles constructing their marital and familial relationships. The tentative nature of the process itself encases marriage more deeply within its own self-absorption of surviving over time, for it can only look to its own success, however defined, to see its future. A marriage, like any other relationship, becomes an artefact of its members' will; an object to be admired (or despised) by individuals as the fruit of their labour. It is telling that Thatcher never justifies his retrieval of betrothal on the basis that it constitutes an essential though neglected aspect of marriage, but argues that it will improve the church's prospects for surviving by making its discourse on sexuality more agreeable to postmodern ears. But when relevancy and survival are the principal forces driving reform, the end product is often deformed beyond recognition. Thatcher has fallen into the same trap as Nelson by failing to differentiate between who is married and who is not in any definitive manner. Marriage is reduced to a process that one can easily enter or leave so long as one remains unencumbered by children, for his intent to marry and remain married is more an emotive plea than a prerequisite. Consequently, he can neither effectively counter the ill effects of absented authority and withheld obedience in respect to marital and familial formation, nor the assertion of unwarranted authority and coerced obedience in respect to childrearing. Thatcher thereby embodies the paradox of late liberal social and political ordering that it must employ illiberal measures to protect its libertine values. It is a paradox that stems from late liberalism's reticence to judge, to pronounce the difference between right and wrong, except when the perceived survival of the civil community is at stake. And in such circumstances the task is not differentiating between right and wrong, but what is required to endure. Such reticence to judge, however, is far more threatening to a civil community, for it represents a political failure at its most basic level, namely, to protect and promote the common good. Yet to speak of the proper relation between judgement and the common good requires that we also inquire into the eschatology informing both a vision of the good and the judgements its enactments inspires, for it is the future desired by civil community that determines its corporate life in the present. But what *should* civil communities desire and judge?

WHAT THE NATIONS (SHOULD) DESIRE AND JUDGE

Jesus Christ is the desire of the nations.[24] This simple confession should not be interpreted as the immodest claim of an imperious Christianity. Rather, it encapsulates the healthy instinct that civil community desires—or at least, should desire—their completion as a society or people. It is, therefore, an eschatological desire, and what other name can Christians confess in this respect than their Lord and Saviour? It may be objected that invoking eschatology is to impose a religious category that violates the secular nature of civil governance. There are two reasons why this objection is misplaced.

First, no civil community can be fully secular in the late liberal sense of being liberated from the influence of any religious beliefs. The secular does not properly denote a sphere of activity free of religious conviction, but a time pertaining to the present age and not the next.[25] Yet no civil community can order its penultimate affairs in the absence of ultimate convictions, however overt or covert they may be. The necessity of making religious decisions and normative determinations is unavoidable, and the 'false self-consciousness of the would-be secular society lies in its determination to conceal the religious judgments that it has made'.[26] The issue at stake is not whether or not religious convictions should inform civil ordering, but which religious and normative convictions are in play. Consequently, care must be taken to discern the difference between true

---

[24] The following discussion draws upon and adapts O'Donovan's central theses of his *Desire of the Nations* and *Ways of Judgment*.

[25] See O'Donovan, *Desire of the Nations*, 247; cf. Milbank, *Theology and Social Theory*, 9.

[26] O'Donovan, *Desire of the Nations*, 247.

and false messianic expectations,[27] and the failure to honour this distinction opens the prospect of 'idolatrous politics' and totalitarian pretensions.[28] The principal tension between Christianity and late liberalism is a dispute over contending eschatologies that are embodied in conflicting claims regarding the nature and purpose of social and political ordering. In confessing 'Jesus is Lord', Christians are attempting to resolve this argument by claiming that subjection and obedience to Christ satisfy the true desire of the nations, namely, that their lives be ordered in preparation for their Sabbath rest in God.[29] The eschatology embedded in this confession does not suggest theocratic governance or the formal establishment of Christianity as the religion of the realm. Rather, it acknowledges that civil governance cannot be genuinely secular in the absence of the sacred, but this does not entitle the church to dictate how the state should conduct its affairs. Even at the height of Christendom a jurisdictional separation was maintained between church and state as promulgated in the doctrine of the two,[30] and their formal separation does not imply that Christian convictions are irrelevant to social and political ordering. The primary complaint with many late liberal regimes is not that they are too secular, but that they are insufficiently so, by often either legislating or regulating in areas where they have no authority to do so, or failing to legislate or intervening in other domains where they are obligated to do so. Marriage and parenthood, for example, are not political rights created and granted by the state, but it does have the rightful authority to regulate who is eligible to marry, and thereby who is best situated to exercise parental duties and responsibilities.

Second, civil community cannot be properly ordered in the absence of limited political authority. To assert the authority to act, an individual or office must also be under authority. Or in O'Donovan's words: 'To be subject to authority is to be *authorized*.'[31] Such subjection should not be interpreted as a severe or unnecessary constraint imposed upon the prerogatives of the state. The purpose

---

[27] Ibid. 215.   [28] Ibid. 49.
[29] See Augustine, *City of God* 22. 30, pp. 1087–91.
[30] See O'Donovan, *Desire of the Nations*, 193–210.
[31] Ibid. 90 (emphasis original); see also O'Donovan, *Ways of Judgment*, 132–4.

of limited political authority is not to diminish the power of the state, but to empower and authorize its acts. If rulers are not subject to the authority of Christ, then they are not free to be obedient rulers, and in turn, nor are citizens free to obey their rulers. The various nations have been elected by God for the task of obedient governance in response to Christ's victory over death. It is only through such obedient freedom that a history may be both safeguarded and evoked out from the created order vindicated by Christ. To deny that civil rulers are subject to Christ's authority is to deny the very nature and end of social and political ordering. There is, in short, a direct correlate among authority, power, and freedom; it is only in and through political acts authorized by Christ's rule that the power to act in particular ways frees civil community to affirm the goodness of God's created order.[32] In this respect, political authority confers freedom instead of granting or withholding it.[33]

The practical application of obedient freedom is embodied in civil community being bound together in a coordinated covenant that perpetuates the tradition of pursuing the good of a vindicated creation. The task of government is to direct the community, as a work of divine providence, towards its destiny in Christ, and in thereby acknowledging its limited authority it embraces its proper social and political identity, namely, that of serving the pursuit of this destiny.[34] This concept of obedient freedom challenges the Aristotelian principle of the state's self-sufficiency, a notion that has become the seemingly unchallenged centrepiece of late liberal social and political thought. Yet if the state is self-sufficient then the authority it invokes is self-referential. But if being in authority requires that one be under authority, then the state's supposed self-sufficiency strips it of any legitimate source of authority. Despite civil religious rhetoric or idealistic allusions to governance under the rule of law, authority is effectively reduced to assertions of power which the state authorizes itself to perform, and is effectively the author, rather than the subject, of the vague religious and idealistic beliefs it purportedly seeks to serve. Consequently, late liberal regimes often fall into the trap of believing that the state may create, reform, or negate the familial,

---

[32] See O'Donovan, *Desire of the Nations*, 30–1.   [33] Ibid. 126–7.
[34] Cf. O'Donovan's three theorems, ibid. 46–7.

ecclesial, and social spheres comprising civil community as it will. Lawful government, for example, may redefine marriage as a contract between any two (or more) consenting persons, or assume parental prerogatives in selected aspects of childrearing. The task of political ordering is not to enable spouses and parents to exercise their proper authority under the authority of Christ, but to construct a civil community formed by autonomous persons who are 'free' to form whatever relationships they choose, and are 'free' to reproduce or otherwise obtain children through a wide variety of means. Such 'freedom' is not free, however, the cost being the surrendering of many crucial parental duties and responsibilities to the state. The net effect is a perception of freedom, stripped of any substantive content, for spouses have not been freed to obey the ways of marriage, parents are not free to obey the ways of parenthood, and neither the family nor the state is free to obey Christ.

The underlying presumption of self-referential authority begs an important question: although the state may have the power to create, reform, or negate marriage and family, does it have the rightful authority to do so? Or to pose the question in a theological manner: under the authority of Christ, what is government authorized to do? In brief, it is authorized to embody the 'practice of judgment'.[35] It is precisely this practice that enables genuinely secular governance, and, according to O'Donovan, it has had a 'decisive effect in shaping the Western political tradition'.[36] The origin of this seminal principle can be traced back to the Old Testament concept of covenant which laid the foundation for both law and authority. The principle is refined in the New Testament by Paul, who contends that the primary purpose of government is to protect the innocent and punish the wicked.[37] This teaching is not minimalist, but it limits the 'role of government to the single task of judgment, and forbids human rule to pretend to sovereignty, the consummation of the community's identity in the power of its ruler'.[38] This task protects the secular nature of political ordering, for the state plays no central role in the unfolding history of creation's redemption. Moreover, it also prevents civil community from incorporating eschatological

---

[35] See O'Donovan, *Ways of Judgment*, 3–4.   [36] Ibid. 3.
[37] See Rom. 3: 14.   [38] O'Donovan, *Ways of Judgment*, 4.

pretensions, for sovereignty is given to Christ, whose final political community is lodged in the New Jerusalem and not in any temporal regime or institution. In the meantime, the task of secular rulers is to maintain penultimate distinctions between the just and unjust through their practice of judgement.

Maintaining this distinction between the just and unjust necessarily entails that judgement is an *'act of moral discrimination*, dividing right from wrong'.[39] A civil community simply cannot exist in the absence of a practice of judgement, however distorted or disingenuous it may become.[40] The late liberal programme of restricting public discourse to procedural issues is thereby untenable, for the restriction itself is an act of moral discrimination; a judgment is made that it is right to forbid the introduction of normative and theological convictions into the public arena, and wrong to try to introduce them in either a covert or overt manner. The late liberal denial that the state should perform acts of moral discrimination effectively strips it of its properly secular role. Ironically, late liberals transform the state into a kind of theocracy, albeit based on agnostic dogma, which they purportedly abhor. More importantly, this denial voids the public context of civil community, for it is in pronouncing judgement on a preceding or present state of affairs that a public space is created and maintained. In judging retrospectively, a space is opened up prospectively, unlike late liberal society in which past and future have no bearing on a vacuous present comprised of private assertions of conflicting wills. Hence the recourse to the threat of state coercion in maintaining the peace of civil society, a threat which is not so much made on behalf of the public, but to protect the private interests of autonomous persons. The alternative to public judgement is not moral neutrality, but 'multitudinous' private judgements.[41]

The practice of judgement, then, is not the exercise of power, but applying the authorized discriminating power of the state to form, maintain, and protect the public space of civil community. In this respect, government through its acts of judgement brings closure to contentious issues, and in its absence there can be no responsibility.

[39] O'Donovan, *Ways of Judgment*, 4.
[40] See O'Donovan, *Desire of the Nations*, 256.
[41] See O'Donovan, *Ways of Judgment*, 23–4.

When it is assumed that no issue is ever resolved, and every decision is open to endless scrutiny, then civil community has surrendered itself to the tyranny of endless moral gridlock which can only be cleared through fiat rather than deliberation.[42] Consequently, the practice of judgement is principally a *descriptive exercise*, for discrimination requires a point of reference in order to determine the difference between right and wrong. Public moral discourse refers to, but does not create, reality. Through acts of judgement, the truth of civil community is revealed, and what is revealed is given rather than manufactured.[43] Contrary to Rawls, a well-ordered society cannot be created *ex nihilo* by deliberating behind a veil of ignorance. Rather, a society is ordered well when the sovereignty of its given constituent social spheres is adequately protected. In faithfully discerning and describing God's judgements as revealed in Christ's vindication of created order, politically penultimate judgements will conform, albeit imperfectly, within a matrix of pluriform social settings and changing historical circumstances. Judgements are thereby constrained, for the authority of government is derived from being subject to Christ's authority, and the state lacks the ultimate authority to pronounce a final judgement; the closure it commands is temporal, not eternal. The state, for example, can neither invent nor abolish marriage and family, but only pronounce judgements which either safeguard or erode the inherent natures of their association.

Law is the concrete outcome of judgement. Law, however, is not the invention or will of the state, but instantiates the truth of civil community. Through law political ordering directs the community away from what is wrong, and is, for good or ill, inescapably a moral statement. Contrary to the late liberal reticence to judge, no substantial line dividing the lawful from the moral can be drawn. As O'Donovan contends: 'The fashion for denying the connection of law and morality was based on a privatized conception of morality as comprising those directive judgments which each person makes for him or herself autonomously.'[44] Yet if judgement reveals the truth of civil community, then its laws cannot evade the task of making moral

---

[42] Cf. Arendt's account of political speech in *The Human Condition* (1998), 22–5, 196–9.
[43] See O'Donovan, *Ways of Judgment*, 19.   [44] Ibid. 23.

judgements, however reluctantly or inattentively it may be undertaken. When law originates in political authority which is under
authority, the necessary limits and constraints which make responsible freedom possible are honoured and supported.[45] Political
judgements embodied in law thereby protect and enlarge the scope
of freedom, for freedom is the power to act within formative social
spheres.[46] In the absence of lawful authority freedom is lost. If there
are no laws governing marriage, or if the statutes are unjust, for
example, women and men are not free to be wives and husbands.
Consequently, the purpose of the state is to defend or promote itself,
instead of defending and promoting the civil community it is authorized by God to govern.

In defending and promoting itself, the state diminishes the obedient
freedom of its citizens by eroding the private and public associations
in which their freedom is defined and expressed. This diminishment is
seen in the liberal corruption of justice in which the sensible principle of
equality is enacted in quantitative rather than qualitative terms—a
penchant for 'making things equal rather than treating them equally'.[47]
This procedural emphasis fails to recognize inherent and formative
differences within various social spheres, resulting in a highly attenuated understanding of freedom and justice. Okin's egalitarian family,
for instance, effectively implements Rawls's suggested abolition of the
family. When individuals are regarded by the state *only* as equal and
inadvertent members of families, then they are not free to be spouses,
parents, children, or siblings in any normative sense which these roles
convey. The familial forms which empower its individual members to
act as such are rendered ineffectual. Late liberalism mistakenly conflates
equal worth with equal treatment. This conflation is unjust, however,
for preserving worth within any association requires treatment that is
pertinent to the structure of the relationship in question, and such
pertinence is based on particular differentiations rather than generic
equality. To assert that each member of a family should be treated in a
strictly equal manner is patently absurd, as well as unjust, for it would
relieve parents of certain duties and responsibilities that are incumbent
upon them, while placing expectations and burdens upon children that

---

[45] See O'Donovan, *Ways of Judgment*, 52–3.
[46] Ibid. 67–83.   [47] Ibid. 33.

are too great to bear. To claim that spouses, parents, children, and siblings should be treated differently in accordance with their respective roles does *not* diminish their equal worth as persons.

Conflating equal worth with equal treatment is a consequence of placing reciprocity as the lynchpin of justice, instantiating a 'totalizing of market-theory' that has dominated late liberal social and political thought.[48] All forms of human relationship involve exchanges, and therefore each party must be treated equally to ensure that the exchanges are just. Yet, as O'Donovan insists, a 'sound theory of justice must recognize that some goods are not exchangeable, and that some transactions are not exchanges'.[49] To insist that the family is based on reciprocal exchange is to destroy its underlying nature and rationale. It is precisely this late liberal assumption that justice is grounded in reciprocity that weakens McCarthy's otherwise astute analysis, for he simply transplants the family from a market economy based on capital exchange to a neighbourhood economy founded on gift exchange. It is far from clear why families are somehow better off being embedded in the latter option since many, if not most, of the familial goods he purportedly wishes to affirm cannot be reciprocally exchanged either as gifts or commodities. In this respect a neighbourhood may be as equally proficient as the global market in eroding the normative roles of the family.

In contrast, O'Donovan argues that the 'search for a fundamental idea of social ethics should lead us not to the idea of reciprocity, but to that of *communication*'.[50] According to O'Donovan: 'To "communicate" is to hold some thing as common, to make it a common possession, to treat it as "ours," rather than "yours" or "mine." The partners to a communication form a community, a "we" in relation to the object in which they participate.'[51] In addition to 'community', the Greek root *koinōnia* can also be translated as 'communion' and 'communicate'. A community is thereby constituted by its shared fellowship rather than the acts it performs. A family, for example, is such a fellowship that makes its consequent acts intelligible, not the outcome of various acts by individuals pursuing their respective interests. Consequently, communication is not synonymous with bestowal. To bestow something means that no ongoing relationship is assumed

[48] Ibid. 36–7.   [49] Ibid. 36.
[50] Ibid. 36. (emphasis added).   [51] Ibid. 242.

between the giver and recipient; what is 'mine' is unilaterally transferred to become 'yours'. Rather, the dispersal of a particular good
creates a relationship or fellowship; the 'ours'. A parent, for instance,
may give a pet to her child, but it becomes effectively the family pet.
Communication is also not synonymous with exchange. To exchange
means what is 'mine' becomes 'yours' and what is 'yours' becomes
'mine'. Although communication is present in an exchange, and exchange is the centrepiece of a market, it is not a crucial characteristic of
a community. A household, for example, is not a marketplace where
goods, services, and gifts are exchanged and consumed. Rather it is
familial communication, not exchange and consumption, which fulfils
the family as such. Consequently, the family, like other communities, is
not founded and maintained for the sake of exchange. 'Human community is not a product of human foundation; it is a condition of being
human, a gift of God.'[52]

We may say, then, that civil community is comprised of *spheres
of communication*, and that government is authorized to order
the relationship among these spheres in ways which promote their
respective communications. Late liberal regimes, however, often perceive these spheres as *marketplaces of reciprocal exchange*. The task of
the state, therefore, is to promote more expansive opportunities for
exchange rather than communication. This raises an important issue:
does the state have the authority to extensively reform or redefine a
sphere of communication in order to create greater opportunities
for exchange? Addressing this question in an exhaustive manner is
beyond the scope of this inquiry, but some of the more salient
features of what is at stake in this issue can be identified by revisiting
Nelson's and Thatcher's proposals favouring same-sex union.

The gist of Nelson's argument is that gay Christians are seeking the
'church's full acceptance'.[53] The church bears a heavy responsibility
for perpetuating anti-homosexual sentiment in Western cultures,
and therefore has a theological and moral duty to rectify discriminatory laws and practices. This mandate for social justice is derived
from Jesus' 'invitation to human wholeness and communion'.[54]

---

[52] See O'Donovan, *Ways of Judgment*, 249.
[53] Nelson, *Embodiment*, 180.
[54] Ibid. 181.

Although this particular biblically based imperative is unconditional and universal, all other scriptural teaching seemingly condemning homosexual acts are dismissed as outdated cultural constructs that have been contradicted by evidence gleaned from more scientific enquiry. Moreover, contemporary theological arguments, such as those offered by Barth and Thielicke, condemning homosexuality must be rejected, because they are based on faulty data, and are 'grounded in an essentially nonhistoricist, rigid version of natural law'.[55] Since there is nothing inherently wrong with homosexuality, Christians should support the civil rights of gays and lesbians. As a concrete demonstration of this support, the church should permit same-sex union for those desiring a lifelong relationship. Since social justice requires equal treatment, any two persons should have the right to marry, so that the church's blessing of same-sex union is the first step in a twofold programme. 'When and if the church moves toward liturgical support of gay union, it should also press toward civil recognition.'[56] This second step is needed to protect the civil rights of same-sex couples, and garner the 'symbolic affirmation' of the civil community.[57]

Thatcher argues that in a postmodern world Christian marriage must be committed to the full equality of spouses. Moreover, since 'heterosexuality'[58] no longer defines sexuality *per se* in any normative manner, the institution of marriage should be extended to same-sex couples. Thatcher admits that his proposal is problematic on two counts. First, there is little consensus within the gay and lesbian communities on whether marriage is an institution they should embrace. For some, marriage would provide a public recognition of friendship, while others counter that same-sex marriage is degrading since it would be tantamount to making homosexuals 'honorary heterosexuals'.[59] Thatcher predicted that, unless same-sex marriage afforded certain advantages such as tax incentives and protecting civil rights, gays and lesbians would not marry in any significant numbers. This reticence leads to the second problem that, given its long and close association with procreation, marriage is widely perceived as a heterosexual institution. This narrow perception,

---

[55] Ibid. 196.   [56] Ibid. 209.   [57] Ibid. 209.
[58] See Thatcher, *Marriage after Modernity*, 295–6.   [59] Ibid. 295.

however, is no longer definitive. As the history of Christianity demonstrates, marriage and family are highly adaptable institutions that have been altered in response to changing historical and cultural circumstances. Children, for example, can now be obtained through a variety of methods that do not require sexual intercourse. Since biology is not the determinative factor of parenthood, there is no reason why the right to form a family should not be extended to same-sex couples. Although the link between marriage and procreation should not be severed, Thatcher contends that marriage as covenant can be extended to include same-sex couples. In addition, since there is no reason to believe that same-sex couples do not find God in their relationship with each other as do many heterosexual couples, there is also no reason to believe that the sacramentality of the marital covenant cannot also be extended to same-sex couples. Consequently, there is no reason why both church and state should not permit same-sex marriage as a twofold affirmation of equality in a postmodern world.

Nelson's and Thatcher's arguments are not persuasive. Nelson contends that the church, and by extension the Western moral and legal traditions it inspired, has perpetuated unwarranted discrimination against homosexuals. To rectify this injustice, church and state should both permit same-sex unions. Assuming that Nelson's contention regarding the church's culpability is correct, and setting aside the morality of homosexual acts *per se*, it does not necessarily follow that justice demands that same-sex union should be permitted. Admitting that discrimination against homosexual acts or lifestyles is wrong can be rectified through laws forbidding subsequent discriminatory acts, but this does not thereby give gays and lesbians a right to marry. In a similar manner, laws forbidding religious discrimination allow individuals to practise their respective religious faiths unhindered, but it does not give Buddhist monks, for example, the right to become Anglican priests. If this were the case, then the rationale of religious tolerance would be destroyed, because particular religious bodies would be unable to preserve the distinctive and exclusive qualities of their respective traditions. Likewise, protecting the civil rights of gays and lesbians does not necessitate a right to marry, for such an entitlement would require a significant redefinition of marriage that would effectively strip it of its distinctive and exclusive tradition of a relationship between a woman and a man. The legitimate issue of equal regard in this instance does not justify Nelson's hasty leap to equal treatment.

Moreover, Nelson's appeal to permitting same-sex union as the symbolic affirmation of the political community is bewildering. Is he really claiming that whatever the state permits is also affirmed by the civil community it governs? If true, then presumably gambling and divorce are goods affirmed by the civil community since they are permitted by many late liberal regimes. Yet is it not the case that both are permitted not because they are good, but in order to protect other goods? Gambling and divorce are permitted, and thereby subject to regulation, in the former instance to protect the public from fraud and in the latter instance to protect the interests and assets of separating spouses. Do gamblers and divorcees really look to the permission of the state to gamble and divorce to have their lives affirmed by the civil community? If Nelson is correct, the answer must be yes, but it is a chilling reply replete with tyrannous implications. In turning to the state to grant same-sex union symbolic affirmation, Nelson not only grants an authority to government that even the late liberalism he embraces is unwilling to bestow, but he fails to recognize that the principal rationale for the state's regulation of marriage is not the sexual and personal fulfilment of spouses, but procreation and childrearing. If this were not case, then why would not the state simply grant any competent adult a licence to pursue sexual encounters with any other consenting adult? The very rationale for the state's regulation of marriage is that it presupposes the birth of children and formation of families which require protection, a presupposition that Nelson is either unable or unwilling to make. This failure could stem from the fact that he makes virtually no mention of children or family, a conspicuous absence in a book purportedly dedicated to analysing the relation between Christian theology and sexuality.[60] But in removing children and family from his theological vision he has also stripped sexuality of any teleological content, and thereby reduced it to a ravenous

[60] In the index of *Embodiment*, e.g. the terms 'child' or 'children' do not appear. There are three references to 'family', and in each instance it is cast in an unfavourable light.

pursuit of self-fulfilment. Consequently, the same-sex union he champions is but a simulacrum of a hollow institution that he has voided of any social and political content.

Thatcher is much more cognizant of the problematic issues at stake, as reflected in his discussion of whether or not marriage is a heterosexual institution. His appeals to non-biological methods of procuring children, friendship, and the history of changing marital practices to justify extending marriage to gays and lesbians, however, remains unconvincing. Recourse to adoption or collaborative reproduction is fixated on the ends to the detriment of the means. The good of *proles* is not measuring the outcome of a reproductive project. Rather, children are an outgrowth of the exclusive one-flesh unity of a couple; more akin to a gift received than a product obtained or produced. What Thatcher is attempting to construct is a parallel system in which marital partners are free to go outside their relationship (if using collaborative reproduction) in order to pursue their respective reproductive interests. And if adoption is used as a substitute method for securing the good of *proles*, then its charitable foundation is effectively discarded. It is curious that Thatcher, who is dedicated to recovering the traditional Christian emphasis on the embodied character of human sexuality, would appeal to these options, for seemingly the limits of the body are honoured *except* when one's reproductive desires are frustrated. This exception is telling, for what he proposes is a workable solution, but it is far from clear why it should be regarded as a distinctly Christian solution.

The inability of same-sex couples to procreate helps to account for Thatcher's heavy emphasis on friendship. He insists that friendship should be the cornerstone of any marriage, for it implies a relationship of equals who delight in each other's company, but in an inclusive rather than exclusive manner. Consequently, gays and lesbians would bring with them a rich set of practices involving friendship that would also enrich heterosexual marriage. Thatcher may be correct regarding this enrichment, but this does not thereby entitle gays and lesbians to marry. Friendship is certainly an important, if not crucial, factor in marriage, and any sources which can enrich its practice are to be welcomed. But marriage is not a formal *recognition* of friendship. Church and state do not perform or recognize a public declaration of friends. If this were the case, then presumably

Thatcher must also be open to the prospect of simultaneous marriages among friends, and consanguineous marriages among consenting adults.[61] In using marriage as a device for ecclesial and civil communities to affirm friendship, Thatcher falls into the same trap as Nelson, for marriage effectively disappears into the marketplace of constructing relationships whose consumers are blessed and licensed by church and state. Marriage ceases to be marriage when it cannot be easily seen as related to but substantially differentiated from friendship, for the very inclusivity and flexibility which gives friendship its inherent appeal cannot alone bear the weight of greater exclusivity and inflexibility which marital fidelity demands.[62]

Thatcher insists that his proposed expansion of marriage is in continuity with the tradition of the church reformulating its understanding of marriage over time. Marriage is not a sacred vessel, but an ecclesial and social construct subject to reform and amendment in response to changing historical circumstances. To a large extent he is correct: the church has altered its teaching on marriage over the past two millennia. But it is misleading to suggest that it has been subjected to periodic radical reformulation, and that he is simply proposing a new chapter in this heritage. What has never been in question for the church is that marriage consists of a covenant between a woman and a man, and its various theological and moral formulations and revisions have been to explicate and strengthen the meaning of this one-flesh core. For the church, like the state, has been authorized to protect and regulate an institution entrusted to its care. Marriage is not an invention or artefact of either the ecclesial or civil communities. Rather, it is a sovereign social sphere ordained by God in the order of creation, an order that has been vindicated and vouchsafed by Christ. In short, what Thatcher, as well as Nelson, fails to recognize is that neither church nor state has the authority to define what marriage is, but only to clarify its meaning through their respective regulations. Again, this regulatory task does not authorize either church or state to discriminate against the civil rights of homosexuals. Nelson in particular is right in his insistence that the

---

[61] Fertile heterosexual couples would presumably be forbidden to reproduce for hygienic reasons.

[62] See Gilbert Meilaender, *Friendship* (1981), 53–67.

church bears a heavy responsibility in perpetuating unwarranted attitudes and prejudices, both within in its own institutions and those of civil society. But its repentance and amendment does not validate or require a wholesale reformulation of marriage of the kind envisioned by Thatcher and Nelson. The legitimate task of protecting the civil rights of gays and lesbians does not necessarily entail dismantling and reconstructing the social institutions of marriage and family. To do so is to remain hostage to the late liberal principle that equal regard is synonymous with equal treatment, an unfortunate scheme in which normative claims are too often dissipated into procedural machinations. Neither church nor state affirms or vindicates the *lives* of its members and citizens respectively through the penultimate acts of judgement that Christ has authorized them to make within their respective spheres. That is an ultimate act of judgement reserved exclusively by God, and failing to honour that reservation is to commit ecclesial and political tyranny.

Given the discussion undertaken in this chapter, the church may be said to uphold and support the family as ascribed in the preceding chapters. In and through such reinforcement the church counters late liberalism's corrosive influence on the created, natural, imposed, social, and political affinities which bind civil community together in its pursuit of the common good. In doing so the church bears witness to the salvific history of creation's providential unfolding, and the destiny of that history in Christ. Such support, however, is neither unconditional nor perpetual. The family is not exempt from legitimate challenge or judgement by the ecclesial and civil communities. When and if the family asserts a loyalty and exclusivity which is not its to rightfully claim, then both church and state are within their rights to judge this unwarranted seizure of authority as an affront against those affinities which order, form, define, and express freedom. For the family too can only assert its rightful, and thereby limited, authority, by being under authority. In the absence of obedience, the family too can become idolatrous, thereby failing to order itself towards broader spheres of human association. Consequently, the church defends or challenges the family in response to changing historical and cultural circumstances. In obedience to Christ such defence or opposition is determined in respect to the extent that familial ordering promotes xenophilia while defraying xenophobia in compliance with God's commands, and it is a task properly shared by the other spheres comprising civil community. For acts which inspire a fear rather than love of strangers are contrary to the gospel, the former being the foundation of tyranny, and the latter of freedom.[63]

More particularly, the church upholds and supports the family within late liberal civil communities to remind its inhabitants of the crucial need to exercise authority by being under authority if the seed of freedom is to enjoy a fertile soil. Yet truth is the prerequisite of the limited authority which makes obedient freedom operative, and late liberalism has largely foreclosed the possibility of truth in political discourse. In the absence of limited authority which truth demands, tyranny displaces freedom as the threat which extracts coerced obedience. As O'Donovan has observed: 'There could undoubtedly be worse tyrannies than that of the regnant liberal secularism, so sensitively averse to overt physical suffering. That much must always be said in its favor.'[64] But having said that, late liberal regimes are nevertheless tyrannical, for in their political totalization of civil society they not only render genuine political discourse irrelevant and impossible, but refuse to embrace a proper authority resulting in withheld obedience that negates freedom. Consequently, despite late liberal claims to the contrary, there is no inherent reason why Christian theological discourse should be forbidden from forming and refining the social and political vocabulary of the civil community.[65] Moreover, there is also no inherent reason why the church should warmly embrace the prohibition in the name of an imperial, though enfeebled, inclusivity which ultimately enslaves rather than liberates. It is only in obediently proclaiming evangelical freedom that the church—to use a term that is in danger of becoming moribund by simplistic overuse—acts *prophetically* by uttering liberating speech instead of demanding a right of free speech, and which in order to be heard must be stated in such palatably correct phrases that it loses any meaning to its addressees. It is for the sake of such freedom that the church is called to uphold the right ordering of the family in the midst of hostile or indifferent civil communities spawned by late liberalism. In doing so, the church also bears witness to Christ

---

[63] See O'Donovan, *Desire of the Nations*, 266–7.
[64] O'Donovan, *Ways of Judgment*, 237.   [65] Ibid. 235–8.

as *the* source of authority from which all other limited authorities are derived and under which they are exercised, and is thereby also the proper object of what the nations should desire in their penultimate ordering of a created order that he has vindicated and redeemed.

Bibliography

Althaus, Paul, *The Ethics of Martin Luther*, tr. Robert C. Schultz (Philadelphia, Penn.: Fortress Press, 1972).

Althusius, Johannes, *The Politics*, tr. Frederick S. Carney (London: Eyre & Spottiswoode, 1964).

Ambrose, *On the Duties of the Clergy* and *Concerning Virgins*, in Philip Schaff and Henry Wace (eds), *A Select Library of the Nicene and Post-Nicene Fathers of the Christian Church* (2nd ser.), x, tr. H. de Romestin (Edinburgh: T. & T. Clark, 1989).

Aquinas, Thomas, *Summa Theologica: Latin Text and English Translation, Introductions, Notes, Appendices, and Glossaries* (Cambridge: Blackfriars, 1964–81).

Arendt, Hannah, *The Human Condition* (Chicago and London: University of Chicago Press, 1998).

Aristotle, *Politics*, tr. Ernest Barker (Oxford and New York: Oxford University Press, 1995).

Augustine of Hippo, *Concerning the City of God against the Pagans*, tr. Henry Bettenson (London: Penguin Books, 1984).

—— *On Marriage and Concupiscence*, in Philip Schaff (ed.), *A Select Library of the Nicene and Post-Nicene Fathers of the Christian Church* (1st ser.), v, tr. Peter Holmes and Robert Ernest Wallis (Edinburgh: T. & T. Clark, 1991).

—— *Of Continence, On the Good of Marriage*, and *Of Holy Virginity*, in Philip Schaff (ed.), *A Select Library of the Nicene and Post-Nicene Fathers of the Christian Church* (1st ser.), iii, tr. C. L. Cornish (Edinburgh: T. & T. Clark, 1993).

Banner, Michael, *Christian Ethics and Contemporary Moral Problems* (Cambridge and New York: Cambridge University Press, 1999).

Barth, Karl, *Church Dogmatics*, iii/3, tr. G. W. Bromiley and R. J. Ehrlich, ed. G. W. Bromiley and T. F. Torrance (Edinburgh: T. & T. Clark, 1960).

—— *Church Dogmatics*, iii/4, tr. A. T. MacKay *et al.*, ed. G. W. Bromiley and T. F. Torrance (Edinburgh: T and T Clark, 1961).

Barton, Stephen C. (ed.), *The Family in Theological Perspective* (Edinburgh: T. & T. Clark, 1996).

—— *Life Together: Family, Sexuality and Community in the New Testament and Today* (Edinburgh and New York: T. & T. Clark, 2001).

Baxter, Richard, *A Christian Directory,* part 2. *Christian Economics (or Family Duties)* = *Practical Works of the Rev. Richard Baxter,* 23 vols (London: James Duncan, 1830), iv.

Beiner, Ronald, and Booth, William James (eds), *Kant and Political Philosophy: The Contemporary Legacy* (New Haven: Yale University Press, 1993).

Berger, Brigitte, and Berger, Peter L., *The War over the Family: Capturing the Middle Ground* (Garden City, NY: Anchor Books, 1983).

Bonhoeffer, Dietrich, *Ethics* (London: SCM Press, 1955).

Borgmann, Albert, *Technology and the Character of Contemporary Life: A Philosophical Inquiry* (Chicago and London: University of Chicago Press, 1984).

—— *Power Failure: Christianity in the Culture of Technology* (Grand Rapids, Mich.: Brazos Press, 2003).

Brown, Peter, *The Body and Society: Men, Women and Sexual Renunciation in Early Christianity* (London: Faber & Faber, 1989).

Browning, Don S., *et al.*, *From Culture Wars to Common Ground: Religion and the American Family Debate* (Louisville, Ky.: Westminster John Knox Press, 1997).

Brunner, Emil, *The Divine Imperative: A Study in Christian Ethics,* tr. Olive Wyon (London: Lutterworth Press, 1937).

Bushnell, Horace, *Christian Nurture* (New Haven: Yale University Press, 1960).

Cahill, Lisa Sowle, *Sex, Gender, and Christian Ethics* (Cambridge: Cambridge University Press, 1996).

Carlen, Claudia (ed.), *The Papal Encyclicals,* ii–v (Raleigh, NC: McGrath Publishing Co., 1981).

Church of England, Board of Social Responsibility, *Something to Celebrate: Valuing Families in Church and Society* (London: Church House, 1995).

Clapp, Rodney. *Families at the Crossroads: Beyond Traditional and Modern Options* (Leicester: Inter-Varsity Press, 1993).

Clement of Alexandria, *The Miscellanies,* in *The Writings of Clement of Alexandria,* 2 vols, tr. William Wilson (Edinburgh: T. & T. Clark, 1869).

Cochrane, Charles Norris, *Christianity and Classical Culture: A Study of Thought and Action from Augustus to Augustine* (Indianapolis: Amagi, 2003).

Congregation for the Doctrine of the Faith, *Instruction on Respect for Human Life in its Origin and on the Dignity of Procreation Replies to Certain Questions of the Day (Donum Vitae),* http://www.vatican.va/roman_curia/congrega-tions/cfaith/documents/rc_con_cfaith_doc_19870222_respect-for-human-life_en.html.

Dooyeweerd, Herman, *A New Critique of Theoretical Thought*, 4 vols, tr. David H. Freeman, William S. Young, and H. De Jongste (Philadelphia, Penn.: Presbyterian and Reformed Publishing Co., 1953–8).

—— *Roots of Western Culture: Pagan, Secular, and Christian Options*, tr. John Kraay (Toronto: Wedge Publishing Foundation, 1979).

—— *A Christian Theory of Social Institutions*, tr. Magnus Verbrugge, ed. John Witte, jun. (La Jolla, Calif.: Herman Dooyeweerd Foundation, 1986).

Ellul, Jacques, *The Technological Society* (New York: Vintage Books, 1964).

Elshtain, Jean Bethke, *Public Man, Private Woman: Women in Social and Political Thought* (Princeton: Princeton University Press, 1991).

Filmer, Robert, *Patriarcha and Other Writings*, ed. Johann P. Sommerville (Cambridge: Cambridge University Press, 1991).

Foot, Philippa, *Virtues and Vices and Other Essays in Moral Philosophy* (Berkeley, Ca.: University of California Press, 1978).

Foucault, Michel, *The History of Sexuality*, 3 vols, tr. Robert Hurley (New York: Vintage Books, 1985).

Grant, George, *Technology and Empire: Perspectives on North America* (Toronto: House of Anansi, 1969).

—— *English-Speaking Justice* (Notre Dame, In.: University of Notre Dame Press, 1985).

—— *Technology and Justice* (Notre Dame, In.: University of Notre Dame Press, 1986).

—— *Time as History* (Toronto: University of Toronto Press, 1995).

Gratian, *The Treatise on Laws*, tr. Augustine Thompson (Washington, DC: Catholic University of America Press, 1993).

Gregory of Nyssa, *On Virginity*, in Henry Wace and Philip Schaff (eds), *A Select Library of Nicene and Post-Nicene Fathers of the Christian Church* (2nd ser.), v (Oxford: Parker & Co., 1893).

Grisez, Germain, *The Way of the Lord Jesus*, ii. *Living a Christian life* (Quincy, Ill.: Franciscan Press, 1993).

Grotius, Hugo, *On the Rights of War and Peace*, tr. William Whewell (Cambridge: Cambridge University Press, 1853).

Gudorf, Christine E., *Body, Sex, and Pleasure: Reconstructing Christian Sexual Ethics* (Cleveland, Ohio: Pilgrim Press, 1994).

Gustafson, James M., *Ethics from a Theocentric Perspective* (Chicago and London: University of Chicago Press, 1981).

Hare, John E., *The Moral Gap: Kantian Ethics, Human Limits, and God's Assistance* (Oxford and New York: Clarendon Press, 1996).

Hauerwas, Stanley, *A Community of Character: Toward a Constructive Christian Social Ethic* (Notre Dame, In., and London: University of Notre Dame Press, 1981).

Hauerwas, Stanley, *The Peaceable Kingdom: A Primer in Christian Ethics* (Notre Dame, In., and London: University of Notre Dame Press, 1983).

—— *Suffering Presence: Theological Reflections on Medicine, the Mentally Handicapped, and the Church* (Notre Dame, In.: University of Notre Dame Press, 1986).

—— *After Christendom?* (Nashville, Tenn.: Abingdon, 1991).

—— *In Good Company: The Church as Polis* (Notre Dame, In., and London: University of Notre Dame Press, 1995).

—— Bondi, Richard, and Burrell, David B., *Truthfulness and Tragedy: Further Investigations in Christian Ethics* (Notre Dame, In.: University of Notre Dame Press, 1977).

Helm, Paul, *The Providence of God* (Leicester: Inter-Varsity Press, 1993).

Hobbes, Thomas, *Leviathan* (Oxford and New York: Oxford University Press, 1996).

Horsley, Richard A. (ed.), *Paul and Empire: Religion and Power in Roman Imperial Society* (Harrisburg, Penn.: Trinity Press International, 1997).

—— *Bandits, Prophets and Messiahs: Popular Movements in the Time of Jesus* (Harrisburg, Penn.: Trinity Press, 1999).

Hugh of St Victor, *On the Sacraments of the Christian Faith*, tr. Roy J. Deferrari (Cambridge, Mass.: Mediaeval Academy of America, 1951).

John Paul II, *Familiaris Consortio* (London: Catholic Truth Society, 1981).

Kant, Immanuel, *Political Writings*, tr. H. B. Nisbet, ed. Hans Reiss (Cambridge: Cambridge University Press, 1991).

—— *The Metaphysics of Morals*, tr. Mary Gregor (Cambridge: Cambridge University Press, 1996).

Lasch, Christopher, *Haven in a Heartless World: The Family Besieged* (New York and London: Norton, 1995; 1st edn Basic Books, 1977).

Locke, John, *Two Treatises of Government* (Cambridge: Cambridge University Press, 1967).

Long, D. Stephen, *The Goodness of God: Theology, Church, and the Social Order* (Grand Rapids, Mich.: Brazos, 2001).

Luther, Martin, *Works*, xliv–xlvi (Philadelphia, Penn.: Muhlenberg Press and Fortress Press, 1962, 1967).

McCarthy, David Matzko, *Sex and Love in the Home: A Theology of the Household* (London: SCM, 2001).

McClendon, James William, *Systematic Theology*, i. *Ethics* (Nashville, Tenn.: Abingdon, 2002).

MacIntyre, Alasdair, *After Virtue: A Study in Moral Theory* (London: Duckworth, 1985).

—— *Whose Justice? Which Rationality?* (Notre Dame, In.: University of Notre Dame Press, 1988).

—— *Three Rival Versions of Moral Enquiry: Encyclopedia, Genealogy, and Tradition* (Notre Dame, In.: University of Notre Dame Press, 1990).

Maurice, F. D., *Social Morality: Twenty-One Lectures Delivered in the University of Cambridge* (London and Cambridge: Macmillan & Co., 1869).

Meilaender, Gilbert, *Friendship: A Study in Theological Ethics* (Notre Dame, In., and London: University of Notre Dame Press, 1981).

—— *The Theory and Practice of Virtue* (Notre Dame, In.: University of Notre Dame Press, 1984).

—— *The Limits of Love: Some Theological Explorations* (University Park, Penn., and London: Pennsylvania State University Press, 1987).

—— *Body, Soul, and Bioethics* (Notre Dame, In., and London: University of Notre Dame Press, 1995).

Milbank, John, *Theology and Social Theory: Beyond Secular Reason* (Oxford: Basil Blackwell, 1990).

Morgan, Edmund S., *The Puritan Family: Religion and Domestic Relations in Seventeenth Century New England* (Westport, Conn.: Greenwood Press, 1980).

Moxnes, Halvor (ed.), *Constructing Early Christian Families: Family as Social Reality and Metaphor* (London and New York: Routledge, 1997).

Nelson, James B., *Embodiment: An Approach to Sexuality and Christian Theology* (Minneapolis: Augsburg, 1978).

Newsome, James D., *Greeks, Romans, Jews: Currents of Culture and Belief in the New Testament World* (Philadelphia, Penn.: Trinity Press International, 1992).

Niebuhr, H. Richard, *Radical Monotheism and Western Culture: With Supplementary Essays* (Louisville, Ky.: Westminster/John Knox Press, 1993).

Noonan, John T., jun., *Contraception: A History of its Treatment by the Catholic Theologians and Canonists* (Cambridge, Mass.: Belknap Press, 1986).

O'Donovan, Oliver, *Marriage and Permanence* (Bramcote: Grove Books, 1978).

—— *Begotten or Made?* (Oxford: Oxford University Press, 1984).

—— *Resurrection and Moral Order: An Outline for Evangelical Ethics* (Leicester: Inter-Varsity Press, 1986).

—— *The Desire of the Nations: Rediscovering the Roots of Political Theology* (Cambridge and New York: Cambridge University Press, 1996).

—— *The Ways of Judgment: The Bampton Lectures, 2003* (Grand Rapids, Mich., and Cambridge: Eerdmans, 2005).

Okin, Susan Moller, *Justice, Gender, and the Family* (New York: Basic Books, 1989).

Osiek, Carolyn, and Balch, David L., *Families in the New Testament World: Households and House Churches* (Louisville, Ky.: Westminster John Knox Press, 1997).

Outka, Gene, *Agape: An Ethical Analysis* (New Haven and London: Yale University Press, 1976).

Passmore, John, *The Perfectibility of Man* (New York: Charles Scribner's Sons, 1970).

Peters, Ted, *God: The World's Future. Systematic Theology for a Postmodern World.* (Minneapolis: Fortress Press, 1992).

—— *For the Love of Children: Genetic Technology and the Future of the Family* (Louisville, Ky.: Westminster John Knox Press, 1996).

Pomeroy, Susan B., *Families in Classical and Hellenistic Greece: Representations and Realities* (Oxford: Clarendon Press, 1997).

Ramsey, Paul, *Fabricated Man: The Ethics of Genetic Control* (New Haven and London: Yale University Press, 1970).

—— *One Flesh: A Christian View of Sex Within, Outside and Before Marriage* (Bramcote: Grove Books, 1975).

—— 'Human Sexuality in the History of Redemption', *Journal of Religious Ethics,* 16/1 (Spring 1988), 56–86.

—— *Basic Christian Ethics* (Louisville, Ky.: Westminster/John Knox Press, 1993).

Rawls, John, *A Theory of Justice* (Oxford and New York: Oxford University Press, 1972).

—— *Political Liberalism* (New York and Chichester: Columbia University Press, 1996).

Rawson, Beryl (ed.), *The Family in Ancient Rome: New Perspectives* (London: Routledge, 1992).

Riley, Patrick, *Kant's Political Philosophy* (Totowa, NJ: Rowman & Littlefield, 1983).

Robertson, John A., *Children of Choice: Freedom and the New Reproductive Technologies* (Princeton: Princeton University Press, 1994).

Royce, Josiah, *The Philosophy of Loyalty* (Nashville, Tenn.: Vanderbilt University Press, 1995).

Russell, Bertrand, *Marriage and Morals* (London: George Allen & Unwin, 1929).

Saner, Hans, *Kant's Political Thought: Its Origins and Development* (Chicago, Ill.: University of Chicago Press, 1973).

Schleiermacher, Friedrich, *The Christian Household: A Sermonic Treatise,* tr. Dietrich Seidel and Terrence N. Tice (Lewiston, NY: Edwin Mellon Press, 1991).

Song, Robert, *Christianity and Liberal Society* (Oxford: Clarendon Press, 1997).

Thatcher, Adrian, *Marriage after Modernity: Christian Marriage in Postmodern Times* (Sheffield: Sheffield Academic Press, 1999).

Theissen, Gerd, *Social Reality and the Early Christians: Theology, Ethics, and the World of the New Testament*, tr. Margaret Kohl (Edinburgh: T. & T. Clark, 1993).

Trigg, Roger, *Rationality and Religion: Does Faith Need Reason?* (Oxford and Malden, Mass.: Blackwell, 1998).

Van Leeuwen, Mary Stewart, *Gender and Grace: Love, Work and Parenting in a Changing World* (Downers Grove, Ill.: InterVarsity Press, 1990).

Wannenwetsch, Bernd, *Political Worship: Ethics for Christian Citizens*, tr. Margaret Kohl (Oxford and New York: Oxford University Press, 2004).

Waters, Brent, Review of *From Culture Wars to Common Ground: Religion and the American Family Debate*, by Donald S. Browning, *et al.*, *Studies in Christian Ethics*, 13/1 (2000).

—— *Reproductive Technology: Towards a Theology of Procreative Stewardship* (London and Cleveland, Ohio: Darton, Longman & Todd and Pilgrim Press, 2001).

—— 'Welcoming Children into our Homes: A Theological Reflection on Adoption', *Scottish Journal of Theology*, 55/4 (2002), 424–37.

—— 'Engineering our Grace: An Old Idea and New Genetic Technologies', in Gerard Magill (ed.), *Genetics and Ethics: An Interdisciplinary Study* (St. Louis, Mo.: St. Louis University Press, 2004).

—— 'Adoption, Parentage, and Procreative Stewardship', in Timothy P. Jackson (ed.), *The Morality of Adoption: Social-Psychological, Theological, and Legal Perspectives* (Grand Rapids, Mich., and Cambridge: Eerdmans, 2005).

—— *From Human to Posthuman: Christian Theology and Technology in a Postmodern World* (Aldershot: Ashgate, 2006).

Webb, Stephen H., *The Gifting God: A Trinitarian Ethics of Excess* (New York and Oxford: Oxford University Press, 1996).

Witte, John, jun., *From Sacrament to Contract: Marriage, Religion, and Law in the Western Tradition* (Louisville, Ky.: Westminster John Knox Press, 1997).

Index

SUBJECTS

NAMES